Import & Export of Apparel & Textiles

Part I: Export to USA

Part II: Import From Pakistan

Nasim Yousaf

First Edition published in 2001

Library of Congress Number: 2001117379
ISBN #:   Hardcover   1-4010-1411-9
                  Softcover   1-4010-1410-0

This book was printed in the United States of America.

Published by Nasim Yousaf
4207 Streamwood Dr.
Liverpool, New York 13090, USA
Fax: 315 622 0205

To order additional copies of this book, contact:
Xlibris Corporation
1-888-7-XLIBRIS
www.Xlibris.com
Orders@Xlibris.com

Contents

PART 1: EXPORT TO USA

PART 2: IMPORT FROM PAKISTAN

ical Sciences, and Oriental Languages) at the Cambridge ersity of England. At Cambridge, he earned many scholarly s including Wrangler in Mathematics, Foundation Scholar, Bachelor Scholar. He was also a Fellow of the Geographical iety (F.G.S.) in Paris, a Fellow of the Society of Arts (F.S.A.) in ris, and a Fellow of the Royal Society of Arts (F.R.S.A).

Mashriqi also authored a number of books. His most famous ork, *Tazkirah*, was nominated for the Nobel Prize in Literature. n addition, he was the first Muslim to be appointed as the Under Secretary of Education in India by the British Government. The British Government also offered him the title of Sir and the position of Ambassador to Afghanistan, both of which he declined.

His contribution and sacrifices toward the creation of Pakistan are unforgettable. The people of Pakistan, including top leaders, paid rich tributes to him upon his death. During a meeting with Mr. Yousaf, the author of this book, the late Prime Minister of Pakistan, Zulifiqar Ali Bhutto, said of Mashriqi, "He was a great leader and his services towards the creation of Pakistan were unparalleled."

The following web site on the Internet has been dedicated to Allama Mashriqi: http://allama-mashriqi.8m.com

Dr. Akhtar Hameed Khan

Dr. Akhtar Hameed Khan was a scholar and renowned social scientist. His works are very well recognized around the globe. He attended Cambridge University in England and later received an Honorary Doctorate (Ph.D) from Michigan State University.

Disclaimer

The author has made the best attempt possible to provide the most accurate information in this book, but he does not take any responsibility for errors, omissions, changes, accuracy of information obtained from a third source, change in laws, variation of laws in different countries, change of addresses, etc. Information may also vary depending on the laws of the respective country. All recommendations and suggestions in this book are the author's personal views based on his personal knowledge and experiences; it is not necessary that all readers will agree with the author's ideas. Information including company names, addresses, contact numbers, and URLs in this book can change at any time, and the author cannot be held liable for such changes. Information and statistics published in this book have been derived from various sources, which the author believes are authentic and reliable. However, he does not take any legal responsibility for wrong information (provided by the source), owing to a misprint, or for any other reason. It is recommended that anyone using the information in this book double-check it with the appropriate authorities for its validity. The author lists organizations/companies in the text, but is not recommending them and does not take responsibility for their dealings. You must check all credentials of the organizations/companies listed in this book before dealing with them.

chan
Univ
title
and
Soc
Pa

Dedication

This book is dedicated to two legends of Pakist devoted their lives to their countrymen: Allama Mashriqi a Akhtar Hameed Khan. Both of these personalities are relat the author; the former was his grandfather and the latter was uncle. The author takes great pride in being a member of a fa ily that greatly contributed to the Muslim cause.

Allama Mashriqi:
One of the Founding Fathers of Pakistan

Allama Mashriqi (Inayatullah Khan) was a scholar and founder of the Khaksar Tehrik in Indo-Pakistan. He had a very large number of devoted followers. He and the Khaksars were an integral part in the appearance of Pakistan on the world map on August 14, 1947.

Mashriqi accomplished many feats during his lifetime. He completed four Triposes (Mathematics, Natural Sciences, Me-

Dr. Khan was a recipient of many prestigious civil awards including Nishan-i-Imtiaz, Sitara-i-Pakistan, Hilal-i-Imtiaz, and the Magsaysay Award (the highest civil award given by the government of Philippines). He was a visiting Professor at Harvard, Princeton, and Michigan State University in the USA. In Europe, he was a visiting professor at Oxford University in England and Lund University in Sweden. He authored a number of books, research papers, reports, and monographs on rural development. Dr. Khan was the founder of two projects, the Orangi Pilot Project and the Rural Academy of East Pakistan. The former is based in Pakistan and the latter in East Pakistan (now Bangladesh). Millions of poor people have benefited from these projects. General Pervez Musharraf, Chief Executive of Pakistan, renamed the National Rural Support Program as the Akhtar Hameed Khan Centre for Rural Development. Because of his tremendous contributions, the Bangladeshi government has also preserved his house in Comilla as a museum. Volumes of his works are available in many universities throughout the world.

The following web site on the Internet has been dedicated to Dr. Akhtar Hameed Khan: http://akhtar-hameed-khan.8m.com

Acknowledgements

This book would not have been possible without the encouragement and support of my family.

I would like to give a special thanks to my wife, Ambereen, who has been very cooperative throughout my life. She has been a source of encouragement and has assisted me in achieving my goals and desires in life. She has always been by my side, and has been a source of strength for me. I would like to say thanks to her from the bottom of my heart.

I also want to express my gratitude to my three wonderful kids, Mehreen, Zain, and Myra, who have been very understanding and helpful. I would like to give my very special thanks to Mehreen. Without her assistance, this book would not have been possible. I also convey my gratitude to my son, Zain, whose help means a lot to me. Finally, my daughter Myra is also very happy and excited to see this book completed.

From a loving husband and father.

Messages

Message to the Pakistani Nation

Self-reliance is the key to progress and growth. A nation's success lies in self-help and hard work; strong nations do not depend on foreign aid.

The survival of Pakistan lies in education. Many of Pakistan's social, political, and economic problems can be resolved by making education a top priority. Through education, Pakistan has the potential to become a very prosperous and affluent nation.

To the Pakistani Women

Women are the backbone and pillar of any nation. The developed nations of the world have attained economic prosperity with the help of women. Fulfill your role by acquiring education and helping the nation achieve affluence. The country cannot succeed without your help. Pakistan needs you, so apply yourself and take on a more active role in society. I salute those who are already actively involved in economic activities.

About the Author

Mr. Nasim Yousaf started his career as a Pilot Officer in the Pakistan Air Force. He resigned after serving for approximately two and a half years. In the late 1970's, Mr. Yousaf began exporting textiles and apparel from Pakistan. As a result of his business acumen, he achieved success at a very young age. One of his companies in Pakistan earned merit certificates, for its commendable performance in export for three consecutive years, from the Rawalpindi Chamber of Commerce and Industry in Pakistan. Approximately, 10 years ago, he moved to the US, and has resided here ever since. His knowledge on trade is a result of his experiences in Pakistan, the US, and his extensive travel across the world.

Mr. Yousaf was a member of the Board of Directors that founded The Pakistan Commercial Exporters of Towels Association (PCETA). He also held other important positions in the PCETA including Vice Chairman (North Zone), Member of the Central Executive Committee, and a Member of the Textile Quota Committee of the PCETA. While in Pakistan, he also represented the business community at different forums. He has attended various seminars on international trade sponsored by reputable organizations such as the United Nations Conference on Trade and Development (UNCTAD), the Export Promotion Bureau of Pakistan, and the Australian Embassy in Pakistan. In the course of his business activity and personal capacity, he has met with many dignitaries, including Pakistani Federal Ministers and Heads of Government. He has participated in various social gatherings within the industry and the business community, including an industry breakfast in the USA where former President George Bush graced the occasion. More recently, Marquis, reputable and renowned publishers of *Marquis Who's Who* directories, recognized the achievements of Mr. Yousaf by offering to include his biography in *Who's Who in the World* and *Who's Who in America*.

In over two decades of being associated with trade, Mr. Yousaf has traveled the world. His knowledge and learning have been a result of his extensive travel and meetings with people from various backgrounds, nationalities, religions, and cultures. His companies have exhibited their products numerous times in Europe, Asia, and the Middle East. Mr. Yousaf's knowledge on international trade is a result of his experiences from across the world.

Mr. Nasim Yousaf's web site address is as follows: http://www.nasimyousaf.8m.com

Foreword

My husband started his career as a Commissioned Officer in the Pakistan Air Force. He resigned and became a business professional, a leader in the business community, and now a writer too. With his energetic and dynamic personality, he attained success at a very young age. But he never becomes complacent with his achievements in life and has always been on the go, even when it's time for relaxation. He believes in working hard in order to achieve one's desired goals.

My husband is greatly impressed and influenced by his grandfather as well as his uncle, Allama Mashriqi and Dr. Akhtar Hameed Khan, respectively. The services of both for the nation of Pakistan are unparalleled. Both were scholars and dedicated their lives to the cause of the Muslims, and they will always be remembered as great patriots. Although he admits that he cannot come close to their level of dedication, he agrees that, in his/her lifetime, one should make a contribution towards society. This thought inspired and motivated him to write this book.

Since the beginning of his adult years, my husband has not agreed with the way Pakistan has been governed. He has always believed that this was not why Pakistan had been created, nor was it the dream that Allama Mashriqi and Dr. Akhtar Hameed Khan had dedicated their lives to. He felt uneasy and disturbed at the deteriorating conditions in Pakistan.

At one time, my husband felt that he should enter politics to bring that change in society. In order to do this, he could have utilized the Khaksar Tehrik and other platforms, but he felt he wasn't suitable to enter politics, keeping in mind the manner in which they were being conducted in Pakistan. Politics had been converted into yet another medium for seeking power and money. According to what he learned from Mashriqi and Dr. Khan, to be a leader is to serve the people with selfless dedication. My husband believes that the leaders should be servants and not the masters of the public and that leaders are like parents and the nation is their child who looks up to the parents for guidance. Thus the leaders today need to ensure proper upbringing of the nation. Sadly, the philosophy in Pakistan is completely different. Keeping this in view, he found himself a misfit in the political environment.

Because he didn't fit into the requirements of the current system and was disheartened by the situation, he decided to leave the country for good. When he finally announced his decision to migrate to the USA, his immediate family and friends were against the move. Many people attempted to stop him or to change his mind. "Pakistan has lost a great exporter." These were the words uttered by one of his friends. Another stated, "This move is not for you. Moving to a foreign country is only for those who are unsuccessful in their own country."

My husband knew that moving to a foreign country meant starting all over again. To reach the social prosperity and affluence that he had achieved in Pakistan would either require an extended period of time or may not be possible at all. For him, moving meant going back down to level one, a step that many people in his position wouldn't dare attempt. He also knew that he would face financial losses that would set him back for many years of his life. He knew that he and his family would have to compromise the lifestyle they had become accustomed to in Pakistan. He knew there wouldn't be any maids to do the house chores or staff to run the office; he would no longer be invited to attend meetings with dignitaries, or business dinners with trade delegations. The only consolation he had was that he and his family would be able to lead a straightforward life. Most importantly, his children would be able to acquire a good higher education.

My husband is an iron man. When it comes to facing such situations, he stands like a rock, takes all criticisms, and faces them boldly. He does not let fear of criticism affect his decisions. He believes in himself, and he believes in the complete independence of thought and action. He takes full responsibility for his actions, whether right or wrong.

Finally, he made the move to the USA. He is now leading a content and happy life, with a goal that his children get the best education possible and learn the real values of life. He also reminds them that although education and material wealth are important in today's world, they should not forget that they have the responsibility of contributing towards their family, their home country, and the country that they live in. Unfortunately in Pakistan, despite some recent changes, women are still enclosed and repressed in their houses. My husband believes that women are an equal and integral part of society and must work shoulder to shoulder with men in order to bring prosperity to the nation. Hence, he wants his son and daughters to play a constructive role in society.

Migrating to the USA and leaving behind a well-established social and economic lifestyle was not an easy step for my husband. It is the biggest decision he has made in his lifetime. The move uprooted his family and resulted in heavy financial losses, but he has never regretted his decision.

The purpose of this foreword is not to merely criticize the nation, but to highlight the problems that plague Pakistan. He regretfully emphasizes the negatives, but only with the purpose of evoking realization in the reader. My husband strongly feels that whatever he is today, he is because of Pakistan. He greatly values his heritage, and hence, he has had a burning desire to make a contribution towards the development of Pakistan. Through writing this book he hopes to help potential Pakistani entrepreneurs enter the export business, thus contributing towards the economic development of the country.

My husband has put countless hours into this book, working tirelessly to include the information that he felt would be useful for an entrepreneur. I am proud to see that he has finally completed this great undertaking, after working so hard for so long.

Ambereen Yousaf

Preface

It gives me great pleasure and satisfaction to see this book finally published. I am grateful to the Almighty God, who provided me with the courage, ability, and the opportunity to complete this book.

This book is helpful for importers as well as exporters of apparel and textiles to the USA. Pakistani exporters as well as businessmen from other countries will hopefully make use of the information I share in this book. The book targets importers, exporters, business executives, textile industry professionals, students, etc.

Before I mention what this book is all about, let me remark on how the idea of writing first came about. I have been associated with international trade for over 20 years. Having lived in both Pakistan and the US, I have been able to obtain a vast knowledge on importing and exporting. I have also traveled extensively throughout the world, which has enabled me to gain a great deal of exposure, knowledge, and information on global trade. Over time, the idea of putting all my experiences together began to develop in my mind. Most importantly, I wanted to give something back to Pakistan and the only way I could make a contribution was to write a book that would be beneficial to Pakistani exporters, ultimately helping the economy. Finally, I am not aware of any other book that serves as a complete guide for importers and exporters of apparel and textiles to the USA.

In the book, I have tried to pass on my knowledge of business to both importers and exporters. The book discusses different steps one needs to take in setting up a business. It explains everything from the advantages of the export business and the production of apparel to making a practical entry into the US apparel and textile market. It also provides valuable information to entrepreneurs in the US and elsewhere, who might be interested in importing apparel and textiles from Pakistan. This information will save a tremendous amount of time for any importer or exporter, especially beginners. It is designed to give a head start to any entrepreneur.

I have tried to keep this book error free to the best of my ability, but I apologize if any mistakes or inaccuracies are found or if there is a disagreement on an opinion.

The book is divided into two parts.

Part 1: Export to USA

This part provides a wealth of information for exporters around the world who want to sell their products to the US. It covers topics in depth, including methods of finding US buyers, market research, important trade shows, options of selling, web sites of designers and large US chain stores, garment production, apparel machinery, fashion and color forecasting information, and much more.

Part 2: Import from Pakistan

This part serves as a guide for importers on how to acquire apparel and textiles from Pakistan. It provides information on how to reach Pakistani manufacturers, exporters, and more.

1 | Chapter One

Exporting: The Best Business!

I am starting the first chapter of my book by expressing my views on exporting. I want to convey the importance and value that I associate with this marvelous business. The intent of this book is to increase awareness of the advantages of exporting. I hope to encourage more people to join the ranks of exporters, so that they too can enjoy the benefits of this trade.

Keep in mind that some people think that selling in the domestic market is a prerequisite for exporting. This is not true. You can start your export business without having sold anything in the domestic market. However, if you are currently selling in your home country, exporting will create additional markets.

In general, getting into business has its advantages. A successful business is not only saleable for profits, but also provides a sense of self-satisfaction, fulfillment, and accomplishment. A business entity is transferable, unlike other professions, such as those of doctors or engineers.

A few advantages of exporting:

- The vast international markets available to exporters allow opportunities for tremendous growth
- In the case in which a company is increasing its scope from a domestic market to an international one, its fixed costs will remain the same. Since more goods will be produced while fixed costs remain the same, the cost per unit will decrease and the profitability will increase
- If a company sells in the domestic market, exporting can help increase its competitiveness in the domestic market
- The dependence on only one market can be eliminated
- Wider markets may allow your company to sell to your production unit's maximum capacity
- Profitability is generally good
- The export business offers opportunities to travel the world, see other cultures, and meet new people
- Trade statistics and information are generally available free of charge in trade libraries of export promotion offices, trade associations, and Chambers of Commerce & Industry
- Government support and incentives are always available to exporters. Incentives may vary among different governments and countries. In general, some incentives that may be available are:
  - ◆ Tax break incentives
    - Lower income tax rates
  - ◆ Tax holidays
    - Export manufacturing plants may be granted tax holidays, which offer them tax-free incomes for a specified number of years
  - ◆ Easier access to loans
  - ◆ Lower interest rates on loans

- Governments may direct commercial banks to provide low interest rates on loans for export; this helps exporters maintain competitive prices
♦ Travel with government sponsored trade delegations
- In order to promote export from their own countries, governments organize trade delegations to other parts of the world; travel opportunities with such trade delegations are available to exporters of that country. This helps exporters develop direct contact with their trading counterparts. Participation in such trade delegations helps establish instant credibility of an exporter. Note: travel may also be subsidized
♦ Subsidized participation in trade shows
- In most countries, governments and trade bodies, such as export promotion agencies, trade associations, and Chambers of Commerce and Industry, provide subsidized participation to exporters in trade shows
♦ Training Seminars/Workshops
- In many countries, the government or trade bodies arrange seminars on export trade. Training seminars are usually free or some times have only a nominal fee. They serve to educate exporters on the export business on both general and/or specific topics
♦ VIP status and recognition
- In order to recognize the achievements of exporters, some countries grant the status of Very Important Person (VIP) to outstanding exporters

- Awards and trophies are presented to exporters in recognition of the best performances; policies vary from country to country
- ◆ Hard currency accounts
  - Countries that do not allow companies or individuals to maintain foreign currency bank accounts may treat exporters as an exception to the rule
- ◆ Duty drawbacks
  - This is a refund of the import duties that may have been previously paid to customs. This refund, which can be either full or partial, may be permissible on the raw materials used in the goods exported
- ◆ Incentives at Export Processing Zones / Foreign Trade Zones / Free Trade Zones
  - Exporters are offered incentives to establish production units in Export Processing Zones (EPZ). EPZ's are secured areas outside a nation's customs territory. They allow exporters to produce, modify, and store their goods without any duties or taxes. See Chapter 19 for more information on Foreign Trade Zones or Free Trade Zones (FTZ)

Since more incentives may be available and policies may differ from country to country, it is advised that you check with the export promotion offices and relevant agencies in your own country.

The advantages of exporting are numerous. However, there are some disadvantages as well.

Disadvantages:

- It can be difficult and time consuming for a novice to gain experience and knowledge of the international market
- Exporting can be challenging, since each market is different in terms of consumer tastes, customs and other legalities, merchandise and price acceptability, etc. Furthermore, language and cultural barriers can be a difficulty
- Extended and frequent travel can be a headache for those who do not enjoy traveling
- An export order may take a long time to materialize
- Payment procedures are tedious and the wait can be longer
- Shipments involve a lot of paper work
- Initially, out-of-pocket expenses for market surveys may be higher than those for a domestic business

Remember that any business has its disadvantages, so don't let these drawbacks discourage you. Overall, the export business has a lot to offer!

The Importance of Export Trade

It is essential for every nation to engage in export trade for its own prosperity and growth. With the passage of time, world markets are becoming increasingly integrated and international trade opportunities are rising across the world. Export plays a vital role in not only one country's economy, but also the world economy. Governments are encouraging their own businessmen to think globally and are providing more conducive environments, policies, and facilities, in attempts to attract more people to enter the arena of export trade.

Characteristics of a Successful Entrepreneur

In order to be a successful entrepreneur, it is important to first take a look at yourself. Entrepreneurs tend to think big and are optimistic about the future. Business can be a lot of fun, provided you love it. Thus, it is important that you are honest to yourself about your own character, to ensure that you are choosing the right profession.

An entrepreneur must possess qualities and attributes such as:

- Honesty and integrity
- Devotion and enthusiasm
- Persistence and focus
- Desire to succeed
- Confidence
- Determination
- Intelligence
- Patience
- A creative mind with new ideas and visions
- A hard working and initiative-taking personality
- Self-control and an even temperament
- A friendly, pleasant, and charismatic personality
- Politeness and good manners
- The ability to handle challenge, take risks, and handle loss
- The ability to assess the future of the market and the business
- Aspirations of being your own boss
- Knowledge of one's product, market, and competition
- Interest in the field
- Love for domestic and international travel
- Organizational, administrative, and management skills
- Decision making, negotiation, and communication skills

Ask Yourself

Some of the many questions that you should ask yourself before starting up a business are listed below. Be honest, as a venture such as this is very demanding, especially in the beginning.

- Do you have enough knowledge of export business?
- Do you have enough information on your possible market(s)?
- Have you acquired enough experience?
- Have you picked the right product?
- Do you have adequate finances or someone who is willing to provide them?
- Have you figured out the roles and responsibilities surrounding your new business?
- Have you set your short and long-term goals?
- Have you looked at the potential of your chosen product in both the domestic and international markets?
- How will you enter the market?
- Have you looked into your competition?
- Have you looked into the pricing and availability of the raw materials?
- How and where will you produce your goods?
- How will you handle fluctuation of orders during peak and off peak seasons?
- How will you handle the logistics of your shipment?
- Will you be able to make timely deliveries?

Experience in the Industry

No one can be successful without having knowledge and experience in the field that he/she wants to enter. One may acquire knowledge through reading books, but practical experience will only come through working. Although the learning process will be faster for a university graduate with a major in the field, there is still no match for practical experience.

If you are interested in apparel export, working in the export department of a sizeable apparel manufacturer/exporter is probably the best way to acquire the necessary experience. The second best choice would be to work with any type of exporter. Although this will not give you the experience you need for the export of garments, it can still provide you with some valuable experience and knowledge on the channels and methods of exporting.

Some key concepts to learn from practical experience:

- Procurement of material
- Running the production department
- Labor management
- Cost control
- Export procedures and preparation of documentation
- Export marketing and sales
- Finance procurement
- Some accounting, including maintaining a positive cash flow for smooth operation
- Problem solving
- Other issues related to the industry

Keep in mind that no one is perfect and competent enough to do everything. Thus, it is not a bad idea to hire someone who can fill in your weak areas. Suppose that you do not have any accounting experience; is there anyone else who could do the job for you, such as your spouse, partner, another director in the company, or an employee?

2 | Chapter Two

Business Planning

Through planning, one can achieve goals for social and/or economic reasons. This is a continuous process that lasts throughout the life of your business. Remember that it is you who will have to run the business, so you must do the planning as well. This process is extremely important in any aspect of life, whether it is business, education, home life, etc. Keep in mind that plans may be revised as the need arises, however, this does not mean that you can change your plan everyday.

There are various steps to business planning. A good planner must assess the market, the industry, the competitors, and the customers. Figure out what your customers might be looking for and how you can fulfill their needs. Look into the strengths and weaknesses of your product and company in comparison to your competitors. This will help you determine the chances of your success. Remember that this is an extremely competitive world, and it is becoming even more so, with advances in technology such as the Internet.

The strategy behind developing a plan differs according to the size of the company and the project. Due to a lack of resources, a smaller company may not be able to afford to plan in a similar manner as their larger counterparts.

Business planning involves two kinds of plans, a feasibility study and a business plan. A feasibility study is conducted in order to determine the viability of manufacturing a product(s) to make profits. This study is generally conducted prior to establishing a business, where as a business plan can be made prior to starting a business or periodically. Business plans are also needed to apply for loans from a bank. Instead of discussing the feasibility and business plan together, I prefer to discuss them separately in order to create a better understanding for the reader.

The Feasibility Study

The aim of a feasibility analysis is to determine the viability of a project. A feasibility study is essential for starting any business. You need to study your market, competition, profitability of the project, etc. The feasibility study will help you determine whether starting a business is workable for you or not. If you are unable to prepare a feasibility study, there are companies who can do the job for you, or at least provide some guidance.

To conduct a feasibility study, take a look at the following areas:

- Financing
  - How much capital is required?
  - Who provides the financing?

- Self financing
- Family, friends, partners or other directors, banks, other institutions
- Foreign partners or joint ventures
- ♦ What is your payoff period for loans and how do you plan to pay them back?
- The product
  - ♦ What do you want to sell?
  - ♦ What are your product's advantages and disadvantages?
- Scope and scale of the operation
  - ♦ Size of the project
  - ♦ Production capacity of the facility
- Target market(s)
  - ♦ Is the project targeted towards the domestic or international market or both?
  - ♦ Who are your target customers? (Low-end, high-end buyers, women, men, children, ethnic markets, etc.)
- Market projections
  - ♦ In your mind, what is the probability of success for your business?
  - ♦ What is the market demand?
    - Sale targets on a yearly basis
    - Sale targets by country/region
  - ♦ What is the potential of your product in the domestic and export market?
- Production facility
  - ♦ Location of the operation
  - ♦ Purchased or rented?
  - ♦ Cost of the building?
  - ♦ Size of the building?
- Machinery and equipment
  - ♦ What domestic or imported machinery is to be used?
  - ♦ Who provides knowledge of the machinery?
  - ♦ Type of machinery

- ◆ Quantity of each type of machinery
- ◆ Production capacity of machinery
- Production
  - ◆ Who provides knowledge of running the factory?
  - ◆ What will be the capacity of the unit?
  - ◆ What type of labor is required?
  - ◆ How will you dispose of sub-standard goods? What will the tolerance of your rejection be? Rejection tolerance must be kept at the lowest level possible, otherwise your cost per unit will increase, resulting in an increase in price
- Raw material
  - ◆ Will raw materials be imported, domestic, or both?
  - ◆ In case of an imported raw material, what will the country of import be?
- Corporate setup and staff training
  - ◆ Who will fill the various positions in your company?
    - Top management
    - Senior management
    - Junior management
    - Administrative staff
    - Skilled laborers
    - Unskilled laborers
  - ◆ How will the staff be trained?
- Marketing channels
  - ◆ What marketing channels will be used?
    - Importers, distributors, agents, sales representatives, branch offices, etc.
- Other
  - ◆ Who is your competition and how will you compete?
  - ◆ What factors will you have to consider when setting prices?
  - ◆ How will you find buyers?
  - ◆ What will be your terms of sale in order to attract buyers?

♦ Are there any textile quotas involved? If yes, how will you procure them? Remember that in many countries, textile quotas can be purchased from the open market and that price is determined by the demand of the category

♦ What delivery schedules will you be able to offer?

♦ Break-even analysis must be performed. See appendix 1-2 for a formula for break-even point

The Business Plan

A business plan explains different aspects of a new or existing business. It discusses strategies in the areas of marketing, finance, operation, and profitability. It provides a plan of action to run your business and helps you anticipate the future to make wiser decisions.

It is my suggestion that you write a business plan regardless of whether you have plans to borrow money or not. However, if you do need financial assistance, banks will require that you submit a well-prepared business plan. When preparing a business plan, you must think competitively, be honest to yourself, and adapt a realistic approach. Do not write a business plan just to attract financial support. Remember that over or underestimating sales may have a negative impact on your business. After you turn in your plan, the bank will study it very carefully and will also run some numbers/ratios to determine the viability of your business proposal. The plan allows the bank to decide whether your proposition is worth the risk of granting a loan. Therefore, your plan must be carefully drawn out or else the loan will be turned down.

Certified Public Accountants/Chartered Accountants or business consultants can also provide guidance or prepare a business plan for you. Other resources that can help include software and books.

In general, the outline of a business plan covers the following:

- Description
  - ◆ Name of the business
  - ◆ Summary of the business
  - ◆ Date of establishment
  - ◆ New or existing business?
- Type of business
  - ◆ Form of business ownership: sole-proprietorship, partnership, limited company/corporation
  - ◆ Trading or manufacturing?
- Potential of the business
  - ◆ Opportunities that will generate business for your company
- Products
  - ◆ Type of products for sale
  - ◆ What is it that gives your product an edge over others?
  - ◆ Are raw materials locally available or will they have to be imported?
- Market
  - ◆ What is your market?
  - ◆ Market share
  - ◆ Current and future market trends; rising, declining, or static?
  - ◆ How do you plan to enter the market?
  - ◆ Who are your customers: domestic, foreign, or both?
  - ◆ Who are your competitors: domestic, foreign, or both?
- Pricing strategy
  - ◆ What will your pricing structure be?
  - ◆ What is your target price?
  - ◆ Are your prices competitive?

- ♦ What edge do your prices have over your competitors' prices?
- Sales projections
  - ♦ What are your business sales projections?
  - ♦ Total sales for the last three years, in case of an existing business
- Profitability
  - ♦ How profitable is your business?
  - ♦ What is your margin of profit?
- Finances
  - ♦ Balance sheet
  - ♦ Profit and loss statement/income statement
  - ♦ Cash flow statement
  - ♦ Bank statement
  - ♦ In case of an existing business, financial and bank statements for the last three years
- Securing the loan
  - ♦ What collateral will you give to secure the loan, personal guarantee, property, securities, Certificate of Deposits, etc.?
  - ♦ Is the amount you have requested genuine?
  - ♦ What is the risk on the part of the bank?
  - ♦ Is your business worth taking a risk?
  - ♦ How do you plan to pay back the loan?
- Management
  - ♦ Background of owners/directors
  - ♦ Experience of management in running the business
- Business facility
  - ♦ Location
  - ♦ Rent or own facility?
  - ♦ Cost of renting or owning
- Advertising
  - ♦ What is your advertising strategy?
  - ♦ How effective do you expect your advertising plan to be?

♦ What mode of advertising are you using, and is it cost effective? (TV, magazines, brochures, etc.)
♦ How will your advertising help you get business?
♦ What will the frequency and timing of advertising be?
• Objectives of your business
  ♦ Short-term goals include
    - What should your sales be in the next one to three years?
    - How will these sales be achieved?
    - How will you acquire raw materials?
    - What criteria will you use when hiring your staff?
  ♦ Long-term goals include
    - Where do you want your business to be in the next ten years or more?
    - Do you anticipate growth in your market in the next period of planning?
    - If you are starting with the domestic market, when will you enter the international market?
    - Will you develop your own brand?
    - Will you add on to your production facility? If so, what are those additions going to be?

Although many aspects of a feasibility study and business plan are similar, it is important to highlight the difference between the two. A feasibility study is only conducted prior to starting a new venture and is generally for large manufacturing projects, where as a business plan can be drafted at any stage of a project.

3 | *Chapter Three*

What is Marketing?

Marketing is a process by which products and services are introduced and sold in a given market. It involves getting to know the customer's needs and fulfilling them with your products and services.

Marketing Strategy

Marketing plays a vital role in trade. Your marketing strategy must be focused around your goals. Before developing a scheme, it is important to gain first hand knowledge of the market. You must figure out how to get market share in the country you want to enter. Keep in mind that, in order to get share, you may have to forgo or reduce your margin of profit.

Your aim should be to produce quality merchandise with unique attributes. This is essential to gaining a competitive edge in the market. You should determine why customers would want to buy your product. Is it because of its quality or cost? Does it increase their prestige? Is it because of customer service? Fulfilling the customer's needs will make your product successful.

Refer to your feasibility study and business plan to develop a marketing strategy. You may also hire the services of a consulting firm to help you out.

Market Research

Before making any investments, it is very important to conduct market research on the product(s) you plan to sell. You must check the size and growth of the market and the demand for your product in the country of export. It is best to start with the one country that seems to be the best potential market. Selecting more than one target country may cause confusion and may not allow you to achieve the desired results. Traveling to the target country to conduct market research is recommended.

The following methods can be applied when conducting your research:

- Consult market survey reports
- Study trends, statistics, and other reports in your trade
- Visit and gather information in the country to which you plan to export
- Meet potential buyers in the country of export
- Visit relevant trade shows in the country of export. Take the following steps:
    - Select the right trade shows
    - Write down the objective of the show; this will help you gather information accordingly

- ◆ Trade shows are held for 3 days on an average; set a goal for each day
- ◆ Be prepared to walk for long hours
- ◆ Walk through the show efficiently in order to get the most out of every exhibit
- ◆ Stay focused
- ◆ Take notes on market information available
- ◆ Stay at the show for its entire duration
- A consulting company can also be hired to do this research for you

Ask yourself:

- Is your market price-conscious? If yes, is there a price point?
- What type of quality do your customers need?
- What type of packaging do your customers need?
- Who are your competitors in the market?
- What services and terms of sale do your competitors provide? Can you meet or beat these terms?
- What do you have to offer in order to attract the customer?

Once an exporter has acquired a good sense of the market, he/she will be able to plan a strategy to make an entry into the potential market.

Sources of Trade & Research Information

Many sources are available to help you in your market research. Some are listed below.

Export Promotion Offices

Export promotion offices, run by governments in their respective countries, provide a wealth of information for starters and existing exporters. These offices get inquiries from importers from all over the world; generally an exporter has free access to such information. See appendix 1-3A for export promotion offices of Pakistan.

Here are some examples of information and services that these offices may provide:

- Information on markets
- Trade statistics
- Market studies/surveys
- Information on the rules and regulations of the importing countries
- Quota information on apparel and textiles
- Regulation of quotas
- Procedures for export
- Information on incentives of exporting available in the respective countries
- A database of exporters
- Information on trade offices in other countries
- Trade leads
- Harmonized Tariff Schedule (see appendix 1-3L)
- Display centers for sample products from exporters
- Receive foreign trade delegations
- Send trade delegations to potential markets in other countries
- Organize and/or participate in trade shows
- Organize single country exhibitions
- Organize training seminars
- Arrange teaching programs on fashion design
- Circulate trade bulletins, apparel magazines, etc.

- Provide web pages to exporters
- Other information and services

Trade Associations and Chambers of Commerce & Industry

Trade Associations and Chambers of Commerce & Industry are recognized trade bodies. They provide similar services; both provide access to information regarding trade. However, one difference is that members of Chambers of Commerce belong to different industries and types of businesses including export, import, etc., whereas members of trade associations generally belong to the same industry. It may be more advantageous to belong to a trade association because it is more specific to your industry. See appendices 1-3B for Trade Associations in the USA, 1-3C for a Chamber of Commerce in the USA, 2-4C for Trade Associations in Pakistan, and 2-4D for Chambers of Commerce & Industry in Pakistan.

The Chambers and Trade Associations:

- Offer membership to companies
- Lobby for the industry at the government level
- Serve as a source of information
- Maintain trade libraries
- Receive trade leads
- Organize trade shows
- Receive and send trade delegations
- Serve as a platform for networking
- Are usually authorized to issue Certificates of Origin
- Circulate trade bulletins
- Act as a liaison between international trade bodies and their members

In addition, textile/garment trade associations in some countries are authorized to disburse textile quotas.

Along with holding membership, it is also advantageous to serve on the executive boards of trade bodies.

Advantages generally available to members of the Executive Board:

- Instant access to useful information; access is available to the Board Members before it is open to the regular members
- Opportunities to meet trade delegates and buyers
- Increased networking possibilities and opportunities for business growth because of increased face-to-face contact with foreign visitors/buyers and top level government officials
- Increased prominence
- Helps establish the credibility of your company
- Opportunities to participate in government trade negotiations with other countries
- Allows you to serve the business community

Trade Libraries

Chambers of Commerce, Trade Associations, and Export Promotion Agencies, usually have trade libraries that are free for everyone to use.

Trade Promotion Agencies in Europe

Exporters from developing countries who wish to export goods to a particular European country can seek assistance of such an agency in that country. These agencies can give you feedback on the market and can also put you through to potential buyers.

Some of the offices may also hold trade shows or have display centers where your samples can be displayed for buyers. See appendix 1-3D for a list of some trade promotion agencies in Europe.

American Embassies: Commercial Section

The commercial sections of American Embassies also maintain trade libraries. Although the purpose of the commercial section of these libraries is to promote export from the USA, there is no harm in visiting these libraries to find trade directories of importers and other relevant information that might be helpful. See appendix 1-3E for a web site listing US Embassies around the world.

American Centers

If there is an American Center in your country, visiting that center may be worthwhile. The trade section of the American Center may be able to provide you with helpful information.

American Chamber of Commerce in Your Country

American Chambers can be found in many countries. It is a good idea to check if there is one in your country. These Chambers of Commerce are based on membership, and their purpose is to improve trade between the two countries. Services of the American Chamber may vary from one country to another. Check out their services, and find out how they can help get you into the US Market.

Visiting the Country of Export

One of the best ways of acquiring first hand information is to visit the country you are exporting to.

Trade Shows

Relevant industry trade shows are an excellent source of information and reaching importers. See chapter 12 for more on trade shows. Also see appendix 1-12A for a list of major trade shows in the US and Europe and appendix 1-12B for other web sites on trade shows.

Seminars and Workshops on Export

Seminars and workshops are a great resource, especially for newcomers. Some are generalized, whereas others are more specialized in the topics that they cover. For instance, a specialized seminar on styling and design can help you in learning how to design and export garments. Seminars are arranged by Export Promotion Bureaus, Chambers of Commerce, trade associations, foreign embassies, banks, the United Nations (UNCTAD), etc. Information about such seminars can be obtained from relevant agencies in your country.

Banks

Banks are another source for acquiring information because they deal with the import/export business and can be helpful in relaying information on market conditions and the potential of your products. For a list of major American and Pakistani banks in Pakistan, see appendix 2-6A.

Trade Magazines on Garments

There are various magazines on fashion and garments. These are published for both consumers and the apparel industry. Magazines on apparel trade could be helpful in seeking information on fashion and color trends, etc. These trade magazines are generally promoted at apparel trade shows. See appendix 1-3F for trade magazines, trade directories, mailing lists, etc.

Web Sites on the Apparel Industry

There are hundreds of web sites on the fashion industry, and new sites are coming up almost on a daily basis. The Internet is a great tool in finding sources for anything. These web sites carry valuable information and can be of great help. See appendix 1-3G for web sites on the apparel industry.

Existing Exporters

Established exporters in your country have extensive knowledge in the field. They can be one of the best resources to get first hand information, provided they are willing to help you. Some might be reluctant since they do not want to raise another competitor, but there is no harm in trying; you might come across a person who is willing to share his knowledge with you, or at least give you some guidelines. They can also provide you with information on fashion trends, marketing options, prevailing prices, hot sellers, etc.

The Office of Textiles and Apparel (OTEXA)

The office of textiles and apparel works under the US Department of Commerce. It regulates textile imports entering the United States of America. The office has a web site with a large amount of information which is extremely useful for textile and apparel importers in the US and exporters from other countries. This source provides information on many topics including trade data, trade agreements, import quotas, etc. Visit their web site for up-to-date information. See appendix 1-3H for the Office of Textiles and Apparel and appendix 1-9C for figures and details on apparel/textile imports into the US.

The following are available through OTEXA:

- Quantity & Value TQs; lists textile and apparel import data by HTS (Harmonized Tariff Schedule) number
- Performance Report
- Trade Balance Report
- Summary of Agreements
- Import, Production, and Market Report
- Export Market Report
- The Major Shippers Report

U.S. Textile and Apparel Category System

According to the HTS, the following numbers correspond with specific textile or apparel categories:

- 200 series are of cotton and/or man-made fiber
- 300 series are of cotton
- 400 series are of wool
- 600 series are of man-made fiber
- 800 series are of silk blends or non-cotton vegetable fibers

See appendix 1-3I for a web site on the US Textile and Apparel Category System.

US Customs

The US Customs controls any cargo entering and leaving its territory. The US Customs web site serves as an excellent source of information on importing into the USA. Exporters are highly recommended to study the information on this web site in great detail, in order to gain knowledge on importation rules, regulations, and other relevant information. See appendix 1-3J for US customs information.

Topics covered on the US Customs web site include the following:

- Quota information
- Current textile status reports
- Rules and regulations regarding import and export
- Commercial importing procedures and requirements
- Trade statistics and importer data
- Foreign Trade Zones
- Generalized System of Preferences (GSP)
- ATA Carnet
- Year-end textile reports
- Month-end textile status reports
- Textile transshipment reports

World Trade Centers

World Trade Centers (WTC) are located in major cities in most countries. These centers get trade leads from different parts of the world. As services may vary from one country to another, you should check on the facilities that your local World Trade Center provides. See appendix 1-3K for a web site listing world trade centers.

In general, World Trade Centers may offer the following services:

- Trade leads
- Market research and conditions; market research for specific needs may also be available
- Advice on business culture and other trade related information on respective regions of each WTC
- Information on local products and services
- Information on government regulations
- Online services
- Profiles of companies
- Business services
  - ◆ Temporary space for display of products
  - ◆ Meeting rooms
  - ◆ Secretarial services
  - ◆ Translation services
  - ◆ Video conferencing
- Organizing trade events
- Promotes business networking
- Organizes incoming and outgoing trade missions

Other Sources of Information for Trade

- The U.S. Census Bureau
  - ◆ Provides relevant data on the economy and the people of the United States
  - ◆ Topics relevant to foreign trade include, but are not limited to the following:
    - Statistics
    - Trade data on US imports and exports
    - Rules and regulations
  - ◆ See appendix 1-9A for the Census Bureau web site

- Foreign Trade Statistics
  - ◆ See appendix 1-3L for a web site for foreign trade statistics
- Standard Industrial Codes (SIC)
  - ◆ Standard Industrial Codes are four digit numerical codes and are assigned to businesses by the US government. These codes classify all business establishments by the types of products or services they provide
  - ◆ See appendix 1-3L for the SIC web site
- The North American Industry Classification System (NAICS)
  - ◆ These numbers classify businesses or services. NAICS businesses are identified by a 6-digit code and are assigned by the US government. NAICS is replacing the U.S. Standard Industrial Classification (SIC) system
  - ◆ See appendix 1-3L for web site
- The United Nations Statistics Division
  - ◆ Provides a wide range of statistical outputs and services for producers and users of statistics worldwide
  - ◆ See appendix 1-3L for web site
- U.S. International Trade Commission Interactive Tariff and Trade Data Web
  - ◆ See appendix 1-3L for web site
- Tariff Affairs and Related Matters
  - ◆ See appendix 1-3L for web site
- Textile and Apparel Quota Embargoes
  - ◆ See appendix 1-3L for web site
- STAT-USA and the Foreign Trade Division (FTD) of the US Census Bureau produce USA TRADE(R) on line. It has monthly import and export data for over 18,000 commodities worldwide
  - ◆ See appendix 1-3L for web site

- The United States Generalized System of Preferences (GSP)
  - ♦ This provides preferential duty-free entry treatment to goods entering the US market from designated beneficiary countries. Eligible countries and items for GSP treatment are listed in the *Harmonized Tariff Schedule of the United States*
  - ♦ See appendix 1-3L for web site
- United Nations Conference on Trade and Development (UNCTAD) web site on Generalized System of Preferences (GSP)
  - ♦ Within the GSP, selected products originating in developing countries can be exported to developed countries at lower or zero tariff rates. Their web site provides all the information the exporter requires to benefit from the various GSP schemes currently in operation. See appendix 1-3L for web site address

4 | Chapter Four

Selecting the Type of Organization

In this section, I will briefly discuss the advantages and disadvantages of some of the different types of organizations. Before deciding on one, you must talk to an accountant and an attorney in your respective country.

Sole Proprietorship

This setup is good for a small startup company.

Advantages

- This is the easiest form of establishing a company
- The proprietor owns the company and is the decision-maker
- The owner keeps all the profits

- The company can be abandoned anytime with very little formalities to fulfill
- Less expensive to form
- Tax benefits may be a possibility; consult your accountant
- Less paperwork

Disadvantages

- All the liabilities of the company are the responsibility of the owner. Personal assets of the owner are at risk in case his/her company is unable to pay the creditors
- Banks might be reluctant to give out loans to this form of ownership
- Possibility of limited financial resources
- Involves high levels of commitment
- Provides few fringe benefits
- Limited ideas and growth
- The proprietor must pay all liabilities and damages if he/she loses a lawsuit
- A sole proprietorship reflects a small business operation
- Total responsibility for the company lies on the owner

Partnerships

Partnerships are formed if two or more people are interested in conducting business together. In order to protect each partner, a proper contract drafted by an attorney/lawyer must be signed and registered with the appropriate agency in your home country. Check laws regarding partnerships in your own country.

Advantages

- More than one person holds responsibility
- Slightly better image than a proprietorship
- Easy to form

- Easier to dissolve than a limited company or corporation
- Availability of finances from more than one source, i.e. the partners
- More minds and energy available to contribute to the growth of the business

Disadvantages

- Conflict between partners
- Less control over decision making
- Unlimited liability of partners
- If one partner fails to meet financial obligations of the business, the responsibility automatically falls on the other
- Division of profits among partners
- The partners must pay all liabilities and damages if they lose a lawsuit

Corporations/Private Limited Companies

A private limited company is a separate entity from its owners. Articles of Incorporation define the rules and regulations for running a corporation. All directors are to abide by the clauses listed in the said document. Shares of the company are sold to the directors, and they are entitled to gain profits according to the number of shares they hold in the company. The directors are the shareholders as well the decision-makers.

Advantages

- Limited liability for all the directors of the company. Private assets are protected due to limited liability
- Banks are more inclined to extend loans to such establishments

- Because corporations/private limited companies are considered to be more sound and stable, this builds up the image of the company.
- The company does not shut down if one or more directors leave
- More financial resources

Disadvantages

- Difficult and cumbersome to dissolve
- Maintenance of accounts is comparatively complex
- More documentation is required
- Comparatively more expensive to form
- Tax rate may be higher
- Conflict among directors

Selecting a Name for Your Company

It is important that the name you select for your company looks and sounds professional. It is the first impression of your company, and it creates an impact on others' minds.

Characteristics of a Company Name

- Short and crisp
- Sounds good
- Easily readable and pronounceable
- Not offensive to any community
- Reflects professionalism

Factors Helpful in Determining the Name of Your Company

Make sure that the name is not used by anyone else.

Consider the following before choosing a name:

- Are you going to be a manufacturing company, a trading company, or a manufacturer's representative?
- Do you want your company name to reflect the type of business you are in? For example:
  ◆ ABC Garment Manufacturing, Inc
  ◆ ABC Garment Industries, Inc
  ◆ ABC Apparel Manufacturers, Inc
- Do you want your company name to be more generalized? For example:
  ◆ ABC Trading Limited
  ◆ ABC Manufacturers' Representatives
  ◆ ABC International Inc.
  ◆ ABC Export Management Company

Selecting Your Company Logo

A logo is not essential, but it is good to have one. Your logo should look professional and should reflect the type of business you are in. It should not be too flashy or gaudy. A nice logo design will make your company look more professional and will create recognition of your company in the minds of the general public.

If you do not want your company names and logos to be used by anyone else in the USA, you must get them registered. See appendix 1-4A for copyright and trademark related web sites.

Selecting a Brand Name / Trademark

It may not be a bad idea to develop your own brand name or trademark. Many American and European businesspeople have been very successful in creating their own brands. These companies are globally known because they have built up their brand names in footwear, apparel, food, and other industries. Many American and European apparel brands are produced in Asian countries and/or developing countries across the world and are sold in the USA and elsewhere. For example, Levi's Jeans and Nike shoes are well known and worn with pride all over the world. It is surprising that many producers in developing countries have been unable to create comparable names. Many manufacturers and exporters do not realize the importance of building their own brands. Keeping in view the value of a name, it may be a good idea to create your own. Although establishing a name is very tough, it can be done. See appendix 1-4A for the International Trademark Association.

Professional companies in the US can help with the creation of a name. See appendix 1-4B for a company that can help in selecting a brand name or trademark.

You should create your own brand if:

- You can produce and maintain quality
- You can back up your quality
- Your product has a warranty
- Your product is well designed
- Your product is innovative and new, and not a copy of another product
- Your product caters and appeals to a specific group of people
- You can invest heavily in an advertising campaign

Advantages

- Name recognition
- Growth of your business
- Loyal customers

In order to protect your brand name or trademark, you must register it with the appropriate authorities in your own country, or in any other country where you plan to sell your products. However, keep in mind that this could be very expensive. In the US, patent attorneys and agents may be used to register your trademark with the US Patent and Trademark Office. See appendix 1-4A for the US Copyright Office web site and appendix 1-4B for a company that provides trademark services.

5 | *Chapter Five*

Setting Up Your Office

A business, whether operated from home or an office, requires basic furniture and equipment to operate efficiently. It is important to note that the appearance of your office does make an impression on any visitor. Keeping this in mind, try to maintain as nice an office as you can, without overextending your budget. The items you will need are listed below.

*Essential Equipment**

- Tables and chairs
- Filing cabinets
- Computer and Printer
- Fastest Internet connection
- Cordless Telephones
- Fax machine
- Separate lines for phone and fax machine

- Calculators
- Book case or a storage shelf
- Office supplies
- Intercoms or a phone system for internal communication

Other Recommended Equipment*

- Photo copying machine
- Scanner
- Digital camera
- Video conferencing facility
- Laptop Computer
- Digital Planner
- Cellular/mobile phone
- Message recorder for leaving messages for the secretary
- Heated/air-conditioned environment

*Expensive equipment may also be leased.

The Internet and Your Web Site

The ways of doing business are changing very fast with the introduction of the Internet. Having a web site on the Internet is becoming indispensable. Clients require prompt information, and this medium is the fastest and most economical way of showing clients what your company has to offer.

Thus, it is important that you have the following:

- A company web site on the Internet
- Company e-mail addresses
- Some type of an instant message program on your computer, which will enable you to communicate instantly with anyone across the world

Many people think that getting on the Internet is all they need in order to do business all over the world. This is true to the extent that clients from anywhere in the world can access your web site, provided that they know the URL. Whether any other potential customer can find your web site, is another question.

Therefore, a company needs to promote its web site in the following ways:

- Include your web site address on all business stationery
- Promote the site on the Internet. For example, get it registered on different search engines and advertise it on other relevant web sites
- Advertise your web site in the media relevant to your business
- Make sure that your web site is on a fast server. If downloading time is too slow, the visitor/buyer will be frustrated and will not waste his/her time browsing your site
- Ensure that your web site is well designed for browsing and downloading

There is a common misconception regarding the number of hits on a web site. A larger number of hits do not necessarily mean greater results for the company. Remember that a site is only good if it is visited by relevant viewers.

Many companies offer web listings, web pages, and banner advertising. See appendix 1-5 for information on a USA based company which offers banner advertising, standard web pages, and listings at highly competitive prices.

Stationery

A company must have excellent stationery and well designed brochures, as these create the first impression. Poorly designed stationery and brochures may immediately discourage a buyer from even looking at them. Get your brochure made by an experienced designer. Professional looking stationery and advertising materials will create a better image of your company. Do not print gaudy or flashy stationery.

Company stationery should include the following:

- Company letterhead, preferably with the company logo
- Matching envelopes
- Matching business cards
- Invoice
- Packing list (see glossary for more information)
- Self-adhesive labels with your company name and address for large envelopes/packets
- Brochure of the company products

Your Workplace

You must first assess how much you are able to invest. Then determine whether your company is to be a trading house or a manufacturing facility. Start with a small decent office, not going over your budget. Then build up your office as you build up your company. The more elegant the office and the set up, the better the image of your company.

A nicely done and well-organized office should include:

- Well lit, clean, and pleasant environment
- Reception and waiting area
- Executive and staff offices with easy accessibility among staff members
- Conference room with a sample display area where buyers can view samples
- A good communication system within the office
- Space for office growth
- Easy access to the office for staff and visitors
- Clean restroom/toilets
- Parking
- Practical set up

An Office at a Trading Center

If circumstances permit, it is better to have an office at or near an established trading center. If there is a trading center available specifically for the apparel/textile industry in your country, then this is the place where you should be situated. An office at a trading center has advantages and disadvantages.

Advantages

- Trading centers are places where buyers and sellers meet
- This increases the opportunities to expand your business
- Allows you to stay up to date with market conditions
- More networking opportunities

Disadvantages

- More expensive to rent or buy
- You may have to pay goodwill to acquire an office

- You may have to compromise on the size of the space due to a higher price/rent
- Commuting during rush hours could be a problem
- Parking problems
- Busy trading centers are generally congested

Home Based Business

An export business can also be started from your home. This has its advantages and disadvantages.

Advantages

- Less expensive to start your business. In the USA and other parts of the world there are millions of successful home-based businesses
- No goodwill fees
- Convenience of working out of your home
- Flexibility; you can set your own working hours
- Relaxed atmosphere
- Less formal attire can be worn, unless you need to meet someone
- Some tax deductions are possible
- You can stay in touch with your clients despite time zone differences, i.e. you can exchange messages even after working hours
- Less loss in case business fails
- No commuting to your office

Disadvantages

- Less interaction with the market
- Less networking opportunities
- Strong disciplinary habits are required in order to operate efficiently

- Professional staff is generally reluctant to work for a home based business
- Does not reflect a positive image of the company, as such people may not have confidence in your company and you may lose some business
- Distractions in the house can make it hard to operate your business
- Office may be less efficient due to limited availability of space
- You may disturb your family life if you do not work fixed hours
- Business visitors feel uncomfortable visiting home offices
- Visits of friends or family members during working hours can disturb your business schedule
- Home life may not provide the environment you need to conduct proper business
- Local laws may prevent you from conducting a home based business

If you decide to work from your home, ensure the following:

- Allocate a separate room(s) for your office
- The office should be away from noise of children, the TV, etc., in case of phone calls and client visits
- If possible, there should be a separate entrance to the office from the outside
- Telephone and fax lines should be separate from home lines
- Set-up must look professional

Production Unit / Manufacturing Facility

In the case of a production facility, it is best to have your office and production facility at an industrial center because the basic infrastructure for setting up production units is readily available.

If you decide to set up your own production unit, ensure the following:

- Easy access to raw materials
- A good transport system
- A good communication system
- Availability of space with the option to expand

The production area should include:

- An office
- A processing and production area
- An inspection room for ready goods
- A warehouse for raw materials and ready goods
- An area for breaks and refreshments
- Clean restrooms

The layout of the production unit should be such that the production manager and supervisors are in position to monitor the quality of production.

Hiring the Right People

Hiring the right people is crucial to your business. Employees with the right mindset and abilities will greatly contribute to the success of your company.

You must look for the following in potential employees:

- Qualifications
- Knowledge and experience

- Motivation and desire
- Devotion and loyalty
- Polite and courteous manner
- Ability to work well with others
- A responsible and dependable person
- A hard worker
- A pleasant personality

Keeping Your Staff Happy

It is important to remember that employees must be kept happy or they will not perform to the best of their abilities. Make sure that employees know what their duties are and what is expected of them. The management should keep in touch with the employees to make them feel comfortable and ensure their happiness. If an employee seems unhappy, try to solve the problem as soon as possible. A satisfied employee will be a more productive one. If employees are not happy with any aspect of their job, they may seek a job with your competitor instead.

To keep your staff happy, you must ensure the following:

- A clean and safe work environment
- A fair number of working hours
- Equal opportunity and fair treatment for all employees
- A competitive salary, raises, bonuses, and promotions
- Performance rewards and incentives
- Holidays, sick leaves, and vacation time
- Opportunities for growth
- A good retirement plan
- A good training program
- A sense of respect for the workers
- A sense of team spirit among everyone, management and production

- A sense of job security
- Easy access to bosses (open door policy)
- A light hearted atmosphere that makes employees feel comfortable and taken care of
- Parties, picnics, and social gatherings for employees

Professional Services for Your Business

Eventually, you will need the services of an accountant, unless you are qualified enough to handle company accounts yourself. Try to work with someone who is familiar with the accounts of exporters and is also aware of the tax incentives and/or other benefits offered by the government. Be sure to maintain proper account records of your business for your use and for income tax purposes. Otherwise, you may have difficulty remembering every transaction, and may face a problem especially when filing tax returns. Maintaining proper and up to date records will also enable you to stay abreast of your business's progress.

6 | Chapter Six

Types of Banks

Commercial Banks

Importers, exporters, traders, manufacturers, and other business people most commonly use these types of banks. The banks must adhere to the policies set by the federal/central bank. These banks finance businesses of all types and sizes. Most of the major commercial banks in any country are capable of conducting any type of international transaction. Commercial banks that are involved in international transactions are always eager to work with importers and exporters because their transactions help the banks make money.

Some of the functions that commercial banks perform are as follows:

- Maintain currency accounts
- Provide loans and overdrafts
- Exchange currency
- Transfer funds
- Issue and receive Letters of Credit and other types of documents
- Provide trade information

Investment Banks

Investment banks finance projects ranging from small to large scale, depending upon the policy of each bank. These banks do not perform the regular functions of a commercial bank. Investment banks finance manufacturing projects, not trading operations. They perform many different types of functions such as arranging mergers, joint ventures, and acquisitions, financing projects, etc.

Development Banks

These banks are usually involved in bigger projects, which require large investments.

Opening a Bank Account

A company can open different types of accounts, such as a checking account (current account) or a savings account. Each bank has its own policy for opening and maintaining accounts. It is advised that you check the terms and conditions in your respective country.

Why Do You Need a Bank?

- To open a business account; business cannot be conducted through personal accounts
- To deposit and withdraw cash
- To send and receive payments
- To obtain a loan
- To open Letters of Credit (see Chapter 18)
- To collect payments for shipments against D/A and/or D/P (see Chapter 18)

Choosing a Bank

An account should be opened with a bank capable of handling international transactions, such as Letters of Credit, remittance of currency, and other international dealings (See Chapter 18 for more details on modes of payment). Some banks entertain small businesses, whereas others are interested only in corporate or large clients. If you find that a bank is not too interested in your account because your business is too small, it is a good idea not to open an account with that institution.

Try to build a good relationship with your bank because you will need its help at every stage of development. Some banks in Pakistan are listed in appendix 2-6A.

Before opening an account, be sure that the bank:

- Is willing to work with you
- Has experience in handling Letters of Credit, collection documents, transferring international payments, etc.
- Has experience in international trade related matters
- Has reasonable fees for handling transactions
- Offers easily approachable decision-makers

7 | *Chapter Seven*

Sources of Financing

A minimum investment is required for running any kind of business. The amount varies depending upon the type of project you wish to undertake. Less investment is needed if you are opening a trading company. I will discuss different sources available for financing your business later in this chapter.

Investment is needed for the following:

- Machinery and equipment
- Office and/or factory expenses
- Traveling expenses
- Salaries
- Business insurance
- Owning or renting property
- Trade Promotion Expenses
- Miscellaneous

In terms of a production facility, it is recommended that you acquire the most up to date equipment. Machinery and equipment can be leased if such a facility is available in your country. There are advantages and disadvantages of leasing. The biggest advantage is that leasing allows you to make a lower investment and the amount is generally tax-deductible. The disadvantage is that you do not own the machinery or equipment.

If finances are limited, purchasing a closed down factory or used equipment is another option. If you choose to do this, make sure that the factory and equipment are not obsolete and in excellent shape.

Financing Your Business

It can take time to establish an export business, due to factors such as long distance and cultural differences. Each situation is different and there are no set rules, however, proper planning and financing play a vital role in the success of any business.

Before starting a business, check out the financial resources available to you. Assuming that you use your resources wisely, have the proper expertise, and possess the qualities of being a good entrepreneur, you will have better chances of success. Some methods of financing are listed below.

Personal Resources

If you are new to business, banks may be reluctant to lend money to you because you lack the credibility of running a business. In this case, financing generally comes from one's savings or from family and friends.

Commercial Bank Loans

Financial support from a bank is very important for any business. In the beginning, getting financial support is very tough. Banks only invest in viable projects. They are reluctant to help finance new businesses because there is no previous record, and they are unaware of a new company's capabilities. However, there is no harm in discussing one's plan with a bank manager from the start. After some time, if you are able to show the bank some progress, then there is a bright chance that the bank will come forward to help you.

A bank will not grant a loan unless you prove that your business is profitable, and that you need assistance from the bank in order to grow. Before granting a loan, banks need to be certain that they will receive their money back. Banks always require adequate collateral, such as property, to secure a loan. They also look at the experience and management qualities of the owners/directors and the equity of investors in the business. Banks also look for detailed business plans. See appendix 2-6A for a list of banks in Pakistan.

In order to review your application for a loan, banks usually require that you submit the following documents:

- Cover letter
- Application with the amount of loan
- Business plan
- Documents of collateral
- Financial statements of your company
  - ◆ Balance sheet
  - ◆ Profit and loss statement/income statement
  - ◆ Cash flow statement
  - ◆ Bank statement

♦ In case of an existing business, financial and bank statements for the last three years

Banks may also require more documents, other than the ones mentioned above.

If a bank decides to grant you a loan, it is better to ask for a line of credit rather than a case-to-case basis loan. This will allow you to borrow funds from the bank as you need them, provided you do not exceed the limit set by the line of credit. Once you pay off your loan, the same amount will be available to you again. Case-to-case loans are a hassle, as you will have to submit new paperwork every time you need funds.

Pre-Shipment and Post-Shipment Loans for Export

Banks grant pre-shipment loans to cover, fully or partially, the costs that you need to produce goods for export. This loan is generally granted if an exporter already has an order. Banks grant post-shipment loans after you have shipped your goods and are awaiting payment from the buyer.

Generally, both loans have easy terms and low rates of interest. Both loans are generally settled against the payments received from the buyer. Terms may depend on how comfortable the bank feels with the exporter. Terms and conditions of such loans may differ among different banks or countries.

Discounting the Letter of Credit (L/C)

A bank can discount the L/C and give you a partial or full payment against it. If, for example, you have a credit L/C according to which you will be paid after 60 days, but you need the money right away, you can request your bank to pay you in advance after discounting the L/C. If the bank agrees, it would discount the L/C and pay you a lower amount than the face value. The rate can vary from bank to bank. A bank is not obligated to provide this facility.

Credit From Suppliers

If you have a good relationship with your suppliers, then they may help you by supplying you with goods on credit. However, this does not mean that you will no longer require financial assistance from any other source. For instance, if you offer credit terms to your clients, and if your client pays you after the credit period offered to you by your supplier is over, then it is understood that you will have to pay your supplier from your own sources. If you delay your payments to your supplier, you will lose credibility. You will have to make cash flow charts in order to ensure that your cash does not fall short at any given time.

Advance Payment from the Importer

This is the best, though not the easiest, way of financing your exports. Under this arrangement, the buyer will send you the payment under agreed terms and conditions, and you, the exporter, are required to make the delivery accordingly. However, getting an advance payment from a buyer is not easy. First, it is costly for the buyer to make a payment in advance. Second, the buyer may not trust you if he/she has not done business with you in the past. Relying on this type of financing is unrealistic, unless the buyer knows you, or if he/she is desperate to buy from you.

Joint Venture Partnerships

Joint venture partnerships with foreign importers or investors can help you finance your business. You and your partner must decide how much each person will invest. This mode of raising finances is also helpful to the economy of your country, as the foreign joint venture partner brings in investment in foreign currency.

Finance Companies / Venture Capital Firms

Private finance companies and venture capital firms may be willing to invest in your business by granting loans, investing in shares, etc. They maintain equity in the business and share your company's profits according to the agreed terms. These firms generally do not invest in start-up companies, but there is no harm in looking into this possibility. Check with the specific firm for terms and details.

Factoring Firms

According to this type of financing, the exporter transfers the title of foreign receivables to a factoring establishment, and gets cash minus a percentage of the face value of the receivables. For example, if your receivables are worth a $100, you may approach a factoring company, which will give you cash in the amount of the receivables after discounting the face value. The factoring company might give you 90% or $90 in cash and then collect the receivables of $100. This arrangement can only be made after the shipment has been sent. Note: the above percentage (90%) is only an example; percentages charged by factoring companies could vary.

In the case that the proceeds are not received from the foreign buyer, the exporter may be required to pay to the factoring firm. Some factoring firms may charge a higher fee if the risk of non-payment has to be borne by them. Check with the specific company for terms and details.

8 | Chapter Eight

Types of Businesses

The following are the most common types of businesses:

Manufacturing Company

It may be better for you to have your own manufacturing facility.

Advantages

- You will have control over production
- Having your own manufacturing facility can help you in making timely deliveries
- You will be able to maintain quality
- Buyers have more confidence dealing with the manufacturers directly

- You will be more confident in regards to what you are selling and the terms you are offering
- You will be self-reliant and have more confidence
- You have more control in planning the future of your business
- Your expertise of production will enable you to engage proper sub-contractors, if you need them

Disadvantages

- You will have to concentrate on marketing as well as manufacturing
- You will have to tackle any labor problems
- Requires more investment
- Closing down is difficult and cumbersome
- More money may be lost if the business does not work
- You have to maintain the equipment and machinery
- Machinery needs to be updated
- It takes more time to set up than any other type of company

Trading Company

You can set up a trading company in order to export products to other markets around the globe. The company buys the product on its own account and then re-sells it. There are various advantages and disadvantages of setting up a trading company or an export house; these are discussed below.

Advantages

- You can run a trading company with less investment
- You can go to different manufacturers to get the goods made; hence you will have more sources to accommodate your orders, and you can provide a wider range of products

- It allows you to concentrate on marketing
- You do not have to deal with labor problems
- You may be able to get the goods on credit from the manufacturers
- Closing down is easier and less money may be lost

Disadvantages

- Buyers always prefer to work with manufacturers, so that they can eliminate the trader's profit
- You do not have control over production
- Manufacturers may delay your deliveries, if they have to give priority to their own work
- Some manufacturers may even deliver inferior quality products in order to make more profit
- Manufacturers may not be very cooperative when asked to fulfill any extra requirements that your buyers may have
- Manufacturers may not understand the needs of your buyer due to a lack of direct contact with the buyer
- Manufacturers generally pay more attention to their regular and larger clients verses new and unsteady clients
- Some manufacturers try to reach your buyers through the back door, so to speak, and hence you can lose your clients
- If you do not understand the product, the manufacturer can sell sub-standard products to you

Agency

An agent may represent one or more manufacturers on an exclusive or non-exclusive basis. Under this arrangement, the manufacturer supplies you with samples, catalogs, and other informative materials about the product; then you contact buyers and sell the products for the manufacturer.

An agent works on a commission basis. The commission can range from 5% to 20% depending upon various factors, which are discussed between the manufacturer and the agent. This type of business requires a minimal amount of investment on the agent's part, as he/she does not have to buy the merchandise on his/her own account. Yet it still has the most of the same advantages as that of a trading company.

Before representing a manufacturer, it is highly recommended that you sign an agreement with the manufacturer specifying all terms regarding your services and the manufacturer's expectations and responsibilities. It is also recommended that you check the reputation and the credibility of the manufacturer. If he/she is not trustworthy or responsible you may lose your customer, and your time and energy will be wasted.

Advantages

- You can represent different companies at the same time
- You can have exclusive selling rights on behalf of a manufacturer
- Your only investment is time and the expenses related to selling or marketing
- The manufacturers generally supply the catalogs and samples for free
- You can work out of a small office, including a home office
- Closing down is easier and less money may be lost

Disadvantages

- Buyers prefer to work with manufacturers, so that they can eliminate commission agents or sales representatives
- The manufacturer may not be very prompt on paying commission or may deny it altogether

- The manufacturer may try to directly approach the buyer that you have found, so as to eliminate you from the picture

Manufacturers use agents if:

- They lack marketing expertise
- They do not have time to devote to develop a market
- They cannot afford employees for marketing purposes
- Their company is too small and cannot afford to establish a separate department for international sales
- They do not feel comfortable dealing with the foreign buyers directly, due to a language or cultural barrier

Importers use agents if:

- They do not have the expertise or the time for finding items for import
- They feel that your services are indispensable
- They have difficulty in quality control
- They sell many different lines
- They feel that you can negotiate better deals for them
- They face a language or cultural barrier

9 | *Chapter Nine*

A Look at the American Apparel Market

The American apparel market is one of the largest markets in the world. It caters for all types of clothing, ranging from the low to the high end. In 1995, US garment imports came from 168 countries around the world. The US imports of apparel grew in current dollars by 171% between 1985 and 1995 reaching nearly US$34.7 billion. In 1999 approximately 46 billion worth of apparel at US wholesale value was imported into the country.

The US has a market for various types of clothing, including attire for winter and summer, with styles ranging from Western to ethnic. The daily attire is Western style and comprises of suits, slacks, jackets, skirts, blouses, shirts, coats, overcoats, T-shirts, shorts, sportswear, etc. Ethnic apparel includes traditional clothing from different cultures. As a result of the different weather patterns across the US, companies import a variety of clothing including those made of light and heavy materials. The market share for each kind of clothing varies depending upon the size of a specific population.

In some cases, American companies import and then re-export apparel to Canada. The large US companies have a huge amount of buying power; they can get better prices from the sellers, and hence, can export to Canada at better prices.

US companies are also producers of clothing and textile made-ups. In 1999, domestic apparel production at whole sale level was US$41 billion. In conjunction with other countries, the US produced US$15 billion in apparel in the same year. Clothing manufactured in the US includes, but is not limited to, blouses, pants, suits, sporting wear, formal and informal wear, bridal wear, tuxedos, lingerie, sweaters, T-shirts, hosiery, knitted, and woven garments. The textile sector produces carpets, rugs, fibers, yarns, towels, fabrics, bed linens, etc.

The textile and apparel industry is the largest US industrial employer with approximately 9% of the US manufacturing workforce. In 1994, this industry employed approximately 1.6 million workers. However, the industry does face problems with growing competition and cheap labor in other countries.

Production of apparel and textiles in the US does not mean that the market for exporters to the US is small. American goods tend to be towards the high-end, which cannot compete with low-end products from developing countries. Furthermore, the US produces many products that are less labor-intensive, which cannot compete against labor-intensive merchandise from other countries, for example machine embroidered vs. hand embroidered goods. American wages are very high in comparison to those in developing countries, and American apparel is generally more expensive than America's imports. Thus, US manufacturers find it hard to compete with cheaper products coming from overseas. In order to provide protection to the industry, apparel and textile imports are subject to quota limitations in the US.

Despite the quota restrictions, there is great potential in the American market. In 1997, total spending on clothing and accessories by people in the US was US $237.90 billion. In the same year, the gross domestic product (GDP) in manufacturing of apparel and textile products was US $28.20 billion.

For more statistical data, visit the web site of the US Census Bureau. See appendix 1-9A for the web site address.

Note: it is important to highlight the fact that information systems in the US are advanced and extensive, hence access to information is easily and readily available.

It is also important to realize that apparel has its own advantages. It is not a high-tech industry, and hence the training of labor is not as demanding as in some other fields, and less involvement of capital may be required.

Sizes of Companies in the USA

Small Companies

Small companies do not have a complex decision-making process. Generally, the president of the company is involved in negotiations and usually acts as the decision-maker. Their policies can also be more flexible than those of larger corporations.

Mid-Size Companies

These companies have few or no departments, and reaching the buyer is comparatively easier than in larger corporations. The decision making process is relatively quicker than that of multi-nationals. In these types of corporations, the president may or may not be directly involved in the negotiations.

Large Companies

As in any other country, the larger companies distribute authority to different departments and individuals at different levels. This ensures a smoother operation.

Sometimes, it is hard to find the right person in a large company. It can be hard to meet or even to find a buyer, as they all are extremely busy. These organizations consist of many layers and as a result, decision making can be very time consuming. The chairman or president generally does not interfere with individuals given the authority to make decisions.

Price Mark-up by US Companies

The mark-up of importers varies, depending on whether they are selling to retailers, wholesalers, or volume buyers. In the US, the common mark-up by retailers is 100% of the US wholesale price. However, mark-ups of big retail chain stores can range from 100% to higher, depending on whether the goods are acquired from domestic or overseas sources, and the demand for the product. Companies mark-up the price keeping in view their marketing strategy and expenses.

Apparel Sizes

American sizes are not the same as in other countries. Since the population in the US is large in number and encompasses people from all different backgrounds, all types of sizes have a market in the country. Sizes range from petite to big and tall. The US does not work under the metric system; all sizes are in inches. Checking sizes is important in order to work out your cost. American apparel size charts are in appendix 1-9B.

Market for Big and Tall Sizes

These sizes are above average sizes in apparel. In the US, there is a special market for big and tall sizes. There are also special retailers who cater for this market and buy products from those importers or wholesalers/distributors who carry such sizes.

Return Policies

In the USA, end consumers can return defective merchandise even after it has been washed. The retailers then return defective merchandise to the seller. In this case an importer might ask for compensation from the exporter for all returned goods.

Sales Tax

In the US, many states have a tax on the sale of apparels, etc. The sales tax may not be applicable in all states and the rate may vary from state to state or area to area. For example, sales tax is higher in New York City than in many other parts of the state. When retailers in the US advertise products and prices, sales tax may not be included in these prices. The consumer pays this tax on top of the retail price. For example, if the wholesale price of jeans is US $10 per piece, the common markup by a retailer will price the jeans at US $20 per piece. If the sales tax is 8%, the consumer ends up paying US $21.60 per piece.

American Garment Import Policies and Data

The Office of Textiles and Apparel of the US Department of Commerce regulates import policy on garments. I highly recommend visiting their web site as it provides some extremely useful information for exporters and importers of textiles and apparel. See appendix 1-3H for the Office of Textiles and Apparel.

Specific figures and details on apparel and textile imports into the US are available on the web sites listed in appendix 1-9C.

10 | Chapter Ten

Information You Will Need on Apparel Export

You will need various types of information for exporting apparel. Staying up to date is crucial to the success of your business. Below are the types of information you will need and the sources to find them.

- Types of goods. Find out what types of goods are already being exported to the US in order to determine what types of goods you are capable of exporting. Sources of information:
  - ◆ Other exporters
  - ◆ Apparel trade shows in your home country and in the USA (see Chapter 12 for more on trade shows)
- Textile quotas. Find out if the items you wish to export fall under a textile quota category. Some apparel items might fall under a non-quota category. Sources of information:

- ◆ Export promotion agencies, apparel trade associations, US Customs web site
- ◆ Harmonized Tariff Schedule (see appendix 1-3L)
- Your competitors' prices. Find out what your competitors' prices are, in order to prepare a competitive price list. Sources of information:
  - ◆ Trade shows in your home country and in the USA
  - ◆ Other exporters
- Fashion trends and colors. Sources of information:
  - ◆ Trade shows in your home country and in the USA
  - ◆ Forecasting books on designs and colors
  - ◆ US Forecasting services for designing and colors. See appendix 1-10A for forecasting services
- Quality in demand. Find out whether the quality of stitching, fabric, and the overall look of the garment are competitive with that of other sellers. Sources of information:
  - ◆ Trade shows
  - ◆ Department stores in the US or country of export
  - ◆ Buyers
  - ◆ Other exporters
- Wholesale and retail prices. Understanding the pricing structure in the US is important to figuring out your strategy for fixing prices. Sources of information:
  - ◆ Wholesale prices can be obtained from apparel exhibitors at trade shows. Be sure to get price sheets from importers only
  - ◆ Discuss your prices with potential customers, their feedback is of great importance
- Mark-up of importers. Find out the mark-up of importers; this can help you quote prices accordingly. Because of the overheads, mark-ups in the US are higher. Sources of information:
  - ◆ Importers
  - ◆ See appendix 1-3B for Trade Associations in the US

- Labeling requirements. Labeling is important for entry into the US as well as for the end consumer. Sources of information:
  - ◆ Labeling requirements can be checked with your buyer
  - ◆ See appendix 1-10B for web sites on labeling requirements
- Packaging requirements. Sources of information:
  - ◆ The buyer/importer. Every buyer/importer has his/her own requirements for packaging
- Importer's channel of distribution. Every importer may have his/her own channel of distribution. Some sell only to wholesalers, while others sell directly to retailers or through agents. Some only cater to mass merchandisers and others sell only to upscale stores. Sources of information:
  - ◆ Ask your buyer/importer about his channel of distribution
- Catalog design. Get ideas on how to design your catalog/brochure. Sources of information:
  - ◆ See competitors catalogs or ask an experienced designer
- Duties. Find out what the duties on your products are. Sources of information:
  - ◆ US custom brokers, export promotion offices, or trade associations
- Mark-up of Retailers (see Chapter 9)
- The Entry Procedure into the USA (see Chapter 17)

Export of Value Added Products

High value added products are those items that require more work and transformation than basic products. Examples of high value added products include jackets, fashion dresses, and beaded and embroidered items. Examples of basic products include yarn and gray sheeting (unfinished cloth). Value added items give your company an edge over many other companies who cannot produce such goods. Furthermore, these products can be sold for higher prices. Basic goods are always more competitive than value added items, and thus leave less money in your pocket. Hence, it is recommended that you work on manufacturing and exporting high value added items.

In order to produce high value items, good quality equipment and materials are needed; for instance special attachments for sewing machines may be needed to produce more difficult designs. If high quality materials are not available in your country, consider importing them. For example, if there is demand for ski jackets, and waterproof material is not available in your country, you could import the fabric/material to make the ski jackets, and then export them to the appropriate market.

Customs provide bonded warehouse facilities to traders who may want to store merchandise for re-export or for temporary storage, without paying any duties. Check policies with Customs in your country. See Chapter 19 for more details on a customs bonded warehouse.

Pricing Your Products

Prices must be carefully calculated, otherwise, the entire exercise of getting orders will fail. You must counter check your prices with the prevailing prices in the market of export. If you sell in the domestic market, make sure expenses pertaining to domestic selling are not included in the export price. If you do not sell locally, you must account for all the expenses related to the manufacturing and selling of products plus profit. When calculating prices, you must take into account materials, manufacturing/labor, packaging, freight, insurance, other variables, such as company overheads, trade show expenses, international advertising, travel, commission, etc. Marginal cost pricing is recommended. Your prices should not be too high or too low.

11 | Chapter Eleven

Finding Buyers

There are many ways of finding buyers. When trying to find buyers, it is advised that you start with one country at a time.

Exhibit in Trade Shows

One of the best ways of finding buyers is to exhibit in trade shows that are most relevant to your products. Visitors including volume buyers, agents, importers, wholesalers, distributors, and sales representatives exhibit at, and attend these shows. If your products, prices, and deliveries are feasible, you can get an order at the show or at least get some contacts to follow up. I will discuss trade shows in more detail in Chapter 12.

Garments are imported in large quantities from parts of Asia, including main China, Hong Kong, and other countries in the region. It is a good idea to check out possibilities of exhibiting in garment trade shows in main China or Hong Kong. These shows will enable you to reach high volume buyers from the USA and other countries. However, it is always better to check the number of visitors from each country with the organizers of the show, so that you are in a better position to decide which show you want to exhibit in. See appendix 1-12A for a list of trade shows in the US and other countries.

Business/Trade Directories

Trade directories can be a helpful resource in finding suitable buyers. In the US, there are highly professional trade directories available. Trade directories can be found in the libraries of export promotion agencies, trade associations, Chambers of Commerce and Industry, the commercial section of US embassies, and world trade centers. You can get directories on importers, wholesalers, distributors, agents, and small or large retail chain stores in the USA. Contact World Trade Venue(sm) in appendix 1-5 for more information.

Import/Export Reporting Services

Such companies in the US collect information from US Customs on all imports and exports to and from the USA. They then compile the data and sell it. You may also request data on specific industries, such as apparel. Some of these companies have web sites on the Internet. Contact World Trade Venue(sm) in appendix 1-5 for more information.

Mailing Lists

Companies in the USA sell mailing lists, which contain information on businesses in your field. In general, these lists consist of a company name, address, phone, fax, type of product, and type of company, i.e. importer, distributor, exporter, etc. Custom designed lists are generally available upon request. Contact World Trade Venue(sm) in appendix 1-5 for more information.

If you need assistance in the USA, contact the following company for help:

Some of the services World Trade Venue (WTV) can provide:

- Internet Advertising
- Trade directories of US Companies
- Mailing lists of US companies
- Liaison office in the USA
- Fashion forecasting and color information for the US market
- Credit report on US companies
- Internet advertising
- Any other service you may require

Contact them for more up-to-date information. Their contact address is in appendix 1-5.

Yellow Pages in the Country of Export

Yellow pages in the country of export are another source of finding buyers.

Exhibitors' Directory

Trade show organizers compile these directories for the benefit of the exhibitors and attendees at the show. This is one of the best sources of reaching target buyers because each directory lists exhibitors that might be relevant to your trade. The prices of these directories are generally lower than regular trade directories. See appendix 1-12A for trade shows in the US and elsewhere. Contact the organizers of these shows for purchasing exhibitors directories. In case of problems, contact World Trade Venue (see appendix 1-5).

Apparel Centers

There are many apparel centers in the USA where importers, distributors, manufacturers, and wholesalers have show rooms and conduct business. The visitors to these centers are retailers/ buyers looking to make purchases from the companies at the center. These centers have permanent/temporary show rooms for importers/distributors/wholesalers. Most of the centers also organize trade shows on an annual or semi-annual basis. The temporary show rooms are usually open during the trade show period.

The centers publish directories that list all the offices contained in the center. If you are visiting the US, it is a good idea to go to some of these centers. Prior to your visit, you should obtain the center's directory and make appointments with relevant companies. Entry into these centers is restricted to the business community only and proper identification is needed upon entrance. If for some reason you cannot make an appointment ahead of time, then a business card, proof of visitation from overseas, and any other necessary proof may be required for entry. Contact the relevant center for requirements of entry, as they may vary from one center to another.

Fashion Center (Garment District) in New York

Fashion Center, located in Manhattan in New York City, is one of the most renowned apparel and textile centers in the world. All types of businesspeople including importers, exporters, distributors, manufacturers, wholesalers, fashion designers, agents, trading companies, fashion color and forecasting companies, pattern makers, fashion book sellers, etc. have their offices here. The garment district is comprised of approximately 34 million square feet and extends from the 5th to 9th Avenues and 35th to 41st streets. See appendix 1-11A for a list of apparel centers in the US.

Export Promotion Agencies in Your Country

Trade leads are received by export promotion agencies from all over the world on a daily basis. These agencies publish trade bulletins that carry information on foreign inquiries. The agencies can be of great help in locating importers. Many of these agencies also maintain trade libraries and web sites on the Internet. Trade delegations visit these agencies in order to find suitable exporters. See appendix 1-3A for the Export Promotion Bureau address in Pakistan.

Trade Associations

A Trade Association is a good place to find information. These associations receive trade delegations from foreign countries and inquiries from importers. Such organizations hold trade shows and publish trade bulletins for circulation. Some associations offer free publications which list buying and selling trade offers. Although these associations charge a small fee, it is worth becoming a member. See appendix 1-3B and appendix 2-4C for a list of Trade Associations in the US and Pakistan, respectively.

Chambers of Commerce & Industry

This is another important trade body for the business community. Becoming a member of a Chamber of Commerce & Industry can be helpful in finding buyers and information on trade. It is also a place where importers send their inquiries.

Trade delegations visit Chambers of Commerce on a regular basis in order to develop trade. In addition, some Chambers also provide trade bulletins for circulation and organize trade shows. See appendix 1-3C and appendix 2-4D for information on the US and Pakistan Chambers of Commerce, respectively.

Trade Delegations

Travel with a trade delegation to meet potential buyers. Traveling with a delegation organized specifically for the promotion of your type of product is best. If there is a trade delegation coming to your country, be sure to meet with members of the delegation who might have come to source your type of product.

Your Country's Trade Offices in the USA

Many countries have trade offices in the US. If a trade office is not available, your country's embassy may have a section on trade. These offices should be able to help you find buyers or at least provide some guidance. Many American importers make inquiries with these offices regarding suitable exporters, so it is in your best interest to contact your country's trade office. These offices may also maintain a list of exporters and have display centers to keep exporters' brochures and samples. Be sure to take advantage of these facilities. See appendix 1-3A for the Pakistan Trade Office address in New York.

RN Number (Registered Identification Number)

This is a number issued by the Federal Trade Commission (FTC) to US companies. All businesses in the US are supposed to include either the name of their company or the RN number on the labels of the garments they want to sell to the end consumer. Businesses can use this number on their labels in lieu of their company name. If you know the RN number of a US company, the company can be easily traced. For a directory of RN numbers, contact World Trade Venue (appendix 1-5) for more information.

World Trade Centers

World Trade Centers (WTC) are located in major cities in most countries. These centers get trade leads from different parts of the world. As services may vary from one country to another, you should check on the facilities that your local World Trade Center provides. See Chapter 3 for services of a WTC and appendix 1-3K for a web site listing world trade centers.

Web Sites on the Internet

The Internet is a great source for finding buyers. Most of the major companies in the US have web sites or are currently working on developing one. These web sites can be found through search engines or on industry web sites. You can also find apparel directories on the Internet.

Buyers are also searching the Internet to find suppliers, as such having your own web site and making sure that it is easily accessible and available through at least the major search engines, is very important. You can also get your company listed on popular web sites. See appendix 1-3G.

Advertising

Figure out how much money you want to allocate for this cause. It is better to start out conservatively and then increase your advertising budget, as your company's sales increase. If you advertise in the right places, you will get the right results. Remember that most of the means of advertising below are just a start; the best results will come from exhibiting in relevant trade shows.

Means of advertising:

- Relevant trade directories and trade magazines/publications. Points to consider:
  - ◆ Talk to people in the country of export about the reputation of different trade directories and magazines/publications
  - ◆ Make sure that the directories/magazine/publications are relevant to your industry and the target audience. Apparel exporters' target audience includes importers and wholesalers of apparel
  - ◆ Ask the publishers for a media kit and let them know whom you want to target. A media kit provides information on different aspects of the publication, such as the number in circulation, target readers, target markets, etc.
  - ◆ Check if the subscribers are getting the subscription for free or if they are paying for it. A paid circulation shows that the subscriber definitely has interest in the products
  - ◆ It is better to advertise in magazines in which your competitors are advertising
  - ◆ Check the frequency of your competitors' advertisements in different magazines. A magazine that has repeat advertisements of your competitors is likely to be a successful one
  - ◆ If you are advertising in more than one magazine, it is important to know which one is generating the best results. Suppose you are advertising in two different magazines. In magazine 1, ask the viewer to respond to the attention of Sales Dept. 1, and in magazine 2, ask the viewer to respond to Sales Dept. 2. The number of

replies addressed to Sales Dept. 1 and Sales Dept. 2 will tell you the number of responses to advertisements in magazines 1 and 2, respectively

♦ Check if the publisher offers any frequency discounts

- Trade bulletins
  ♦ Contact the Chambers of Commerce and trade associations in the country of export to check if they publish trade bulletins. Free advertisement in these bulletins may be available

- Classified and display advertising
  ♦ Display advertising is great and gets the audience's attention quickly, but classified advertising can have its own impact too. Classified advertisements allow one to test the market, while paying a comparatively small amount. I remember opening the newspaper every morning and seeing just a three line advertisement for a distributor. These small advertisements were very successful for this company because its strategy was to advertise in the classifieds daily, and put in an occasional display advertisement as well. The key is to select the right publication, which will reach your audience

- Direct mailing
  ♦ Prepare your own mailing lists from contacts that you get at trade shows or through other promotional methods. You can also buy mailing lists from US companies. See appendix 1-5 for the contact address of a company that can provide mailing lists. Occasionally, send mailers to potential clients; this will keep your name in the customer's mind. You never know when a buyer might decide to place an order with you
  ♦ Remember that mailing information to the wrong companies is just a waste of money, so make sure that your mailing list is up to date and relevant

Trade Promotion Agencies in Europe

There are import promotion offices in different countries in Europe where exporters from developing countries can get help in accessing the market. Countries such as Norway, Sweden, Denmark, the Netherlands, and Germany all have such agencies. See appendix 1-3D for trade promotion agencies in Europe.

Networking

It is very important for any businessperson to have networking skills. Networking can help you establish new connections with buyers and suppliers. Through networking, you can find new sources to reach domestic and foreign buyers. Domestic buyers can be helpful when you have surplus inventory. Industry breakfasts/lunches/dinners, trade conventions, trade shows, etc. are just a few of the places to develop friendships and increase your network.

Exporters in Your Country

An exporter might suggest a buyer who may be looking for items that you can supply. Generally, this type of information is not released by your competitors, but there is no harm in asking.

What Are Buyers Looking For?

Before they place an order with your company, buyers will generally look for the following:

- Who is the exporter? What is the capability of the exporter?
- The country of export
- Can the exporter provide any references?

- Does the exporter have a quota for shipping to the US?
- What merchandise is the exporter offering?
- Uniqueness of the product or service
- What are the terms of payment?
- What is the delivery schedule?
- What is the quality and packaging of the merchandise?
- What is the mode of shipment?
- What is the foreseen profitability?

Options of Selling

Selling to Importers

There are all kinds of importers in the US, ranging from small to very large. Selling directly to importers helps to maintain closer contact with the buyer and the market itself. Importers generally do not sign a contract; they tend to work on a shipment to shipment basis. They keep buying from you as long as they are able to sell your products. In order to sell to importers on a continuous basis, ensure that the quality of your products, delivery timings, and prices are competitive.

Some importers sell directly to retailers; others sell to wholesalers who then sell to retailers. Some importers do both.

Selling to Distributors

Generally, distributors are appointed by the manufacturers to sell on an exclusive basis in a designated area. The exclusivity is awarded because a distributor promises to generate a certain amount of sales with an increase every year. An agreement is negotiated and signed between the seller and the distributor. A distributor buys products from a company, stocks them, and then sells them to make a profit in his/her territory. If your products, prices, and other terms are good, your chances of finding a distributor who would like to work with you will increase. If you find a good distributor, try to work with him/her on a long-term basis. Also try to accommodate his or her needs as much as possible.

An established distributor is very knowledgeable on issues revolving around the domestic market as well as on the sources of suppliers. Established distributors are in great demand, and many exporters try to appoint them to sell their products in the US.

Requirements of a Distributor

In my opinion, appointing a distributor is the best route for getting into the market. A strong distributor will want to know the full capabilities of your company, including its financial strength. An exporter should also look for certain qualifications before appointing a distributor. Both parties must consider the viability of working together. I have discussed some of the requirements of both parties below.

Cooperating With A Distributor

A distributor must be given full cooperation and must be made aware of the capabilities of your operation. He/she must also have complete and updated catalogs and price lists on your merchandise. You must stay in touch with him/her for mutual benefits. If your distributor makes a suggestion, listen to it carefully and try to accommodate his/her suggestions to the best of your ability. Regular visits to your distributor must be made, and the distributor should also visit you in order to see the workings of your establishment. If the distributor has knowledge of the system you operate under, he/she will be in a better position to market your products.

Remember, for a new business, everything will seem difficult at first; from finding buyers, to appointing distributors/agents, to getting financing. However, if you are serious about becoming successful, you must work hard to attain that success. Slowly but surely, things will start turning in your favor, and everyone from buyers to banks to distributors, will be looking to work with you.

The sales targets you set for the distributor must be workable and mutually agreed upon, or else they will not be achieved. In order to determine targets, getting feedback from your distributor is essential. Also be sure to study the market and competition.

General Criteria Used by an Exporter When Selecting a Distributor

If you decide to work through a distributor, it is very important to pick the right one, or you may have problems. A strong and established distributor can get your company a share of the market, but a bad distributor can damage your business. Thus, the selection process should be done very carefully.

Keep the following points in mind when considering potential distributors:

- The time period that the distributor has been in business
- Stability of the distributor
- Credibility and financial strength of the distributor
- Advertising, marketing, and distribution channels used by the distributor
- The time and energy contribution toward your products
- Number of people in marketing staff
- Area of distribution
- Potential sales the distributor can generate for you
- Benefits to the exporter for providing exclusivity rights

- The right to terminate the agreement in case of poor performance
- A no-compensation clause in case of termination of agreement
- Knowledge of the market, current laws, custom regulations, import policies, and other procedures
- Product price range covered
- Short and long-term selling plans for your products
- Number and location of branch offices of the distributor
- Make sure that there is no conflict of interest if the distributor represents other companies, especially those with similar products

General Criteria Used by a Distributor When Selecting an Exporter

- The time period that the exporter has been in business
- Quality of products
- Competitive prices
- Incentives for the distributor
- Credibility and financial strength of the exporter
- Capability of making timely deliveries
- The capacity and capability of the manufacturing unit
- Contribution required towards advertising your products
- Contract with minimum binding clauses
- Experience of the exporter
- References provided by exporter
- Exclusivity rights for the distributor
- Warranties on the product

Advantages of Appointing a Distributor

- The distributor buys on his/her own account
- The distributor agrees to meet the sales target
- Allows you to concentrate on your production

- Experienced distributors are well versed with export and import rules and documentation
- Distributors in the country of import will keep you updated in regards to the market conditions

Disadvantages of Appointing a Distributor

- It is hard to engage a distributor as a new business with new products
- Termination of a distributor agreement can create problems for you, and you may have to compensate the distributor before canceling the contract
- A bad distributor can destroy your reputation
- A distributor may be very demanding and press you on prices and other terms

Selling Through Agents / Export Management Companies

An agent is based in the country of import and an Export Management Company (EMC) is based in the country of export. Both are appointed by your company to sell your products, and follow the same general procedures.

An agent / EMC uses a company's samples, brochures, flyers, and other promotional materials, and presents these to potential clients. Agents / EMC's do not buy on their own account. They are only responsible for arranging orders and will charge commission on all the orders placed through him/her. The commission generally ranges from 10% to 20% depending upon the value of the product and/or the volume of sales. If the products can generate a high volume of sales, generally the percentage of commission is lower, in some cases it can even be lower than 10%. The services of agents / EMC's can be exclusive or non-exclusive for a certain territory.

In my opinion, it is a little easier to engage agents / EMC's than distributors, because they do not use their own finances to stock your merchandise. An agent / EMC may have less requirements when agreeing to represent an exporter. However, remember that there are some very well established agents / EMC's, and they have certain requirements you must meet before they will agree to represent you. Agents / EMC's must also determine whether the amount of time, energy, and travel expenses incurred when looking for buyers for your product, are worthwhile. Hence, they will want to know the full capabilities of your company, including its financial strength, before making any agreements.

General Criteria Used by an Exporter When Selecting an Agent / EMC

A good agent / EMC can get your company established in the market, but a bad one can damage your business. So the selection process is important.

Keep the following points in mind when considering potential agents / EMC's:

- The time period that the agent / EMC has been in business
- The kind of market the agent / EMC is selling to
- The strength of the agent's / EMC's connections
- Number of people in agent / EMC's staff
- Potential sales the agent / EMC can generate for you
- Benefits to the exporter for providing exclusivity rights
- The right to terminate the agreement in case of poor performance
- A no-compensation clause in case of termination of agreement
- Knowledge of the market, current laws, custom regulations, import policies, and other procedures

- Make sure that there is no conflict of interest if the agent / EMC represents other companies, especially those with similar products
- References may be requested and checked

General Criteria Used by an Agent / EMC When Selecting an Exporter

- The time period that the exporter has been in business
- The capacity and capability of the manufacturing unit
- Quality of products
- Competitive prices
- Promotional material
- Rate of commission
- Credibility and financial strength of the exporter
- Capability of making timely deliveries

Advantages of Appointing an Agent / EMC

- The agent / EMC looks after your interests
- The customer's payments for the goods are generally the responsibility of the agent / EMC
- Allows you to concentrate on your production, especially if your company is a small operation
- Experienced agents / EMC's are well versed with export and import rules and documentation
- Agents / EMC's are paid on a commission basis and only get paid after sales materialize
- You will incur a lower startup cost and less expenses of overseas travel
- No staff needed to maintain your export department
- Agents / EMC's can add to your knowledge about the import process; helpful especially if you are new to the business

- If something goes wrong during the process, such as a delay in shipment, you do not have to face the customer directly
- Possibility of generating fast sales; this can be especially helpful in the beginning of your operation
- Many US importers prefer to have contacts in the USA and feel more comfortable dealing with a local agent versus talking to suppliers in foreign countries
- If there is a language barrier, an agent / EMC can be of great help

Disadvantages of Appointing an Agent / EMC

- You are dependent upon the agent / EMC
- You do not see the buyer
- You do not get first hand exposure to the sale of your products and export markets
- You make less money because you pay commission to the agent / EMC
- An agent / EMC may not pay full attention to the promotion of your products, if he/she has too many other hot selling products
- Termination of an agency agreement can create problems for you, and you may have to compensate the agent / EMC before canceling the contract
- A bad agent / EMC can destroy your reputation

Agreements Between the Exporter and Distributor/Agent/EMC

After you have appointed a distributor or an agent / EMC, it is better to sign an agreement for clarity of obligations and duties on both parts. A qualified attorney should be hired to draft the agreement. Perhaps you can start off with a trial period to see if the relationship between the two companies is working out.

Remember building relationships takes time, and nothing will be done overnight. Strong relations between the two companies will lead to a prosperous business. Both sides have to make an effort to build up the relationship; however, it is more important for an exporter to be on the giving side, because the distributors or agents / EMC's are the ones building up your business.

Some of the items that should be incorporated in the agreement are as follows:

- Exclusive or non-exclusive agreement
- Types of goods/services covered
- Territory covered
- Obligations and duties of both parties
- Sales target, if any
- Annual percentage of increment in sales
- Details and rules of termination
- Trial period
- Renewal period

Export Trading Companies (ETC)

In your home country, you can contact established ETC's to sell your products overseas. These companies are experienced in international marketing and can get your goods in the international market very quickly. These companies will only buy from you if your goods match quality or price points. The advantage of this selling method is that you will be dealing with an experienced local company, and thus procurement of an order might be faster. The disadvantage is that you may not earn a large profit; ETC's will buy goods from the manufacturer at the lowest possible price and will try to retain a major portion of the profit for themselves.

Buying Agents

These agents are based in either the country of import or export and are appointed by buyers to find products that they are looking for. Because they generally deal with high volume buyers, it is not a bad idea to work with them. The buyers rely on these agents for reliable suppliers. These agents keep in contact with and visit the exporter's manufacturing facilities to ensure that the goods meet the buyer's required standards.

These agents charge commission and are responsible for maintaining quality control and timely deliveries on behalf of the importer. They arrange a Letter of Credit (L/C) for the exporter. The L/C may include a clause stating that a Certificate of Acceptance is to be issued by the buying agent, upon approval of the quality of the merchandise. Orders, with such clauses attached, should only be taken if you feel that you can produce the goods as per the agreed specifications. Otherwise the agent may refuse to issue a Certificate of Acceptance and the bank will not release any payment if such a certificate is required according to the L/C. Letters of Credit are discussed further in Chapter 18.

Buying agents can be reached by contacting the importer and asking if he/she has a buying agent in the country of export. They can also be reached by contacting export promotion offices, trade associations, Chambers of Commerce and Industry, etc. Distributors of apparel machinery in your country might also know of buying agents. You can also request that buying agents contact you by advertising in relevant trade publications or popular newspapers. Some names and addresses of buying agencies in the US and Pakistan are given in appendix 2-6F.

Selling to Large Retail Chain Stores

There are many large chain retailers in the USA. Some own hundreds of stores across the USA and many have branches in Canada. Their sales can range from millions to billions in US dollars per year. Many of these chain stores carry imported merchandise; hence, it is in your best interest to see if you might be able to sell to them.

Large retailers purchase goods directly from the exporter and through buying agents or intermediaries. They also buy from importers and wholesalers based in the US. Buyers of large retail stores are very knowledgeable about consumer needs as well as the availability of suppliers across the world. They regularly visit reputable trade shows around the globe in order to stay in touch with the latest in the market. These buyers receive offers from many exporters from different countries on a daily basis. Hence, in attempts to get an order, exporters offer them the best possible terms.

Information on large apparel chain retail/department stores and designers is available in appendix 1-11B. On these web sites, you can get ideas about the type and styles of merchandise and any other information that may help you learn about the US market. For a list of chain stores, contact World Trade Venue(sm) in appendix 1-5.

Mail Order/Catalog Companies

All types of companies ranging from small to large can be found in the mail order business. They send catalogs to end consumers, and the orders are placed over the telephone or by mail. The mail order companies ship the merchandise by mail or courier service. Exporters should try to find catalog houses/companies that might be interested in importing their products.

For directories of US mail order companies, contact the company mentioned in appendix 1-5.

Television Sales

In the US, garments are also sold on television networks. There are TV channels that sell merchandise directly to the consumer by showing the products on their network. This is another area where exporters can find a market.

Selling to Group Buyers

Small retailers sometimes form a group, which buys products on behalf of them. In this manner, small retailers can get the price advantage by buying in larger quantities directly from the manufacturer.

Establish Partnerships in the US

You can form a partnership with a buyer in the US. A buy back agreement may be signed between the buyer and the seller, under which the buyer agrees to purchase all or a partial quantity of production. In this case, both parties may share profits and investments. A detailed contract will specify duties and obligations of each party, thus eliminating any misunderstandings. It is recommended that you work with an experienced attorney who has knowledge and experience of these types of agreements. In addition, a good understanding and relationship between the two parties is very important.

In order to find partners, you can advertise in relevant trade magazines, seek help from banks, Chambers of Commerce, trade associations, consulting companies, or from the commercial section of the American Embassy in your country. Also, consulting companies can be one of the best ways of finding a partner. Make sure you check the reputation of the consulting company before assigning the job of finding a suitable partner.

Advantages

- A partner is based in the US to sell on your behalf for mutual financial gains
- The exporter will have more time to concentrate on production and improving quality
- Joint growth will be mutually beneficial
- A partnership with an overseas company will increase credibility of the exporter's establishment
- Both sides will exchange trade information
- Capital investment, profits, and losses will be shared
- Language and cultural problems will be less of a barrier
- Production and selling can be well planned
- Mutual interest of the two parties will bring desired results
- Foreign investment is good for your country

Disadvantages

- Your decisions cannot be independent
- Terms of the contract can be binding
- In the case of a new company, it is hard to arrange a partnership
- Income tax matters can be complicated

Forming Partnerships with Other Countries

If you cannot find a partner in the US, establish partnerships in another area such as Hong Kong. Many buyers from America, Europe, and other countries visit Hong Kong to get all types of garments. Hong Kong designers have successfully developed their reputation, and their products are being sold in some of the most prestigious chain stores in the USA as well as in other developed countries. In Hong Kong, advanced clothing technology such as CAD/CAM, marker making, robotic spreading, and automatic cutting is being used. In addition, it is important to mention that during my many visits to the Far East, I have found that the businessmen from the area are intelligent, polite, and humble, and know the art of conducting business.

In 1998, Hong Kong's apparel industry's gross output was HK$ 45,742 billion (manufacturing), and their value-added items were worth HK$11.503 Billion (manufacturing). China is the largest exporter of apparel in the world. Manufacturers and exporters from Hong Kong and the rest of China exhibit in different renowned trade shows in the industry. They display their products in cities like New York, Las Vegas, and Miami in the US, Dubai in the United Arab Emirates, Dalian in China, Dusseldorf and Cologne in Germany, Buenos Aires in Argentina, Sao Paulo in Brazil, and Poznan in Poland. The Hong Kong Trade Development Council (HKTDC) also organizes one of the best trade shows in the industry, which is attended by a large number of buyers from all over the world. The show is held at the Hong Kong Convention and Exhibition Center, which is one of the best and most prestigious trade show centers and is equipped with the most modern facilities in the world. See appendix 1-11C for the Hong Kong Convention and Exhibition Center web site.

Due to a local labor shortage and rising production costs in Hong Kong, manufacturers are expanding their production facilities into many other countries. Although Hong Kong companies prefer to set up facilities in main China, they are also moving to many other countries such as Vietnam, Nigeria, and Mexico. Hong Kong companies are making use of their remarkable sales and marketing, designing, and quality control techniques and abilities, while outsourcing from other countries.

Exporters from Pakistan and other countries should seek partnerships with companies in places such as Hong Kong. Exporters can learn from these companies' expertise and both can work for mutual benefits. These companies may be willing to invest in and become part of your business.

Hong Kong companies get the following benefits by developing manufacturing facilities in other countries:

- Through partnerships, they can use textile quotas of the manufacturing countries
- They make use of cheap labor and lower overheads in other developing countries
- They increase the volume of sales
- They can meet quantity demands
- They can meet delivery schedules by sub-contracting with your company

As a result, all parties are able to make money.

Licensing

Licensing means an established company grants rights to a company to produce goods under their trademark, such as 'Disney'. The licensor may provide complete or partial know-how along with granting the rights. This can allow quick entry into the market due to the already established name. The licensing arrangement can also bring expertise and transfer of technology to you. The disadvantages are that a royalty has to be paid, interference of the licensor in marketing is possible, and the extra costs related to finalizing the agreement can be incurred (i.e. the fees of an attorney).

Selling Directly to the End Consumer Over the Internet

Using the Internet, a company may sell directly to the end consumers. The Internet is creating a limitless environment for doing business. You can reach customers directly, avoiding all middlemen. As such this method of selling may be beneficial to you.

Advantages

- You can sell globally
- You can reach your customers directly
- You can sell under your own brand, thus establishing your brand
- You can build loyal customers
- You can offer custom designs to your customers
- Customers can communicate with you through e-mail
- Better profitability is possible

Disadvantages

- You may not be able to cater to individual needs
- Higher freight charges may not allow you to offer attractive prices
- You will have to keep up with the latest designs in demand
- Reliable mailing services may not be available from your country
- Having a return policy for defective/unacceptable goods, etc. is extremely important in the case of US Customers
    - ◆ Returning the merchandise may be a hassle for the customer
    - ◆ Returns may incur additional costs for you, such as shipping fees, etc.

♦ In the absence of a return policy, you may face difficulties in selling your product

To provide better service to customers in the US, appointing a customer service representative in the US may also be considered. Setting up a customer service arrangement can produce better results, because US customers are more comfortable in dealing with local companies.

Marketing Through Relatives or Friends

The United States of America is a multinational country. There are people from every corner of the world who live here. You may have a relative, friend, or acquaintance in the US who might like the idea of representing your products in this country. They may even want to import your products on their own account. This is probably one of the easiest and quickest ways of getting started. Before you begin, ensure that the person has adequate finances, knowledge of the market, and the capability of selling your products.

How Long Does it Take to Get an Order?

There is not a defined time period in which one might obtain an order. There are many variables that affect how long it will take to get an order. These include your experience, market conditions, the right product, marketing strategies, etc.

Realistically speaking, it takes at least six to eight months, before an order might materialize. If you have picked the right product with the right price, and you have the necessary experience, then there is no reason that you should not be successful.

Keep in mind that large corporations in the US have very complex operations. Every corporation has its own structure, and different tasks are assigned to different individuals or departments. Hence, in larger corporations, it may be hard to contact or to even find the right buyer. Thus, it may take even longer to get an order from larger US companies.

12 | *Chapter Twelve*

Trade Shows

A trade show is a place where buyers and sellers meet to conduct business. Different companies put up booths and display their products. The exhibitors include importers, exporters, traders, distributors, manufacturers, wholesalers, agents, and sales representatives. Visitors to international shows include both small and high volume buyers. Exhibiting in an international trade show is an excellent method for finding buyers.

Even if you do not wish to exhibit in the beginning, it is a good idea to travel and visit relevant trade shows in order to survey the market. During your visit, talk to the exhibitors. You may be able to find a company willing to work with you or at least give you feedback and steer you in the right direction. One word of caution, exhibitors spend a lot of money in exhibiting at trade shows. They are there to do business for the season and may not be willing to entertain any sales inquires from an exporter at the booth. So as an exporter, you will have to use your own judgement on approaching exhibitors.

The USA is a very big country and there are many fairs in different cities. Some very reputable trade shows are held in the US. These fairs are held regularly and dates are announced well in advance. It is important to find out the type of the show before attending one. Some trade shows are geared towards domestic selling and tend to attract small retailers. These shows are not the place to find volume buyers. However, there are shows where large and small buyers come to see the latest merchandise and conduct business with international and/or domestic exhibitors.

Trade shows are strictly for trade buyers and are not open to the general public. Entry into a trade fair requires registration, and visitors are required to prove their business affiliation before entry is allowed.

For the convenience of the visitors, the organizers publish a directory of exhibitors. If you are exhibiting, make sure your company is listed in this directory because it is used by the visitors during and after the fair. Some organizers also sell these directories to anyone interested in finding information on the exhibitors. It is an excellent source for reaching potential buyers.

During the show, the organizers also distribute free bulletins carrying information/news relevant to the industry for the interest of the exhibitors.

Many trade shows offer educational seminars and fashion shows to educate visitors about the coming trends. Fashion shows are generally more common in European trade shows, such as those held in Germany, France, Italy, etc. There is, generally, a separate fee for attending these seminars and fashion shows.

Reputable fashion shows by many famous designers are also held in US cities, such as New York.

Some organizers arrange an opening ceremony to which exhibitors, government officials, and media personnel are invited. It is advisable to attend such functions to benefit from the exchange of ideas and networking.

Reputable organizers do a lot of advertising before and during the show in order to attract buyers. Trade show organizers use different types of media to publicize their fair. They make special arrangements for the press and for television coverage. The better the show, the more media coverage it will receive.

To gather a list of shows, ask export promotion agencies in your own country. Another resource is the embassy of the target country. Trade show directories and web sites can be helpful as well. See appendix 1-12A for a list of trade shows and appendix 1-12B for other information on trade shows.

Exporters interested in exhibiting in trade shows must contact the organizers well in advance for complete information on availability of space, charges, dates, types of visitors, etc. It is hard to get into some fairs, as space is limited. For this reason, a newer company may be placed on a waiting list.

What Will You Find at a Trade Show?

At trade shows, you will meet importers, distributors, wholesalers, agents, manufacturers, trading companies, and sales representatives.

The following information can be obtained at the show:

- Fashion trends
- Wholesale prices
- Sources of buying fashion magazines, books, and trade directories
- Sources of forecasting services (see appendix 1-10A)
- Potential of the show
- Information on your competitors and their products

The following can be found at apparel shows:

- The Women's Wear Show: active wear, handcrafted apparel, sportswear, bridal dresses, career suits, casual wear, dresses, evening wear, nightwear, hosiery, intimate apparel, hats, gloves, knitwear, leather garments, fur garments, sweaters, scarves, shawls, street wear, T-shirts, swimwear, jackets, coats and other outerwear, jewelry, handbags, hair accessories, footwear, gifts, etc.
- The Men's Wear Show: suits, shirts, neckwear, pants, formal wear, gloves, jeans, headwear, leather apparel, outerwear, rainwear, robes, knitwear, shorts, socks, sportswear, sweaters, T-shirts, sport coats, swimwear, underwear, vests, etc.
- The Children's Wear Show: active-wear, coordinated sportswear, jeans, outerwear, pajamas and robes, sport coats and suits, sweaters, swimwear, christening wear, communion wear, costumes, dresses, hosiery, gloves, hand painted clothing, infant wear, headwear, knitwear, neckwear, preteen clothing, rainwear, T-shirts, etc.

Benefits of Exhibiting at a Trade Fair

- Staying updated
  - ♦ Every time you attend a trade show, you will see new items, designs, colors and some new ideas, clients, and suppliers to the industry. Keeping yourself up to date about the market and any changes in it is very important in order to conduct a successful business
- Gaining knowledge of your competition
  - ♦ You will also get to see what your competitors are doing and how and why their sales are increasing or decreasing. You will be able to assess what they are doing to attract customers to their booths
- Meeting buyers
  - ♦ This will give you the opportunity to meet clients. If you are a regular exhibitor, you will meet your old as well as some new clients. This will help increase your business
  - ♦ You will have access to buyers from many different areas, all at one location. This will save you the money, time, and energy of having to go to different places to meet each buyer in their respective locations
- Learning about new ideas and techniques
  - ♦ Attending seminars and fashion shows at the trade show will enable you to get new ideas. Some seminars will discuss techniques to increase your sales
- Building the credibility of your company
  - ♦ Some buyers like seeing you at a trade fair every year before they will place an order. People will have more confidence in your company if you are a regular exhibitor

- Able to display all products
  - ♦ At a trade fair, you will be able to display your entire product range. If you were traveling to visit each buyer, it would be cumbersome for you to carry samples. Furthermore, you may not be able to carry samples of all of your products
- Getting listed in the trade fair directory
  - ♦ You will be listed in the exhibitors' directory. Interested companies use this directory both during and after the trade show

Selecting a Trade Fair to Exhibit Your Products

Selecting the right show is extremely important for finding buyers. A trade fair can be very effective if the proper selection and planning is done. A company must allow several months to prepare for a trade show. Exhibiting is a sign of your readiness for selling in the market.

It is important to note that not all shows are good for everyone. If, for example, a trade show is exclusively meant for high-class garments or is specialized for bridal dresses, and you are exhibiting casual wear, then the show may not be successful for you.

First select the target country in which you want to export. Then decide which trade shows you should go to in order to find buyers from that country. There are two ways you can access buyers from your target country.

First, you can exhibit your product in the country to which you wish to export. Make sure that the show you choose attracts volume buyers. Visitors to US fairs will mostly be from the USA,

Canada, and South American countries. Visitors from the US include small to large retailers and volume buyers.

Second, you can attend a trade show in a third country. Because there is intense competition in the US, American buyers travel all over the world to find the best sources and products. Hence, it is also in your interest to exhibit in shows in other countries that have proven to be popular for buyers. You should talk to the organizers of the trade fair to find out the full details on the visitors, including the total number and a breakdown by country. A large number of US buyers attend far-Eastern trade shows, such as in Hong Kong, mainland China, and Taiwan. Reputable fairs in the Far East attract high volume buyers from across the world. European buyers attend trade shows in Germany, Hong Kong, France and other countries. If you plan to export to either the US or Europe, check if any of those shows are appropriate for you. Some trade shows are listed in appendix 1-12A.

Make sure that the show that you plan to exhibit at does not conflict with any other shows. If it does, then make the proper arrangements to attend both fairs.

Keep the following in mind when picking a show:

Type of Fair

There are various types of garment fairs. Make sure that the fair has an international appeal and attracts volume buyers. The show must also be relevant to your products and price point.

Specialized shows are generally better than non-specialized ones. For example, for a garment exhibitor, an apparel show may be better than a consumer product (general merchandise) show.

Reputation of the Show

It is advised that you get full details on the fair from the organizers. Check on the number of years the show has been running; if the show has been around for a long time, it is likely to be popular enough to attract a large number of trade buyers. Also, be sure to check on the reputation from other exporters in your country, export promotion offices, garment trade associations, and/or previous exhibitors and attendees.

Visitors

- Number of visitors
  - ◆ This number can give you an idea as to how big or small the show is. Be sure to check the ratio of foreign to domestic visitors. This information is available from the organizers
- Type of visitors
  - ◆ Make sure that the visitors to the show are not small retailers only
  - ◆ Make sure that the trade show is exclusively for trade buyers and is not open to the general public

Exhibitors

- Number of exhibitors
  - ◆ This number can give you an idea as to how big or small the show is. This information can be obtained from the organizers
- Type of exhibitors
  - ◆ If the same international companies are exhibiting at a show year after year and they represent a varied range of countries, then the show is most likely a good one. Check the brochures for the trade show and/or ask the organizers for the following information:

- How many international exhibitors are attending the show?
- From how many countries?
- How long have those exhibitors been participating in that show?
- What percentage of the exhibitors are repeat exhibitors?
- Are products exhibited similar to your products?
- If possible, obtain a trade directory from the previous year's show to check statistics from that year, such as the number of exhibitors, countries, and products

♦ If you are visiting the show before applying for a booth, talk to other international exhibitors at the show who are displaying products similar to yours, and find out the following information:
- Are they regular exhibitors at that show?
- If so, then how long have they been coming to that particular show?
- What kind of results have they seen at the show?

Cost and Payment of the Booth

The cost of exhibiting varies depending upon the show and the country. Different booth sizes are available. The organizers may also be able to provide a special size if needed. Check on the cost of different booth sizes and see if they fit your budget.

The policy on payment for the booth varies. A partial payment is required at the time of booking the booth. The remaining balance is payable before the start of the show. Note that payments are mostly non-refundable.

Is Space Available?

The more popular trade shows sometimes have waiting lists and space may not be available. You need to check on the availability of space before you plan to exhibit at a particular show.

Location of the Booth at the Show

The number of visitors to your booth will depend on the number of visitors passing by your booth. As such the location of the booth is extremely important. Try to get a booth in a high traffic area. Booths near the main entrance, restaurant, and rest rooms are in high traffic areas. A booth that opens into two aisles or a corner booth will be better than a booth squeezed in between two. Keep in mind that everyone wants to be located in a high traffic area, and thus it is hard to get such a booth, especially in the case of a first time exhibitor. There is no harm in trying though; you might just get it because of reasons such as cancellations. Keep in mind that there may be a higher price for a better location.

While you are at the show, if you are unsatisfied with the location of your booth, it is a good idea to discuss next year's location with the organizers. If they agree to provide you with a new location for the following year, you may want to book it right there. It is not a good idea to wait, because somebody else might book it.

If you pick the wrong show, you may face any of the following situations:

- No visitors to your booth
- Loss of money
- Waste of time and energy

Prior to the Trade Show

Listed below are some helpful tips:

- If you are sending your samples to the location of the show through another carrier, make sure they arrive in time. Show organizers give you deadlines for setting up your booth. You will not be allowed to set up your booth on the date that the exhibition starts
- The *ATA Carnet* (see glossary) is an international customs document, which is used for the temporary import of goods into a country without paying any custom duties, provided that the goods leave the country within the specified time. If you are carrying a substantial quantity of samples for the trade show, it is good to arrange for a carnet. The ATA Carnet can be used for commercial samples, professional equipment, etc. The International Chamber of Commerce or an authorized issuing office can issue this document
- You should plan your trip keeping in mind how long it will take to set up your booth. If you are coming to a trade show for the first time, give yourself an extra day or two so that you can familiarize yourself with the location and have enough time to make necessary arrangements for the setup
- Check the timing and days for setting up and closing the booth. Exhibitors are required to set up and dismantle booths according to the date and time set by the organizers
- Check exactly what is included in your contract for the booth. If anything you need is not included in your contract, bring it with you or buy it upon arrival. Examples include spotlights, shelves, racks, etc.
- In the US, quota compliance may be required on samples of apparels, depending upon the quantity
- Electrical equipment in the US operates at 110V, and does not work at 220V.

Success at the Trade Show

Success at Your Booth

Success at your booth is a function of the following:

- Number of buyers to your booth
- Availability of information for the buyer
- Attractive display
- The right product at a competitive price
- Prompt delivery period
- Attractive terms of payment
- Company listing in the show's directory of exhibitors so that buyers can find you
- Look into the possibility of advertising in the directory of exhibitors or other trade publications. Free publicity, with media covering the show, may also be a possibility

Pre-Show Campaign

It is advised that you run a pre-show campaign inviting customers to your booth. Let them know what you plan to exhibit and what new products you will be introducing. Give them an incentive to come to your booth. For instance, offer them a discount if they bring your invitation with them. Ask your trade show organizers whether they offer any services to the exhibitors to help them arrange pre-show campaigns.

Organizers may offer the following:

- VIP entry passes, this makes your client feel important
- Free entry to your clients, if there is a fee to attend the trade show

Planning Your Display at the Booth

This is one of the most important aspects of your planning. You are going to a trade show with a mindset to get orders, so you must plan a strategy to attract visitors to your booth.

To attract customers:

- The styles, material, and colors of your products must be in line with the latest fashions
- The display of your products must be attractive in order to lure visitors to your booth, since you only have a few seconds to grab their attention

At Your Booth

If possible, more than one person manning a booth is always better. This can help in receiving more than one customer at a time. It can also give you some breathing time if your booth is too busy. The persons managing the booth must be knowledgeable about the product and must be ready to answer any questions that they may encounter. The persons working at the booth should also be able to make quick decisions.

At the booth, you need to have the following:

- Product samples
- Company brochures and flyers
- Sufficient supply of business cards with full particulars. Visitors will generally maintain a file of cards that they collect from the trade show and will refer to them in the future
- FOB Price sheet; also keep C&F and CI&F (see glossary) prices readily available, if possible

- Display materials, such as spotlights, adhesive tape, hangers, pins, posters, etc.
- Basic office supplies, such as a notebook (very important!), pens/pencils, stapler, garbage can, etc.
- If possible, samples to hand out to potential customers
- Small gifts for the visitors to your booth such as pens with your company name
- Candy or coffee/drinks for your visitors
- Snack foods for yourself

The standard booth package provided by the organizers generally includes the following:

- Bare walls
- Carpeted floor
- A few spotlights
- One table
- One or two chairs
- One or two shelves
- A standard sign

Check to see if you need the following:

- Extra spotlights
- Mannequins
- Extra shelves
- Models
- Hangers
- Pins
- Music
- Adhesive tapes and double-sided adhesive tape
- Posters of your products
- Computer connections
- Fax/Phone connections
- TV/VCR to run a video of your product range
- Interpreters

You can get additional equipment for an extra price. Remember that anything sold at the venue of the show will be much more expensive than buying it from outside sources or stores. Even food is sold at much higher prices than at the market.

Some exhibitors make their own arrangements to obtain equipment and accessories because ordering them from the show authorities is generally very expensive.

Note: the organizers do not allow nails to be used for hanging purposes.

Dress Code

If you are visiting/exhibiting in a trade show or attending a business meeting, you must be dressed nicely in proper, conservative business attire. For men, this is usually the Western suit and a tie. The color of the suit could be black, gray, or navy blue with a matching tie. White shirts go best with any conservative colored suit and tie. Plain, matching socks and black polished dress shoes work fine with black, navy blue or gray colored suits. Wear a suit according to the weather; light suits in the summers and woolen suits in the winters. Do not be over or under dressed. A light cologne is fine, but do not wear heavy or strong scents. A clean-cut appearance and professional attire are very important.

Women generally wear coordinated skirts or pantsuits. Light jewelry and light perfume are also ok. Foreign nationals who may not wish to wear Western attire, may wear any clothing so long as it is professional.

Language of Your Brochures/Flyers

The language of the brochures/flyers must be geared towards the target market. For example, if your target market is the USA, the brochure must be in English. If you are exhibiting in Japan, it is preferred that you print a brochure in English and Japanese.

Interpretation and Translation Services

If you are not good at speaking English, it is recommended that you hire the services of an interpreter. You can either arrange one yourself or through the trade show organizers. Private companies in the US can arrange such services. These companies can also be located on the Internet, see appendix 1-12C for interpretation and translation services. Be sure to arrange for this facility before arrival at the show.

Keep in mind that the interpreter may charge by the hour or per day. Check the prices and terms before hiring one.

Greet Your Customer

Greet every customer who walks inside your booth and welcome him/her with a pleasant smile. Try to qualify the customers by asking key questions, without offending them or letting them know that you are trying to judge their buying potential. You need to qualify each visitor because you do not want to lose another serious customer who may be waiting for you.

Remember that the buyers also have very little time because they have to go to other booths to place orders or to find new products/suppliers. If there is more than one visitor in your booth, make sure that no one feels neglected.

Taking Notes

Take notes on all conversations and exchange of information you have had with each customer. Be sure to hand your business card to the visitor and do not forget to take a card from every visitor to your booth and file it in along with your notes. The card and your notes can be helpful for future reference.

Taking Photos

Take photos of your booth for your record. This will help you improve your booth for next time. Taking photos of booths of other companies is generally not allowed. Be sure to ask organizers before taking any pictures.

After the Show

Post-show tips:

- Give samples to potential buyers
  - ♦ Try to sell any remaining samples. Generally bargain hunters come to different booths during the show; offer to sell the samples to them after the event. Keep in mind that selling during the show is strictly prohibited at most shows, hence you may only sell after the fair
  - ♦ It is a good idea to leave as many of your samples behind with your potential clients as possible, as it will be a hassle and may be an extra expense for you to carry all the samples back home
- Follow-up on appointments
  - ♦ If you made any appointments during the show, be sure to meet your buyers and try to finalize the deal before leaving for home
- Get all necessary information from clients

♦ Check to make sure that you have all the information you need from your clients (i.e. information needed for completing an order)
- Try to get back to your home country as soon as possible so that you can proceed with the inquiries received at the show
- Write a report about your experience at the show
  ♦ This report will help you in future shows. Be honest in your report and evaluate positives and negatives of both your performance and the show itself. Discussing your report with others who are involved in exporting in your company is also a good idea. Also refer to any suggestions made by your visitors. If you do not write a report, it will be hard for you to remember everything, and you may end up repeating the same mistakes

Exhibit in Trade Shows on a Regular Basis

In order to stay in business and to make your company grow, it is recommended that you exhibit in trade shows on a regular basis. At the trade fairs, you will meet your old clients and will also come across a few new ones. Be sure to give adequate attention to both. Aside from building your clientele, attending trade shows will keep you updated on your competition, new trends, and much more. It will also establish the credibility of your company and will help generate confidence in your buyers.

Other Modes of Displaying Your Products

Shared Space at the Trade Show

If you are on a tight budget, see if you can share a space with another exhibitor. This will allow you to reduce your costs and test your market at the same time. Some organizers do not allow sharing of space, so be sure to check with them first.

Your Hotel

You can also invite your customers to your hotel.

At the hotel you may have the following options for displaying your products:

- Renting space
  - ◆ Prior to your arrival, ask the hotel if they can arrange a space where you can exhibit your products and invite customers
- Booking an extra room
  - ◆ Book an extra room where you can exhibit your products and show your buyers what you have. Always book a room or space in a 5 star or luxury hotel

World Trade Centers in the Target Country

Ask the World Trade Center in the target country if it will rent out space where you can display your products and invite potential customers. This may not be a great option, as there could be a lack of visitors. See appendix 1-3K for a web site listing world trade centers.

13 | Chapter Thirteen

Business Travel to the USA

Communication today has reached very advanced levels; we can talk and exchange documents instantly from almost anywhere in the world. Video conferencing is becoming very popular. However, a face to face meeting with a client cannot be replaced by any other means of communication. The shaking of hands is still important in conducting business. Business executives should travel in order to locate and cultivate relationships with current business counterparts overseas.

Traveling to exhibit at trade shows or to meet buyers will be a part of your business. Business related travel and exhibiting expenses are usually tax deductible. However, every country does have its own laws, so be sure to check with your accountant as to what tax deductions are allowed in your country.

Make Appointments

Before traveling, decide on the objective of your trip and plan your agenda accordingly; set your goals and priorities. Do not overload your schedule. It is better to have some time between appointments, so that you can relax or reach another location. Well-planned arrangements are productive and bring more desirable results.

You can also make appointments with your potential customers at your hotel. This will save you a considerable amount of time and will allow you to make more appointments during your stay. Allow at least one hour for each appointment and take a break for at least an hour during the day. Sometimes buyers may be reluctant to come to your hotel, especially if they do not know you or know of your company. In this case, it is better to meet on their premises.

Before Departure From Your Home Country

- Preparing for business travel
  - ♦ Find out about working days, business hours, and national holidays in the country you are visiting. In American and European countries, the working hours are generally from 9AM to 5PM. In the US, corporate offices are closed on Saturdays, Sundays, and national holidays. Banks open at 9AM and some are open as late as 7 PM. Banks and post offices are open Monday through Friday, with some hours on Saturday. Large grocery stores are generally open 24 hours a day and 7 days a week. Many retail businesses are open almost every day of the year except for Thanksgiving and Christmas. Avoid traveling during holidays, especially near Christmas. It is hard to catch people from December 20th until the first week of the next year. Major holidays in the US are listed in appendix 1-13A

- ♦ Arrange appointments with perspective buyers prior to travel
- ♦ Be sure to bring copies of any previous correspondence with the buyer. These may be needed to finalize a business deal
- ♦ Bring an invoice for US Customs showing the value of your samples
- Passports and Visas
  - ♦ Get a valid passport. For entry into the USA, your passport must be valid. Most countries require that your passport be valid for at least 6 months from the date of travel, or you might face problems at the airport
  - ♦ Get a valid visa for entering the USA. Nationals of some countries may not be required to get a visa for entry into the US; check with the US Embassy in your country
  - ♦ Make photocopies of your passport and visa. Also keep at least 6 passport size photos with you, in case you lose your passport
  - ♦ If you plan to travel to other countries, obtain visas for all the countries that require them prior to departure from your country
- Money matters
  - ♦ Bring U.S. currency in the form of cash, travelers' checks, or major credit cards
  - ♦ Currency conversion rates will be better in the country of origin so try to convert money before departure. Keep approximately US $100-200 in cash for use upon arrival for taxi, tips, meals, etc. Then, figure out how much cash you need for day-to-day expenses and keep enough accordingly

- ◆ If you are bringing in or taking out US$10,000 or more, under current regulations, you must declare this amount at US Customs upon arrival. For the most current rules and regulations, check with the American Embassy before departure or with Customs upon arrival
- ◆ Like any other country in the world, pick pocketing and theft does take place in the USA, especially in very large metropolitan cities like New York. Thus, it may be risky to carry too much cash
- ◆ If you intend to use credit cards issued in your country, make sure that the cards are usable in the US. The most widely used credit cards in the US are Mastercard, Visa, Discover, and American Express
- ◆ Carry sufficient local currency for use when returning home
- • Travel
  - ◆ Make flight reservations with an airline. If you are stopping at more than one location, ensure that your entire itinerary is confirmed
  - ◆ If you have a medical condition that requires special care during the flight and may cause discomfort to you or fellow passengers, inform the airline at the time of the booking and the flight attendant before departure, so that necessary arrangements can be made
  - ◆ If possible, travel business or first class for more comfort and less fatigue. If traveling economy class, request a seat with extra legroom for more comfort. These are generally available near the exit doors
  - ◆ If possible, take a direct flight to your destination to cut down on the hours of travel
  - ◆ In general, wide-bodied planes, such as the jumbo jet, are more comfortable to travel in; you will experience less turbulence or other shocks

- ◆ Keep in mind that you may experience jet lag as a result of the time difference
- Packing and baggage
  - ◆ Travel as lightly as possible
  - ◆ Make sure you bring the appropriate clothing for the season. In winters, it is bitterly cold in many cities of the US, as such heavy clothing including long winter coats (overcoats) are needed. The temperatures can fall below the freezing point at any time during the winter in some parts of the US, so one must be prepared for the weather
  - ◆ Do not forget any prescription medication and medicines for small ailments such as headaches, etc.
  - ◆ Do not forget to bring extra eyeglasses if you wear them for reading, in case one breaks
  - ◆ Do not forget an umbrella in case of a rainy day
  - ◆ Check baggage rules with the airline. Under current regulations, a passenger to the USA is allowed two pieces of checked-in baggage. Some airlines allow first class and business class passengers to carry extra baggage
  - ◆ Make sure you have a small cart for hand baggage; at some airports you may have to walk long distances to change terminals or to reach the baggage area. Bring suitcases with wheels for easy movements
  - ◆ Never put your valuables in luggage which is to be checked in
  - ◆ Do not overload your bags. In case of an inspection by customs, you may find difficulty in re-packing your bags at the airport
  - ◆ Put tags with your name, address, and phone numbers on your luggage, including your brief case/handbag
  - ◆ All important addresses and phone numbers from home and from the foreign country must be kept handy

- Other
  - ◆ It is a good idea to get travel health insurance before departure, as medical care in the US is extremely expensive
  - ◆ If you intend to drive in the USA, bring an international license. AAA or other relevant authorities in your home country can issue international drivers' licenses. Check current regulations with the American embassy in your home country or auto rental agencies in the country of arrival
  - ◆ If you are carrying a large quantity of samples to exhibit in a trade show, they may be subject to textile quota restrictions and may require you to obtain a quota certificate/visa for clearance. Check with the export promotion agencies in your country or US Customs for current regulations
  - ◆ Get a hair cut before departure. This will save you time and hassle when looking for a hairdresser to suit your needs. The rates for a basic hair cut in major metropolitan cities such as New York can range between US $20 to $40 for men and US $25 to $65 for women, plus tips
  - ◆ Seek travel and other tips from people who have visited the USA

Your Flight

The Classes

If possible, try to travel in first or business class.

- First class
  - ◆ First class is the most comfortable of the different classes. Most airlines provide wider, more comfortable, sleeper seats. The service in first class is more

personalized. Almost all airlines offer more meal and drink options. Other services include priority check-in, first class lounges, extra baggage privileges, etc.

- Business class
  - ◆ This is less comfortable than first class, but is also less expensive. The facilities and services offered to business class passengers are pretty good and fall between first class and economy class. Generally, sleeper seats are not offered to passengers, but seats are wide enough to relax and enjoy the journey. The services are personalized. Priority check-ins are available, and generally airlines offer use of the same lounges as available to first class passengers. Although business class is not first class, it is still quite comfortable and enjoyable
- Economy class
  - ◆ If you are on a tight budget, then traveling in economy class is the best option. The seats are not as comfortable as those in the other two classes, especially for people who are tall/large. If you have to travel in economy, try to get an aisle seat with extra legroom. The extra legroom seats are located next to the emergency exit doors and offer enough space for you to relax and enjoy the flight

Your Seats

Some airlines can reserve a seat for you at the time of the booking; others will ask you to check the availability at the time of check in. In that case, try to be at the airport well in time to request a good seat.

Avoid taking the center or window seat as these restrict your movement. The center seat is the worst, as you might feel cramped in between two people.

If a flight is empty and you prefer to have more space for yourself, see if you can get a seat with no one sitting next to you. The airline staff at the check-in counter will know if the flight is fully booked. Otherwise, you can always move around within your class once you are on the plane, provided empty seats are available. Flight attendants are generally helpful, and you can approach them with any requests.

In the US, most flights are non-smoking flights. However, in the case of a long flight, some airlines do allow smoking in designated areas. It is better to get a seat in the non-smoking section even if you are a smoker, so that you do not have to inhale second hand smoke during the entire flight. If you need to smoke, you can go to the designated area, and then return to your seat.

Meals

Different meal options are available depending upon the class you are traveling in. More options are available in first and business class. However, even in economy class, the food is fairly good and caters to all types of needs. At the time of reservation, you can also request special meals such as Muslim, kosher, vegetarian, nonfat/low calorie, and special diet meals. At the time of check-in, be sure to reconfirm your special meal request.

Jet Lag

Some of you might not have had the experience of a long flight, and as such have never experienced jet lag. Jet lag is caused by an imbalance in our bodies' natural clocks when traveling between different time zones.

Jet lag can cause some of the following problems:

- Sleepless nights
- Fatigue and exhaustion
- Headaches
- Indigestion
- Irritability and depression
- Constipation or diarrhea
- Body aches and swollen feet
- Disorientation

How to Avoid Jet Lag

This is how I have been avoiding jet lag when traveling to Hong Kong from the US:

If I am on a flight that is scheduled to arrive early morning in Hong Kong, I try to sleep as much as possible in the last 8 to 10 hours of the flight. This keeps me fresh upon arrival. After arrival in Hong Kong, I do not sleep during the daytime and go to bed close to 11:30 PM. By the next morning, I am refreshed and ready to go. However, upon my return to New York, my flight usually arrives in the evening. I avoid sleeping during the last few hours of my flight so that when I get home, I am ready to go to bed. This system may not work for everybody, but it is worth a try. For more information on jet lag, you can read articles on the subject or consult a professional.

Listed below are a few other tips for avoiding jet lag:

- Move around on longer flights. Walk as much as you can during and after the flight
- Apply lotion to avoid dehydration of the skin
- Drink lots of water and juices during and after the flight
- Spend time under daylight upon arrival

- Avoid consumption of alcohol, caffeinated, and carbonated drinks during your flight
- Eat less during the flight

Arrival

On the flight, customs forms are distributed to passengers who intend to enter the USA. Fill out the form before landing in order to save time. This form is self-explanatory. If you need help, ask any of the flight stewards or the flight purser. Customs forms are also available at the arrival hall before immigration.

Upon arrival, keep your passport and traveling documents handy. First you will need to go to immigration. Next, collect your baggage and then pass through US Customs. If you have declared any dutiable items on the form, you will be charged customs duties according to the prevalent rate. If there is nothing to declare, the customs officer may allow you to go. Customs officers reserve the right to inspect your baggage, even if you have nothing to declare. If you are not sure whether something in your possession is dutiable, do not hesitate to ask a customs officer.

Note: do not discard your tickets; you will need them as proof of your business travel for company accounts.

Upon arrival, if you have not yet converted your currency, it is best to find a bank or money exchange at the airport. You can exchange money, provided it is convertible currency (hard currency). Currencies from developing countries are not easily convertible. Hard currency can also be exchanged within the US cities, at banks, money exchanges, and luxury hotels. Because you will need US dollars for transportation, meals, etc., you must have some US dollars in hand. Travelers' checks in US dollars are acceptable at many places, but taxi drivers and smaller businesses may not accept them. Credit cards are heavily used in the US. Car rental agencies, hotels, and airline bookings can be conveniently made with the use of credit cards. In the absence of these cards, bookings over the telephone for car rentals, hotels, airlines, etc. are hard to make.

If you are visiting the country for the first time and no one is picking you up from the airport, then go to the information desk and ask about the modes of transportation to get to your hotel, or wherever you need to go. If you made reservations with the hotel prior to departure, at the time of the booking, check if the hotel provides a shuttle service from the airport. This shuttle service could also be free.

Upon arrival, obtain a local city map. Maps for subways, trains, and buses are also easily available. Calculate the distances to and from anywhere you need to go. If you are on a tight appointment schedule, getting a taxi will be a better idea than trying out other public transportation systems. This way you can avoid being late. Becoming familiar with public transportation systems may be a little confusing for the first time visitor. Paying tips to taxi drivers and waiters is common and ranges between 10-15% of the total.

If you are planning to drive in the US, and in your home country you drive on the opposite side of the road in relation to the USA, then try not to go on roads with heavy or high-speed traffic. Get some practice in low traffic areas, before attempting to drive elsewhere. Do not pick up hitchhikers or strangers at any time.

It is important to note that different time zones exist *within* the USA. See appendix 1-13B for a listing of World Time Zone web sites.

Your Safety

As in any other country, there is crime in the USA. Major metropolitan cities generally have higher crime rates than smaller or suburban cities. For example, New York City is considered a high crime area. Certain areas may be dangerous even during the daytime, but those areas are in small pockets. Other than that, it is ok to travel around provided you use common sense and follow basic rules of safety.

Anything can happen in any big city anywhere in the world; whether it is New York, London, Paris, Hong Kong, or Tokyo. I am going to tell you about two incidents, one in London and the other in Paris.

I was leaving the London airport with a client who came to pick me up when I saw a man hit a pregnant woman in the stomach and run away with her handbag. The woman screamed and collapsed as the thief sped away. I was shocked to see the woman collapse and was extremely upset by the situation.

In Paris, I was inquiring about a taxi at the information desk at the airport, and there was a man from another country standing behind me. The man was very well dressed and was carrying a nice brief case. In an instant, another man came and grabbed his brief case, and ran with it. He was screaming and started crying. He had lost his passport, money, and some other valuables.

What I am trying to convey is that crime does exist in every part of the world, and precautions must be taken to prevent such incidents. Millions of visitors come to New York and other cities of the USA, and such bad incidents happen only to a very small number of people. Nevertheless, it is important to be careful.

Take the following precautions:

- Your valuables
  - ◆ Do not leave your bags unattended at any time. Keep all belongings in view, if not in touch, and be alert at all times
  - ◆ Avoid carrying cash or valuables, but if you do have to carry them, do not show any cash or valuables to avoid inviting trouble
  - ◆ Do not keep all your cash in the same pocket or wallet/bag
  - ◆ Keep your passport, airline ticket, other valuables, and documents in a safe place
  - ◆ Do not put your handbag on your side or on the floor, especially if you are at a counter talking to someone
- Be aware of your surroundings
  - ◆ Be vigilant and alert. Purse-snatchers and briefcase thieves are known to work at busy airports or in busy downtown areas. Also keep in mind that criminals who are caught at the airport are often not prosecuted, because it is hard to produce witnesses and ask victims to travel for prosecution purposes
  - ◆ Watch out for criminals such as pickpockets, unauthorized taxi drivers, baggage thieves, and unauthorized tour guides. Do not get into an unauthorized taxi or hire an unauthorized tour guide. Authorized workers wear some kind of identification or a uniform
  - ◆ Keep an eye on your belongings and your surroundings when using pay phones or Automated Teller Machines (ATM) for money transactions
  - ◆ Do not talk to strangers unless it is necessary
  - ◆ Watch out as pick-pockets sometimes create diversions

- They might approach you with questions and then try to take the opportunity to steal from you
- Watch out for groups of people who approach you. One person might keep you busy while the other does the job
- They may use tactics such as, throwing their own money on the floor and diverting your attention by saying that you dropped some money or spilling a drink on your clothing and then helping you clean it up. While your attention is diverted, they make their move and disappear with your purse or brief case

◆ Do not go jogging or walking in deserted and unfamiliar areas, especially after dark. Avoid going to desolate places but if you have to, it is not a bad idea to carry some cash; if you come across a person who demands money from you, it is better to give it to him than to antagonize him. There have been incidents where people have been killed when they have refused to pay small amounts of cash like US $10 to $20

- Your behavior
  ◆ Do not look absolutely bewildered or lost if you are new to the area
  ◆ Do not look worried when trying to find places
  ◆ Do not act under-confident
- Ask others
  ◆ For assistance and guidance, talk to your friends or your business associates
  ◆ Ask for guidance regarding safe areas around the city from who ever is picking you up at the airport, or upon arrival at the hotel, talk to the concierge, bellboy, or front desk

Staying in a Hotel

If you are traveling for business purposes, it is recommended that you stay in the finest hotels, especially if you are planning to hold meetings at your hotel. This makes a good impression on the buyer.

The average hotel prices in Manhattan, New York range from US$ 150 to US$ 400 plus taxes per night, for just the room. Hotels in New York are generally more expensive than in other metropolitan cities. Do not hesitate to ask if breakfast is included in the hotel prices.

If you are traveling to a trade fair, hotel reservations can be made through trade show organizers at a convention rate, which is much lower than the regular rates. A hotel reservation must be made well in advance, as hotels are heavily booked during the trade show period. Some hotels are even booked one year or more in advance. Arriving at your destination without making a prior hotel booking is not recommended, especially during a trade fair.

Once at the hotel, check to see if they provide a free shuttle service to and from the hotel and the trade show venue.

Wherever you are traveling in the USA, make sure that you have easy access to transportation so that you can easily get around. Hotels in the downtown area (main city) are generally more expensive than others, but that does not mean that if you book a hotel in a suburban setting, that it will be cheap. It is best that you shop around before making any reservations. Hotel reservation sites are also available on the Internet. See appendix 1-13D for a list of hotel reservation web sites.

All five star or luxury hotels cater for the needs of a businessman or businesswoman.

These hotels generally have the following facilities:

A concierge provides you with help and information on:

- How to get around
- City tours and attractions
- Shopping areas, restaurants, etc.
- Other entertainment
- Flight arrangements

A business center equipped with the following:

- Fax machines
- E-mail facility
- Photo copiers
- Typing secretaries/receptionist

Some also offer the following:

- Internet access in the hotel or in individual rooms
- Video conferencing

Rates for long distance calls are available from the hotel operator. Check if the hotel offers free local calls from your room. Generally, local and long distance calls from a hotel cost more than the normal rates.

Refreshments and drinks in rooms are always available for guest use. Remember that the hotel provides you with luxury, but they charge a higher price for the service.

Remember to do the following:

- Keep the hotel address card in your wallet so that you can come back to the hotel easily. If you do not know how to get back to hotel, you can show it to the taxi driver and he can bring you back. Taxi drivers are supposed to be familiar with the area. If you do not know the language, an address card will be of great help in reaching the hotel
- Get a map from the concierge and mark landmarks around the hotel. If you do not know the language of the country, ask the concierge or bellboy to draw a map and/or write directions to and from the hotel in the local language
- Learn how to place a call, since telephone systems vary from one hotel to another. Also learn how to use the pay phones that are available in the hotel lobby or public areas

Safety Precautions at the Hotel

- Ask for a safe deposit at the hotel and keep all your valuables, including your passport, traveler's checks, cash, flight tickets, and any other important documents in these lockers. These are available near the reception of the hotel or are provided in each room. Some hotels charge for this service
- Keep the keys to your room with you at all times for safety
- Upon check-in, let bellboys open the hotel room door for you; in case someone is hiding inside, the bellboy will be able to handle the situation better
- Upon entry, quickly survey the room and bathroom to make sure that no one is hiding
- Keep the room door locked, preferably with the privacy latch, at all times
- If somebody knocks at the door, use the viewer provided at the room entrance door to identify the person before opening it

- Keep your baggage locked whenever you are out of the room
- Check emergency exits in case of a fire or other emergencies

For hotels in the USA, see appendix 1-13C. For other hotel and reservation related information, see appendix 1-13D. For car rental companies, see appendix 1-13E. For major airlines in the USA, see appendix 1-13F.

14 | Chapter Fourteen

Meeting the Buyer

You must be ready for your meeting with the buyer at the appointed time and place. Keep all materials, such as samples, catalogs, price lists, and other relevant information, ready. Delays of any sort should be avoided, as they will create a bad impression in the buyer's mind.

When meeting face to face with the buyer, greetings are first exchanged. Common greetings in the US include "Hi, Hello, Good Morning, or Good Evening." Generally, Americans are not as formal as Europeans, but addressing a buyer with his/her first name, at the first meeting, is not recommended. However, you must let them set the tone and adapt yourself to the situation. Avoid addressing a woman with the title, "Madam." Address her with the title "Ms." followed by her last name. A handshake with a smile and eye contact are also important. Unlike in some other countries, physical contact or a kiss on the cheek is not appropriate in the USA.

Following the initial greetings, business cards are usually exchanged. If there is more than one buyer present, do not forget to exchange cards with each one of them. After the exchange of cards, be sure to read the contents of the cards so you know exactly whom you are talking to. Putting the card away immediately, without even a glance, is considered impolite.

At this point, it may not be a bad idea to engage in small talk, like discussing the weather, to create a friendly atmosphere. Remember to maintain eye contact while talking. Not making eye contact implies that you are hiding something or are not confident in yourself. Try to stay pleasant and keep the atmosphere light and friendly. A nice friendly conversation will lead to developing a good business relationship. If a buyer invites you to a luncheon or a dinner, do not hesitate to accept the invitation.

Finally, take notes at each meeting so that you remember all that was discussed when exchanging correspondence in the future.

Communicating/Negotiating With the Buyer

Communications skills are very important. The primary language in the USA is English. If you are good at English and put your message across properly, your chances of success are greater. Americans are generally easy to converse with because they are casual and open in their attitudes and behavior. They like to keep the atmosphere light-hearted.

An entrepreneur must have excellent communication skills in order to negotiate and materialize an order. The purpose of negotiation is to get a better deal for your company, but it must be done in a manner in which you do not lose a customer.

A few tips on negotiation:

- Put yourself in the shoes of the buyer and think of questions that the buyer would ask you
- Be prepared with answers to possible questions
- Try to be as flexible as possible in order to obtain the order
- Do not "throw all your cards on the table"
- Avoid using the word "No"
- Stay calm and composed at all times

Selling the Products

These factors are important to the sale of the product:

- Up to date designs, styles, and colors
- Workmanship
- Quality
- Pricing
- Presentation
- Terms of payment and delivery

Points to Consider when Selling

- Offer credit terms if you can
- Offer your best price
- Offer quantity discounts, if possible
- Try to offer better terms than your competitors
- Finalize a safe mode of payment
- Keep your promises
- Build trust between you and your client

- Do not boast unnecessarily about yourself or your company
- Be humble and polite
- Develop a relationship where both parties respect each other's opinion
- It is better to deal with one person within a company. Some of the advantages of dealing with one person are as follows:
  - ♦ Helps avoid confusions
  - ♦ Helps build an understanding relationship with the buyer
  - ♦ Helps you work closely with the buyer
  - ♦ Buyers generally become more helpful if you develop a personal touch in your dealings

15 | Chapter Fifteen

Corresponding With Your Buyer

Correspondence is an important aspect of any business. Different mediums, such as, airmail, courier, fax, and email are being used today for the exchange of correspondence. Be sure to maintain a record of all correspondence in a proper filing system, which will allow you to retrieve all correspondence and information without any loss of time. Keep the following in mind:

All correspondence should:

- Be neat
- Be well written and well organized
- Be professional in appearance and in language
- Be polite and show courtesy
- Be to the point and stress the most important selling features to get the buyer's attention

- Be typed on a letterhead and printed on a high quality printer (if sending a letter by mail)
- Be signed
- Not have any grammatical, spelling, or typing errors
- Avoid negative comments, such as "We can't do this"
- Address the customer in a formal manner and not by his/ her first name, unless a relationship has been established
- Include "Attention:" followed by the full name and title of the receiver
- Be precise

Avoid sending pre-printed letters, since these are not personalized and do not leave a good impression. Most of these are thrown in the trash without even being read.

Since Americans commonly use first names, they sometimes do not write "Mr." with someone's full or last name, so do not get offended if you get a letter which does not address you as "Mr."

Your first letter to the buyer should contain the following information:

- Brief introduction to your company; a detailed introduction should be in the brochure, in case a buyer needs more information
- Should briefly establish the credibility of your company
- List of products
- Any references, if necessary
- Terms of payment and delivery period
- Attach the following with your first letter:
  - ◆ Business card
  - ◆ Price sheet
  - ◆ Company brochure

The company brochure should carry the following:

- Introduction to the company
- Company profile
- Capacity and capabilities of production facilities
- Information about the equipment in the production facility
- Total sales figures
- Number of employees
- Markets served
- Product details
- Photos of the products and production facility

If you are enclosing a sample, ensure the following:

- The sample is tagged with a reference number and specifications
- It is neatly packed
- A tag is attached stating "Not for Sale"
- The sample is presented in the form in which it is ultimately going to be shipped
- The invoice and packing list for US Customs is included with the sample. On the invoice, type "Free samples of no commercial value"

Buyers, especially at large corporations, are extremely busy, and you may find that they are not as prompt as you expect them to be. However, if they are interested, they will certainly reply to you as soon as possible. Nevertheless, do not forget to follow-up.

Building Up Your Business

Build a Strong Relationship With Each Customer

Make sure that all existing clients are completely satisfied with your product and service. If there have been flaws in the past, make sure you overcome those problems and do not repeat them. This will help you in building a strong relationship with your customer.

Another important factor in good marketing is not to overcharge your client. For instance, if you manage to get an order at a higher price, the second order may not follow because the buyer might switch to one of your competitors who may be quoting lower prices.

Do not work on a one-time basis; develop long-term strategies. Be cooperative with your buyers and listen to their needs, as they are the ones who are selling your product. Develop good communication channels and a good relationship with your buyer.

Customer Service

Treat your customers like kings; they will make or break your business. Be prompt, courteous, and accommodating to the best of your ability; accept your mistakes and compensate for them, if necessary. Put yourself in the customer's shoes. If you keep this in mind you will never go wrong.

Do not forget the end consumer, who will be using your product. If you provide them with good products, they will be loyal customers, especially if you sell under a brand name. Even if the product is not under any name, the customer will check the label and will at least be able to tell where the product came from. A bad product will damage the reputation of your business and your country. Remember that the US is a very competitive country, and its consumers are very demanding. If they are not completely satisfied with the merchandise, consumers do not hesitate to return it, even after it has been worn and washed. In general, the seller has to refund the money in full, regardless of the reason that the product was returned. Remember that the satisfaction of the customer is the primary goal of a business.

Tips:

- Treat your customers fairly, make them feel important
- Provide prompt service at all times
- Deliver goods as per your promise
- Keep customers informed of new products and offers; send them brochures/flyers of new products
- Make sure you are easily accessible
- Send Thank You letters after every order
- Send greeting cards at Christmas, New Year's, or on any special occasion
- Invite them to visit your booth at trade shows
- Encourage feedback from your customer
- Pay a visit to your customer when possible
- Stay in touch with your customer, even if orders are not repeated; this will tell them that you are in business and they may decide to come back to you at some point

Increase Your Customer Base

Building up a customer base is very important for the growth of your business. The more customers you have, the more sales you will generate. Furthermore, you will not be dependent upon one customer.

Avoid Substandard or Late Shipments

Remember that shipping substandard goods or making delayed shipments can jeopardize the business of your buyer and adversely affect your relationship with him/her.

Substandard Shipments

It is very unprofessional to ship substandard merchandise. This will damage your relationship with your buyer. It also damages the reputation of your country.

Late Shipments

Delayed shipments can create a tremendous loss for the importer. The buyer orders merchandise based on a certain schedule. If he/she does not receive your shipment in time, the buyer can face losses.

Many items such as garments are seasonal. Since garments are seasonal, as such they must arrive well in time so that they can reach the end consumer during that season. For example, shorts sell very well during the summer, but after that season there is no demand for such items. Furthermore, certain colors are more popular than others in a particular season, and the same color may not sell as well or at all in the next season.

In the case of a late shipment, importers will face problems such as:

* Being stuck with extra inventory, thus blocking their finances
* Having to sell the garments at a lower price
* Having to pay extra storage charges

Before sending a late shipment:

- Inform the buyer of the problem as soon as possible
- Ask if he/she can accept the goods
- Compensate the buyer if necessary

Regularity

You must have a carefully planned strategy to maintain control over your business and to market your product. If you maintain regular orders from your buyers, you will be in a better position to plan your production. This will help you produce quality products and make timely shipments. If your business is running on an irregular schedule, it will be hard to become an established exporter.

Before you enter the business of exporting, you should know the art of doing business. This comes from experience in the field. Even if you have a business degree, I still highly recommend that you work with an established exporter, preferably in a manufacturing company, until you feel confident in your ability. If you have the necessary experience, it is less likely that you will make mistakes.

16 | Chapter Sixteen

Buying the Latest Equipment and Machinery

The type of garments you plan to manufacture will determine the machinery and equipment you will need. Various types of machinery, tools, and computer software are available. The right type of equipment will help you produce quality garments.

Dealers set up by major machine and equipment manufacturers in your own country can supply you with the machinery you need. An advantage of purchasing from a local dealer is that he/she will be able to supply after-sales service. This is very important for running your unit in an efficient manner. If the local dealer does not stock the latest machinery, ask him/her if he/she can get it for you.

Another source for buying equipment is trade shows. To buy the latest equipment, machinery, accessories, and computer software for the garment industry, it is a good idea to visit a relevant trade show to acquire the appropriate knowledge and information. I recommend visiting a specialized show that is geared towards the garment industry. Such shows are held in the US, Europe, and the Far East. In the US, the *Bobbin Show* is one that exhibits the latest apparel tools and machinery. Attending shows such as these will help you stay abreast with any new developments in this area. If you decide to buy machinery from another country, make sure you have made adequate arrangements for after-sales service. See appendix 1-16A for machinery manufacturers and suppliers.

Products you can find at good apparel machinery shows include:

- Industrial sewing machines and attachments, boilers, CAD/ CAM and design systems, computer systems, closures, cutters, embroidery equipment, fabric inspection and finishing equipment, heat transfers, knitting machinery, label printing equipment, pleating equipment, pressing and fusing equipment and supplies, quilting machines, screen printing equipment, trade publications, etc.

Some brand names of apparel machinery are:

- Baratto, Brimato, CRA, Durkopp Adler Ag, Eastman Machine, Fasco, Gerber, Her Yeh, Juki, Kannegiesser, Kansai Special, Kennedy, Melco, Naomoto, Ngai Shing, Paris, Pegasus, Perfecta, Tajima, Treasure, Union Special, Wastema

Manufacturing for the Domestic and/ or International Market

Domestic

Although you can start manufacturing for export from the very beginning, I recommend that you begin by manufacturing for the domestic market; I call this "phase one." You can manufacture apparel and sell in the domestic market through locally appointed distributors or sales agents, or by selling directly to the retailers. You can also act as a sub-contractor by producing goods for large exporters based in your country. Sub-contracting is sometimes referred to as CMT (Cut, Make, and Trim).

By manufacturing for the domestic market, you can:

- Have the domestic market as your base, and then develop your export market
- Learn everything from procuring the fabric to the actual production and packaging of the garments
- Gain marketing and selling experience
- Sharpen your overall skills in manufacturing and selling
- Establish contacts with suppliers and buyers in the domestic market
- Establish credibility
- Create a brand name, and ultimately use it in the international market
- Learn how to manage day to day problems connected with the business, including labor problems
- Learn to maintain accounts and a positive cash flow
- Supply to exporters in your country on a CMT basis (sub-contracting). Under this arrangement, the exporters supply you with all materials, designs, etc. and you are responsible for putting the garments together. This will help you

learn what other exporters are selling in the international market

International

In the second phase, you can manufacture and export on your own account. Phase one will give you the appropriate experience needed for exporting. You will now know the steps of manufacturing. You will also have the experience of dealing with different situations and solving problems in order to deliver your final product efficiently.

How to Prepare Your Sample Range for the International Market

Once you have attained sufficient knowledge and experience about your product, the best thing to do is to get access to publications or to contact design and color forecasting companies. Both will forecast information about future trends and styles in the country you wish to export to. The best thing to do is to discuss your target market with these companies before purchasing their services or publications. For the American market, it is better to get such books from the USA. For export to Europe, there are some reputable companies based in Europe that can be of great help. These companies can be found at apparel trade shows. Once you have access to these publications and forecast color information, develop your products accordingly for your target market. See appendix 1-10A for forecasting services.

Once an Order is Placed

Import orders are placed well in advance. Orders can be placed from six months to a year or more in advance, depending upon a number of different factors. You must remember that a long process is involved between the date of the order and the time that the merchandise goes out on the sales-floor.

Before accepting an order, make sure that your production facility is capable of producing the quality required. If not, make the proper arrangements to obtain the equipment, material, skilled labor, etc. that is needed. Also make sure that your production facility has the capacity to meet delivery schedules.

An order follows these steps:

- Buyer selects the item and its design
- Buyer selects the manufacturer or supplier
- Buyer checks the delivery schedule
- Buyer places the order
- Supplier manufactures the order
- Supplier ships the order
- Buyer receives the order
- Buyer sells the merchandise
- Merchandise is put out for sale to the end consumer

Production of the Order

This is a very important aspect of your business. Make sure that goods are produced as per the samples shown to the client. Always keep the satisfaction of your client and end consumer in mind. Also make sure that you make timely deliveries. Garments are seasonal, as such timely deliveries are extremely important.

It is very hard for a buyer to sell a garment after the season is over, and he/she may face a big loss if the delivery is not made on time. If you maintain your commitment to the buyer and your product sells well, then buyers will place repeat orders. In this manner, both you and the buyer will achieve growth together. Always keep in mind that the buyer's success is your success.

Stages of Garment Production

There are various stages of garment production, but in general the steps are as follows:

- Designing
  - ◆ Designs play a vital role in the sale of your products
  - ◆ The buyer provides most of the information on styles and color
  - ◆ You can use books on design and color and the services of forecasting companies in the USA
  - ◆ If you are preparing a range of products for a presentation to an importer or in a trade show, you can use the services of a professional fashion designer
- Procurement of fabrics
  - ◆ Ensure that quality fabrics have been procured as per the specifications of the samples approved by your buyer
- Inspection of the fabric and accessories
  - ◆ Each yard or meter of fabric must go through the inspection process in order to avoid the production of damaged garments. This also reduces the amount of wasted fabric, accessories, time, energy, money, and labor. Remember that with every damaged good produced, your cost per unit rises

- ♦ If you are procuring fabric from another source, it is recommended that you inspect it at the place of procurement in order to avoid any complications associated with returning or replacing the cloth
- ♦ Make sure that colored fabrics have fast colors and that printed fabrics do not have printing defects such as misprints or faulty design
- ♦ Make sure that the fabric, whether woven or knitted, is pre-shrunk or that the shrinkage margin has been catered for prior to cutting the fabric. Keep in mind that knitted fabrics are prone to more shrinkage, as such complete control may not be possible, unless new technology is developed in the future
- ♦ Any other accessories including laces, buttons, appliques, etc. must be inspected ahead of time
- Patterns and cutting
  - ♦ First, the patterns are made, keeping in mind the sizes, design of the garment, and shrinkage of the material. Proper patterns will save you from wasting fabric, thus keeping the cost per unit low
  - ♦ The fabric is cut according to the pattern made
- Distributing the material
  - ♦ The fabric is distributed to each worker for stitching. Make sure that relevant materials are available to each worker to avoid delays in production or misuse of materials
- The production line
  - ♦ Here, the material is sewn together to make the garments
- Cropping / Threading
  - ♦ This department ensures that all loose threads are cut, and that the garment is ready for inspection
- First inspection
  - ♦ Qualified inspectors should check every aspect of every piece. The main areas to be checked include:

- Correct size and stitching
- Correctly placed labels stating the contents of the fabric, care instructions, and size. See below for labeling requirements
- No lose threads
- No stains
- Properly placed tags, if any
- Garments are as per the specifications of the buyer
- Ironing
  - Garments are ironed and folded
- Putting the garments in bags
  - The garments are packed in printed or plain bags as per the requirements
- Final inspection
  - The garments must be checked one last time to make sure that they have been properly ironed and placed in the bags and that the bags are not torn, stained, or misprinted
- Preparing the packing list
  - A packing list must be included with your shipment; it will be needed for customs and the buyers
  - This list states the quantity of goods in each box/package; discrepancies or shortages can negatively affect your relationship with the buyer
  - Do not send hand written packing lists to the buyer/customs
- Packing the boxes
  - Sturdy, quality boxes should be used to avoid breakage during shipping and handling
  - Boxes must be sealed properly
  - Goods should be packed in boxes as per the requirements of the buyer
- Marking the boxes

♦ Boxes should be neatly and properly marked for easy recognition by the shipping company, customs, and the buyer. This helps keep the shipment from getting misplaced

♦ Mark the boxes on at least two sides for easy identification

♦ Use stencils for any marks on the boxes

♦ Make sure that all marks and numbers are legible and waterproof

♦ Use international symbols if special handling is needed

♦ The following items are generally printed on the outside of packages/boxes:
  - Name of the item
  - Box number (i.e. 1 of 200)
  - Order number
  - Quantity
  - Design number
  - Color
  - Country of origin
  - Weight (net and gross)
  - Pictorial symbols for handling if necessary
  - Cautionary markings such as "Do not Bend" or "No Hooks," if necessary

• A note on packaging
  ♦ Shipment by sea takes a long time to get to its destination and is exposed to different weather conditions. It is necessary to prepare seaworthy packaging, so that merchandise is not exposed to water and moisture

  ♦ It is recommended that the boxes are wrapped in sheets of gray or jute fabric to provide extra protection, particularly if the shipment is LCL (Less than a Container Load) and is not placed on pallets and shrink-wrapped

- ◆ Garments
  - Each garment is inserted into a poly bag, and then a suitable or designated number of garments are packed in each box. For extra protection, wrap all garments with a poly sheet. The poly sheet must be kept inside the box before packing the garments
- ◆ Textiles
  - Fabric rolls are wrapped in poly sheets, and then a suitable or designated number of rolls can be placed in hessian cloth or polypropylene in order to convert it into a bale
- ◆ Make sure that the packages are not very heavy and can easily be moved by humans

Note: Qualified inspectors/supervisors must oversee the entire process, from qualifying the fabric to packing the final garment. They should monitor every stage of production in order to obtain the best quality.

Quality of Raw Materials

Be sure to check the quality of materials that are available in your own country. It is ideal if you can find materials in your own country that are comparable to, or of better quality than, those in other countries. However, if the exact raw materials required by your buyer are not available in your home country, you can import materials from another country and then re-export them in the form of a garment. You must ensure that your product stays competitive after going through the exercise of importing and re-exporting. Also, check with authorities on the use of a custom bonded warehouse facility to store the imported goods. This would allow you to avoid paying customs duties. The duties paid on the material may be refundable if the material is used in the product exported. Each country has its own laws for importing under bond; check the laws in your country.

Before importing materials, consider the following:

- Have you found the right manufacturer/supplier of the material?
- Is the landed price (includes the cost of goods, freight charges, insurance, duties, and other related expenses) competitive after the materials arrive in your country?
- What is the delivery schedule and is it workable for you?
- Is the supplier reliable?
- Is the quality acceptable?
- Do you need an import license?
- Is a bonded warehouse facility available? Is it workable for you?
- If you need to pay an import duty, can it be easily re-funded after the goods have been re-exported? If the duty is not refundable, is the final product still competitive?

Labeling Requirements

The Federal Trade Commission (FTC) regulates labeling rules for the benefit of end consumers. These rules are to be followed by manufacturers and importers when putting information on the labels. You can get information on labeling requirements in the USA from many sources. It is best for an exporter to get the labeling guidelines and requirements from the importer.

Details on labeling requirements are also available on the FTC web site. The FTC web site provides information on labeling as well as on other areas including the Textile Fiber Identification Act and the Wool Products Labeling Act. In addition, the Textile Industry Affairs (TIA) unit of the Clorox Company assists US apparel/textile professionals in understanding and implementing the FTC Care Label Rule. If you need assistance in this regard, they may be contacted. Check if they can send information to your country directly. If not, ask your buyer to contact them. See appendix 1-10B for web sites on labeling requirements.

Apparel Testing Laboratories

Testing laboratories that can check the construction of the fabric and color fastness are located in almost every country. It is cheaper to get your goods tested in your own country, but if your country does not have such labs, you may want to hire the services of some of the apparel testing laboratories listed in appendix 1-16B.

Working With Suppliers

You will always need some suppliers, even if your facility is relatively self-sufficient. For instance, if you have a stitching factory, you will need suppliers of cloth and accessories. It is recommended that you work with more than one supplier so that you are not dependent on one. However, sometimes you may find it hard to work with multiple suppliers because there is only one who can make the product as per your specifications.

It is also recommended that you draft a written agreement with your suppliers, so that both parties understand the working relationship. This helps to build long-term relationships. In certain situations, verbal agreements are enough and if you ask for a written agreement, the supplier may take this request in the wrong way. To avoid creating such awkward situations, use your best judgement. Remember that a good businessperson must always honor both verbal and written agreements. That is the key to ultimate success.

17 | *Chapter Seventeen*

Shipping Cargo

Freight Forwarder & Custom Broker

A freight forwarder is a shipper's agent who moves the cargo. A custom broker clears the shipment through customs on behalf of the shipper. Some freight forwarders specialize in sea or air cargo. Custom brokerage and freight forwarding are two different types of operations. However, many companies perform both functions.

A large freight forwarding and custom brokerage company can generally handle air, land, and sea cargo. Before choosing a company, ensure that the company is knowledgeable about freight charges, preparing shipping documents, booking space for cargo, packaging, cargo insurance, moving and keeping track of cargo, the best modes of shipping, the requirements of customs for clearance of the shipment, any duties involved, and the laws of all countries involved. The company must ensure the safe and timely arrival of the shipment. It should also be able to use the most cost-effective method of shipping, whether by land, air, or sea.

Finally, be sure to discuss the mode of transit, freight charges, delivery period, weight and size of the cargo, destination, and requirements of the buyer, with your freight forwarder.

Freight forwarders/custom brokers generally need the following information when quoting prices:

- Mode of transportation (i.e. air, land, or sea)
- Type of commodity
- Number of packages
- Size of packages (to calculate the volume of the cargo). Using this information, they can determine if the shipment is to move on a Full Container Load (FCL) or a Less than Container Load (LCL)
- Weight of each package (net and gross)
- Destination
- Is local transportation required before the cargo is placed in the carrier?

Make sure that the company is experienced enough to handle your shipment.

An inexperienced freight forwarder and customs broker may not be able to:

- Arrange the most cost effective freight charges
- Arrange the fastest mode of shipment
- Handle your shipment properly
- Prepare the proper documents for customs, thus delaying your shipment

- Prepare the proper documents according to the Letter of Credit (L/C), thus resulting in the following:
  - ◆ The bank may refuse to pay you because of improper documents. Also, you may not have enough time to rectify the documents as per the L/C. If the L/C expires, then the bank is not going to pay you unless an extension of the L/C is received from the opening bank upon instructions from the buyer
  - ◆ The company may be incapable of removing discrepancies from the L/C. Again, a bank will not pay you if the documents are not corrected and submitted within the time allowed in the L/C
- Send the shipment out on time, resulting in the following:
  - ◆ A negative affect on your relationship with the buyer
  - ◆ Loss of future business from your client

Note: In order to make a timely shipment, you must hand the shipment over to the freight forwarder/custom broker well in advance. It is best to discuss a date with your freight forwarder and work accordingly to get the goods ready on time. See appendix 1-17A for a freight forwarder in the US, appendix 1-17B for customs brokers/clearing agents, and appendix 2-6H for information on shipping.

Your Customer's Freight Forwarder

Check if your customer has a freight forwarder that must be notified to handle the shipment upon arrival. Some companies in the USA provide global logistics services on behalf of the importer. They can also provide customs clearance and freight forwarding services in the US.

Documents Needed for Customs Clearance/ Shipping

At the time of shipping, you must prepare certain documents for customs clearance in your home country. You will also have to send documents to the importer, which will be needed for customs clearance in his/her country. The number of documents depends on several different factors: the type of merchandise, the country of origin, the mode of payment (L/C, D/A, or D/P), the laws of the country of import/export, etc. The freight forwarder can prepare a complete set of documents on their own, but they generally charge you extra for this service.

In general, the following documents are required by the exporter for customs clearance at the port of departure:

- Invoice
- Packing list
- A copy of the order (L/C, etc.)

In general, the following documents are required by the importer for customs clearance at the port of arrival:

- Invoice
- Packing list
- Bills of Lading (B/L) or Airway Bill (see below)
- GSP Form (Generalized System of Preferences)
- Certificate of Origin: Form A
  - ♦ The Certificate of Origin (see glossary) must accompany other documents in order to get preferential treatment when paying duties. It is issued by the authorized agencies in the country of export, including the Export Promotion Agency, the Chamber of Commerce and Industry, or a trade association

Note: Items under textile quota will require other specific documentation such as a quota certificate.

It is important that you prepare a checklist and verify all the documents before sending a shipment to your client. This must be a standard procedure in your company. You can make a checklist with the help of your custom broker and freight forwarder, your bank, an export promotion agency, or an experienced exporter.

Bills Of Lading (B/L)

When goods are shipped by sea, the shipping company issues an Ocean Bill of Lading.

The Ocean Bill of Lading is a very important document because:

- It is a receipt issued by the shipping company verifying that the goods have been received
- It confirms the condition of the goods (see clean or dirty B/L below)
- It is a promise by the carrier to deliver the goods to the appropriate destination
- It controls the title of the merchandise

Ocean Bills of Lading are prepared in two or three originals, each signed by authorized officers of the shipping company. Unsigned copies of the B/L are also issued for record keeping purposes. In the case of a L/C or documentary draft, the originals are sent to the importer's bank and the exporter keeps copies. The bank releases the documents to the importer in accordance with the terms of the payment. The shipping company releases the cargo upon receiving the originals from the importer or his/her agent.

Note: Most L/C's require "Shipped On Board" written/stamped on the B/L. Even if the cargo is sent against any other mode of payment, make sure that your B/L is stamped "Shipped On Board" or "On Board." This means that the cargo has been loaded onto the ship.

There are five types of endorsements on the Bills of Lading:

- To the order of the applicant, which means that the importer/applicant has the title of the goods
- To the order of the shipper, which means that the exporter/shipper has the title of the goods
- To the order of the negotiating bank, which means that the advising bank has the title of the goods
- To the order of the opening bank (the one who opens the L/C), which means that the opening bank has the title of the goods
- A blank endorsement on the B/L means that the title can be transferred to anyone

Types of Bills of Lading (B/L)

- Clean B/L
  - ◆ Issued only if the shipping company receives non-damaged cargo
- Dirty/Unclean B/L
  - ◆ Issued if the shipping company receives damaged cargo
- Through/Combined Transport B/L
  - ◆ Issued if more than two carriers are involved in the shipment, for instance, if your cargo has to travel on land and then sea, to get to its final destination
  - ◆ Eliminates the preparation of a separate B/L for the inland and the ocean component of the journey

- Shipper's Order (Negotiable) B/L
  - ♦ The shipment is delivered to the company or anyone designated in the B/L
- Straight (Non-negotiable) B/L
  - ♦ The shipment is delivered to only the company/person named in the B/L

Airway Bill (AWB)

When goods are sent by air, the carrier issues an Airway Bill instead of a B/L. An airway bill is a receipt issued by the airline. Originals are sent to the importer's bank, which then releases the documents to the importer. The deliveries are made by the airline upon receiving an original airway bill from the importer.

Modes of Shipping

To select a carrier check on the following:

- Reliability and reputation of the carrier
- Transit time
- Will your shipment be going directly to the port of destination?
- Is there more than one carrier involved before delivery to the destination?

Air

Shipments of garments and textiles to the USA can be delivered by air or by sea; in the case of Mexico and Canada, shipments can also be delivered on trucks and trains. Air shipments from Asia reach the USA within an average of seven days. Air freight is much more expensive than ocean freight. Your customer will specify the mode of shipment, keeping in mind how fast he/she needs the merchandise. Air cargo is moved either by weight or by volume, and airlines charge whichever amount is greater. Generally high value added items or time sensitive items are sent by air. Very large shipments can also be sent through chartered flights. Airlines use a formula to calculate freight charges. See appendix 1-2 for the dimensional weight formula.

Sea

Heavy or large shipments are moved by sea. This is less expensive than air, although it is much slower. It can take 3 weeks or more before the shipment reaches its destination, depending upon the distance and the type of service available. If trans-shipments are involved, then the shipment will take longer. See appendix 1-17C for a list of web sites containing shipping schedules and other information.

Types of Ocean Carriers

- Conference Lines
  - ◆ Independent shipping lines are members of a consortium called Conference Lines
  - ◆ Reliable; offer standard tariffs and a regular schedule
  - ◆ An exporter can get better rates if he or she signs a contract to use a conference line for all of his/her shipments
- Independent lines or non-conference lines
  - ◆ Operate independently
  - ◆ Usually cheaper than conference lines
  - ◆ Do not offer the same services and may not be as reliable as conference lines
- Non Vessel Operating Common Carriers (NVOCC's)
  - ◆ Ship small volumes
  - ◆ Consolidate the cargo and offer better rates to their customers

- ◆ NVOCC's can issue their own B/L
- Tramp vessels
- ◆ Can be part of conference lines or independent
- ◆ Generally used for moving bulk cargo

The Postal Service

Small or sample shipments up to a value of US$1250 per day can be sent to the US through the postal service. Customs duties shall apply as per the laws of the USA. Check with a relevant agency in your country to see if a quota certificate/visa is needed.

Air Courier Service

Most of the courier services can bring shipments from overseas. Their services are excellent and shipments can even be tracked before arrival at their destination. Services like UPS, FEDEX, DHL, and others are operating worldwide. They also offer discounts if you use their services on a regular basis. Discounts depend on how often you use their services. See appendix 1-17D for a list of courier services in the US.

LCL and FCL

If a shipment is small, then it is transported on a LCL (Less than Container Load) basis. It may be consolidated with other cargo. Shipping companies generally accept cargo on a LCL basis if it is at least one cubic meter. If the cargo is less than one cubic meter, the shipping company may accept it, but will still charge for at least one cubic meter. Since you will be paying for higher than the actual dimensions of the cargo, this will increase your cost per unit. This should be kept in mind when accepting a very small order. The most secure and economical way of moving large shipments is on a FCL (Full Container Load) basis.

Some advantages of FCL:

* Cargo is secure
* More economical than LCL for large shipments
* Faster transit time
* Easy handling
* Can be brought to the place of loading/unloading (i.e. your warehouse)
* Theft and pilferage is difficult

Types of containers:

* 20x20x20 cu ft
* 20x20x40 cu ft
* 20x20x45 cu ft
* 20x20x48 cu ft

The most popular and standard sizes used in the industry are the first two. Containers 20x20x45 or above in size are also called high cube containers and are generally offered at the same price for shipping as that of the smaller containers. Special containers for garments are also available. These are equipped with a movable track system, so that the finished garments can be shipped out on hangers. This system helps keep the garments in shape and makes them easy to handle.

When preparing the size of the boxes, remember to get the inner dimensions of the container so that the maximum amount of goods can be loaded into a container. By utilizing as much space as possible, you can keep the cost per unit of the merchandise low. The formula used to convert cubic inches to cubic meters is in appendix 1-2.

Shipping and Handling

Make sure that your packaging can sustain all types of handling. During the course of shipment, the packages are handled by persons, slings, hooks, conveyors, forklifts, etc. Sea shipments are exposed to rain, storms, unexpected weather conditions, careless handling, dampness and moisture, and theft. Proper packaging keeps the shipment from being damaged, and proper marking helps keep the goods from being stolen or lost.

Smaller shipments are generally placed on wooden pallets and then shrink-wrapped, before the forklift moves them onto the carrier. This way the cargo is not thrown around during loading or unloading. This keeps the shipment from being damaged and prevents it from getting lost or stolen.

A professional freight forwarding company generally provides a sheet of questions, asking the exporter to specify all details about the shipment. On that sheet, you can specify if any special care is needed in order to avoid damage.

If you are concerned about the handling of your shipment during the transit period, you should discuss any of the following with the freight forwrder:

- If you want your shipment to be placed and moved on pallets
- If you want your shipment to be shrink-wrapped
- If the boxes carry any delicate or fragile items
- If the boxes are to be kept upright at all times, with the opening side on top

Customs Clearance at the Port of Departure

Generally, it is the responsibility of the exporter to get the shipment cleared through customs before loading the shipment on the carrier. The exporter should hire the services of a customs broker. The documents required for customs clearance in the country of export are available at your local customs offices, export promotion agencies, or with custom brokers.

Customs Clearance at the Port of Arrival

It is the responsibility of the importer to get the shipment cleared through customs upon its arrival. A US importer can clear the shipment by him/herself or through a licensed customs broker. Usually, all tariffs and duties are borne by the importer. The shipment can generally be kept at the port for a few days, without any storage fee or port charges. After the expiry of the free storage, the port authorities levy demurrage for each excessive day.

The Entry Procedure into the USA

Knowing the procedure of entry of goods into the US can help you understand the requirements of an importer. It is recommended that you ask the importer what documents Customs require for entry into the US. Proper documentation will help the importer attain a smoother clearance from Customs. Generally, the importer or his/her agent has five working days, from the date of arrival of the shipment, to file entry documents at the port of arrival.

These documents generally include:

- An Entry Manifest
- Evidence of the right to make entry

- Commercial invoice
  - ◆ A Commercial Invoice (see glossary) should carry all information about the shipment including: names and addresses of the importer/consignee and exporter, prices (FOB, C&F, CIF), quantity, mode of shipment (sea or air), terms of sale (Consignment, D/A, L/C etc.), complete description of the goods, unit and total prices, currency of sale, weight and measures, marks and numbers, country of origin, and port of entry
- Packing list
  - ◆ Make sure your packing list includes all relevant information, such as the total number of boxes, exact quantity in each package, and clearly written marks and numbers
- Quota/Visa Certificate
- GSP form and Certificate of Origin
- Bill of Lading/Airway Bill
- Other documents, if required

All documents must be error free. GSP, Country of Origin, and quota/visa certificate must all be issued by a competent authority in the country of export. Any discrepancies can cause problems for your customers and entry may be delayed or refused by US Customs. You may consult the importer in regards to preparing the documents. These problems can be easily avoided if proper care and attention is paid while the documents are prepared.

Discrepancies can cause the following:

- Unnecessary delay of the entrance of the shipment into the USA
- Demurrage will be applicable after a certain number of days, leading to extra expenses for the importer
- Your customer will be frustrated

- An unnecessary waste of time, energy, and expenses is involved in getting everything in order
- A delay can result in loss of sale to your client, if the sale is time sensitive
- Customers may lose faith in your capabilities
- You can also lose a client if the difficulty has caused enormous problems for your customer

If problems do occur for unforeseen reasons, then an exporter must pay full attention and give priority to the problem of his/her customer. Be sure to maintain constant contact with your customer until the problem is resolved. Take responsibility if problems are caused as a result of your negligence. Do not hesitate to compensate your customer, if the demand for compensation is genuine.

Some reasons why US Customs examines shipments:

- To ascertain the value of the goods for duties/taxes
- To make sure that the goods are legally allowed to enter the US
- To make sure that they do not contain prohibited goods, such as narcotics
- To make sure that the goods are in conformity with the documents submitted, in terms of their value, quantity, etc.

Helpful Information on the Internet

The IATA (International Air Transport Association) provides information on seaports, airports, time zones, carriers, schedules, tracking, country data, export-import directory, trade news, etc. See appendix 1-17C for web sites containing shipping schedules and information.

Marine Insurance

All shipments must be covered by insurance. If the terms of sale are on a CI&F or CIF&C basis (see glossary), then the exporter arranges for the insurance. The importer arranges for insurance if the terms of sale are on a FOB or C&F basis (see glossary). The most common insurance used is the all-risk coverage. More information on this type of insurance is available from any company that deals in marine insurance. See appendix 2-6K for Pakistani insurance companies.

Keep in mind that the goods must be insured from the moment they leave your warehouse until they arrive at their final destination. If the cargo is not insured and is damaged or lost, you can lose a lot of money.

Claiming Insurance in Case of Damage

In order to claim insurance, proof of damage must be provided as per the requirements of the insurance company. Proof may be needed from the trucking company or from the shipping company, depending upon where the goods were damaged. If the importer or his/her agent receives damaged goods, he/she must notify the shipping or trucking company and get a damage report in writing before accepting the goods.

Be sure to follow any deadlines that may be set for filing a claim.

Steps to take After the Merchandise Has Been Shipped

- Inform the customer of the date that the merchandise was shipped on

- Ask your customer to give you feedback about the merchandise as soon as it is received
- Try to work closely with your customer, without overdoing it. Because people are quite busy, do not pester your customers unnecessarily or you will turn them away

18 | Chapter Eighteen

Modes of Payment

Cash in Advance

This mode of payment is very attractive to the supplier because the money for the merchandise is paid up-front. However, advance payment is very difficult to get, especially if it involves a large amount of money.

Buyers generally avoid making advance payments because they create cash flow problems and increase risk for the buyer.

Letters of Credit (L/C)

A letter of credit is the most commonly used method of payment and is recognized internationally. It is a document issued by a bank, which allows the importer to provide secure terms of payment to the exporter. It also assures the importer that the issuing bank (importer's bank) will release the payment only if the exporter meets the conditions stated in the L/C. In short, the bank guarantees the payment to the exporter provided he/she submits the documents in accordance with the terms of the L/C. Transactions made against L/C's are complex but are considered safe for both importers and exporters.

Opening an L/C

First, the importer (applicant) and the exporter (beneficiary) agree on all the terms of sale. The exporter then sends a pro forma invoice for final acceptance by the importer. Upon acceptance of the pro forma invoice, the importer instructs his/her bank to open the L/C in favor of the exporter. The importer's bank, or the opening bank, sends the L/C to its advising bank, generally based in the country of the exporter. The L/C is sent via mail/telex or SWIFT (Society for Worldwide Inter-bank Financial Transactions). The advising bank then forwards the L/C to the exporter after verifying the L/C. The advising bank could be any bank, not necessarily the bank where the exporter maintains his business account. Upon receipt of the L/C, the exporter reviews the conditions in the L/C, and if everything is as per the terms agreed, the exporter accepts the L/C. If the exporter doesn't agree to the terms in the L/C, he/she contacts the importer in order to make the necessary amendments to the L/C.

Once the exporter accepts the L/C, he/she sends the shipment as per the L/C. After the shipment has been completed, the exporter submits shipping documents to the bank designated in the L/C, which is generally the advising bank. This bank checks the documents submitted by the exporter, and ensures that they are in conformity with the terms of the L/C. Upon acceptance of the documents, the bank arranges the payment to the exporter as per the terms of the L/C. Finally, the original documents are forwarded back to the opening bank.

Note: It may not be a bad idea to request a copy of the L/C application from the importer to ensure that all terms are acceptable to you before he/she applies to the bank for opening the L/C. Either the importer or the exporter can pay the charges involved in opening a L/C. However, generally the charges of opening the L/C are borne by the importer. Also, L/C's can either be restricted or unrestricted. In the case of a restricted L/C, the negotiating bank is listed in the L/C. In the case of an unrestricted L/C, the exporter may choose any bank as the negotiating bank. Generally, it is better to have an unrestricted L/C. The charges for opening or negotiating the L/C documents vary from one bank to another. The bank terms regarding L/C's may also vary from one country to another; check with the banks in the country of export and import.

Types of Letters of Credit

- Irrevocable L/C
  - ◆ This is the most commonly used L/C
  - ◆ This is the safest type of transaction, and provides protection to the buyer and the seller
  - ◆ Once opened, this type of L/C cannot be canceled or altered without the consent of the seller and the buyer
  - ◆ Confirmed Irrevocable L/C
    - This is the safest option, but is more costly than the unconfirmed irrevocable L/C
    - The exporter may request either an opening bank or an advising bank to confirm the L/C
    - After the shipment has been sent, the exporter presents the shipping documents to the negotiating bank. The bank examines the documents very carefully, and if there are no discrepancies, it releases the payment to the exporter on the date specified in the L/C. The

advising bank can confirm the L/C. Sometimes the opening bank asks the advising bank to add confirmation. If the advising bank adds confirmation, it is also responsible for releasing the payment. If the issuing bank fails to make the payment for any reason, the advising bank is still liable to release the payment to the exporter

◆ Unconfirmed Irrevocable L/C
   - This form of L/C is also very commonly used and is less expensive to open than the Confirmed Irrevocable L/C
   - The negotiating bank checks the documents for compliance with the terms of the L/C, and if no discrepancies are found, it forwards the documents to the opening bank for final acceptance and release of payment. The negotiating bank usually waits to make the payment to the exporter, until it receives the funds from the opening bank
   - This L/C is a good option if issued in a low risk country by an established and reputable bank. If the exporter is not sure of the reputation of the opening bank, he/she should seek guidance from his/her bank. Banks have information and credit histories/reports on other banks

The Letter of Credit can be either at Sight or a Time/Deferred Payment L/C. In the case of an L/C at Sight, the negotiating bank pays the exporter at the time of negotiation of the L/C documents. L/C's at Sight are more desirable than Time/Deferred Payment L/C's because the exporter's payment is released immediately without a waiting period.

In the case of a Time/Deferred Payment L/C, the negotiating bank releases the payment on the date specified in the L/C. Buyers prefer these because they do not have to make the payment up front. Most common L/C's allow up to 90 days before the payment is due. If the exporter needs the money before the due date of a Time L/C, the negotiating bank may be willing to discount the L/C and make the payment immediately. In other words, the bank shall pay less than the face value of the L/C and retain a certain amount as a fee for early release of payment to the exporter.

Other Types of Letters of Credit

- Revocable L/C
  - ◆ Can be revoked or changed anytime by the importer without the exporter's consent
  - ◆ Not a good form of payment and is not commonly used
- Revolving L/C
  - ◆ This L/C is automatically restored after the completion of each L/C. It can be used if the same merchandise is being imported on a regular basis. If the importer is comfortable with the exporter and his/her dealings, he/she may open a revolving L/C, saving him/herself the bother of opening L/C's repeatedly
  - ◆ Rarely used as it involves a tremendous amount of risk for the buyer
- Back to Back L/C
  - ◆ This is arranged when there are more than two parties involved. In the following example, Company A is the buyer, B is the middleman, and C is the seller. Company A sends the L/C to Company B, and then Company B opens an L/C for Company C. This way all the parties feel comfortable in making the transaction. The L/C opened by Company A is used as collateral by

Company B for opening the L/C in favor of Company C. Company B adjusts the price in the second L/C for its own profits

♦ Back to Back L/C's must be opened with almost identical terms

♦ Good for intermediaries who cannot or do not wish to involve their own funds

♦ Consult your bank for more details before asking for such an L/C

- Standby L/C
  ♦ This is used as a secondary payment method in case the buyer fails to make the payment using the original/ primary method of payment. This L/C will only be executed if the original payment is not made within the specified time
  ♦ Good way to secure your payment if your buyer insists on sending shipments on an open account
- Installment L/C
  ♦ This allows an exporter to make multiple shipments within specified date ranges. The exporter can draw a payment at each installment of the shipment
- Transferable L/C
  ♦ Typically used by middlemen/intermediaries
  ♦ The buyer opens the L/C, then the middleman transfers the L/C to the supplier

There are other less common kinds of L/C's, such as a Red Clause L/C; check with your bank to find out more about different kinds of L/C's.

Advantages to the Exporter for Working Against an L/C

- The bank guarantees payment so long as the documents submitted to the bank by the exporter do not have any discrepancies
- The banks are generally willing to finance against L/Cs

Advantages to the Importer for Working Against an L/C

- Much safer than working against advance payment
- Bank will ensure that the documents submitted by the exporter agree with the terms of the L/C before releasing the payment to the seller. This provides some security to the buyer
- The buyer can get a deferred payment L/C which enables him/her to sell the goods, and then make the payment within the time allowed in the terms of the L/C
- A bank can open a L/C against margin, meaning that the importer doesn't have to deposit the full amount of the face value of the L/C in order to open the L/C. For example, if the face value of a L/C is $100,000, the importer may only have to pay $10,000 up-front. However, if the bank doesn't trust the importer, then it will require that the full amount be paid up-front for opening the L/C

Discrepancies in Documents Submitted by the Exporter

It is very important for any exporter to know that banks deal in documents, not goods. Banks do not physically check merchandise nor do they enforce the terms of the L/C, rather they ensure that the documents presented by the exporter are as per the terms of the L/C. Banks do not monitor different aspects of production or shipments. If there is a discrepancy in the documents submitted, the exporter is allowed to correct the discrepancy and re-submit the documents before the expiry of the L/C. If the discrepancy cannot be removed for any reason, the negotiating bank can refuse the payment or may ask the opening bank if it will accept the discrepancy. If the opening bank agrees, the negotiating bank can release the payment. The opening bank may discuss the discrepancies with the importer before agreeing to the acceptance of documents, which are not in accordance with the terms of the L/C.

The most common discrepancies are as follows:

- Spelling errors
- Incorrect company name or address
- Description of goods does not conform to the L/C requirement
- Omissions and misprints
- B/L or Airway Bill is not issued as per the L/C
- Incomplete documents are submitted

Word of caution:

Banks are extremely cautious in checking L/C documents and will return the documents to the exporter even if a minor discrepancy is found. For example, if the description of the goods in the L/C is "100% cotton blouses", but the exporter's description in any of the shipping documents (invoice, packing list, etc.) is "one hundred percent cotton blouses" or "blouses of 100% cotton", the documents would probably be returned for correction. You must ensure that you fulfill all the requirements of the terms of the L/C. Do not make any type of error, no matter how small it may seem. Otherwise, you will be at the mercy of the opening bank or importer. Some unscrupulous importers could also take advantage of the situation and deny acceptance of the documents, even with minor discrepancies, because they are no longer interested in the shipment. It is extremely important that you study the terms of the L/C upon receiving it. If you feel that all the terms cannot be fulfilled or are not as per the agreed terms, ask for an amendment before shipping the goods.

Upon receipt of the L/C, the exporter should check the following:

- All the terms and conditions of the L/C (description of the goods, quantity, price, date of delivery, etc.) are as per the terms agreed
- Is the L/C confirmed or unconfirmed?
- Is it irrevocable?
- Make sure that there are a few days between the date of shipment and the expiry of the L/C. A time of three weeks is preferable and should be available so that an exporter has sufficient time to submit the documents to the negotiating bank after the shipment
- Is trans-shipment/part-shipment permitted? Ask for it, if required
- Are there any restrictions on using a particular shipping carrier? If so, can you comply with those restrictions? Make sure the restrictions are not problematic
- Is the L/C payable on the currency mentioned in the pro forma?
- Points of origin and destination are correct
- Is there any allowance for a small shortage of goods?
- The documents required in the L/C are securable

Amendments to the L/C

It is essential for the importer and exporter to make the terms absolutely clear before a L/C is opened. Once the L/C is opened, it cannot be amended without the consent of both the exporter and the importer. In case of a discrepancy pointed out by the exporter, the importer requests a change in the L/C to its bank, which then forwards the amendment to the advising bank. The L/C is then sent to the exporter.

It is important to note that banks charge a fee for making amendments to a L/C, and those charges are either borne by the importer or the exporter, depending upon their mutual agreement. If the discrepancy is the importer's fault, then generally he/she pays the charges.

Tips for Exporters When Requesting an L/C

- Make sure you understand all terms of the L/C. Remember that an irrevocable L/C cannot be amended without the importer's consent
- Request an irrevocable confirmed L/C from the importer
- In the case of an unconfirmed L/C, be sure to check the credibility of the opening bank
- Read every clause of the L/C very carefully and make sure you understand and agree with all the terms and conditions, including description of goods, amount, date of delivery, company names and addresses, etc. In case of a discrepancy, or if you do not agree with the clauses, contact your buyer immediately and ask him/her for an amendment

Tips for Importers When Opening an L/C

- Make sure you understand all terms before opening a L/C. Remember that an irrevocable L/C cannot be revoked or amended without the exporter's consent
- Make sure that you understand all the terms sent in the pro forma invoice.
- If necessary, make the pro forma invoice an integral part of the L/C. Ensure that everything you agree upon is mentioned in the pro forma invoice, including the description of goods, date of delivery, price, mode of shipment, etc.

- L/C's are not foolproof. An unreliable exporter will be paid even if he/she sends sub-standard goods, provided he/she submits documents in conformity with the L/C. Banks only check to see if the documents are correct, and do not actually check the merchandise
- Make sure all the documents which are needed for customs clearance, are listed in the L/C
- A clause in the L/C authorizing you or your agent to issue a Certificate of Inspection (see glossary) may be added, provided it is acceptable to the exporter

Collection Basis/Documentary Draft/ Documentary Collection

Another mode of payment is a documentary draft.

There are two types of documentary drafts:

- Documents Against Payment (D/P)/Sight Draft
  - ♦ The title of the goods remains with the seller until the buyer makes a payment to get the goods released. Once the payment is made, the buyer's bank endorses the documents and hands them over to the buyer to obtain the shipment
- Documents Against Acceptance (D/A)/Time Draft/Date Draft
  - ♦ These are signed when the exporter sends the merchandise to the buyer on credit. The buyer signs the draft to make a payment on a specific date. The buyer takes possession of the goods after signing the time draft. Title of the goods remains with the seller until the draft is accepted and signed by the buyer

There is some risk involved for an exporter using a D/A or D/ P. The importer could refuse to accept the documents and the exporter's shipment could just be lying at the port of arrival. This can only be remedied if the exporter is able to sell the goods to someone else, and this new buyer agrees to make the payment to get possession of the goods, or if the exporter asks for the shipment to be returned. In case of a return shipment, all freight and other charges have to be borne by the exporter. If the importer has accepted the documents and promised to pay on a specified date but fails to abide by the commitment, the bank will exert pressure on the importer to make the payment but cannot automatically release the payment to the exporter. In other words, the bank is not obligated to make the payment.

Word of Caution to the Exporter

You should only sell against D/A or D/P if the buyer is well known to you and has the ability to make the payment as per the agreed terms. Check on the credit history of the buyer with companies such as Dun & Bradstreet (see appendix 1-18), or ask for references if you have any doubts.

Advantages for the Exporter When Using a D/A or D/P

- Preparation of documents is comparatively easier than shipments made against a L/C
- More buyers are willing to buy using this mode of payment

Disadvantages for the Exporter

- Exporter's funds are at risk until the payment is received
- If the importer refuses to pay, the goods must be sold immediately to someone else. Otherwise, all port charges will have to be borne by the exporter
- If goods are left at the port for longer than the time allowed, the port authorities/customs reserve the right to auction off or destroy the goods without any compensation

Advantages for the Importer

- The importer does not have to invest his/her own funds up front
- The importer can save money that would have been spent on opening a L/C
- The importer has the option of asking for a Certificate of Inspection before signing the draft
- The Time Draft allows the importer to sell the goods and make the payment later
- In the Time Draft, the importer can ask for a partial payment to the exporter
- The Time Draft gives the importer a specified time to make the payment. If he/she manages to sell the goods before the due date of the payment, he/she can use the funds for other transactions

Open Account

Under this arrangement, an agreement is established under which the importer attains the goods from the exporter. The exporter sends the shipment, along with the bill, to the importer. The importer is supposed to pay the exporter upon receipt of the shipment or at a later date as per their agreed terms. Remember, if the importer fails to pay according to the agreed terms, it can be very difficult and costly to recover the payment for the shipped goods. This arrangement is risky for the exporter. An unreliable importer may not send the payment in full or at all, or might delay the payment, even after receiving the goods.

Consignment

In this case, an importer receives the goods on credit. However, he/she does not have to pay the exporter until he/she sells the products. The title of the goods remains with the exporter.

This method is disadvantageous for the exporter, since he/she is at the mercy of the importer and may have to wait a long time to get a payment.

Note: For cash in advance, open account, or consignment basis, the banking system is not involved, except when a bank is used for the purpose of remitting the payment.

Refusal of Payment by the Importer

If an exporter is shipping his/her goods to the importer on credit such as an open account, consignment basis, or through documentary drafts, he/she may be at risk of refusal of payment by the importer.

The importer may refuse the payment for the following reasons:

- Importer's inability to pay for the goods
- Late arrival of shipment
- Importer's inability to sell the goods
- Importer finds another supplier with better products, prices, or terms
- Importer is dishonest
- Exporter did not comply with the instructions of the importer

Take the following steps if the payment is refused:

- First, find out the reason for the refusal
- If it is your fault, correct the problem if possible, otherwise offer compensation
- If it is not your fault, you may the contact the bank to see if they can help

- Exert pressure on the buyer through whatever means possible
- Contact a payment collection agency. They charge a fee for the collection of a payment. See appendix 1-18 for credit reporting services/debt collection agencies.

To avoid such a situation, it is best to do a good background check on the importer before sending the goods.

The following are the means of obtaining information on buyers:

- Use credit reporting services (Credit Bureaus) in the USA. See appendix 1-18 for credit reporting services/debt collection agencies
- Banks may be willing to provide credibility reports on the importer
- Ask the importer to provide references, two or more
- Use other exporters, who do business with the same buyer, as references

If you are unsatisfied with the amount of information you have received, then be sure to ask for a Confirmed Irrevocable L/C.

Export Credit Guarantee Insurance

This insurance provides protection to the exporter, in case of non-receipt of payment from the importer. There are insurance companies in most exporting countries who issue Export Credit Guarantee Insurance to the exporter. This type of insurance is worth considering when an exporter is offering his/her products to the importer on credit.

Insurance companies will check the credibility of importers before issuing a policy. Thus, the exporter does not have to worry about the credit check on the importer. If the credit report of the importer is good, an insurance company will want to issue a policy in order to make money. Hence, this policy works for all parties involved, and everyone can make money.

19 | *Chapter Nineteen*

Foreign/Free Trade Zones

Foreign Trade Zones or Free Trade Zones (FTZ) are secured areas outside a nation's Customs territory, which allow exporters to store their goods for an unlimited time without any duties or taxes. This program is designed primarily for importers and exporters. For complete details, you are advised to check with the local authority controlling the FTZ.

Such FTZ's are also available in the US. They help to promote international trade. Foreign companies can join hands with their counterparts in the USA to take advantage of this program. Companies planning to expand in the American or nearby markets may store their goods in Foreign Trade Zones. The community also benefits from this, since FTZ's stimulate economic activity and development, thus retaining old jobs and creating new ones. This helps to attract new business and investments.

A company may attain the following benefits by using an FTZ:

- Merchandise in an FTZ can be graded, sorted, manufactured, exhibited, assembled, altered, repacked, cleaned, mixed with foreign or domestic goods, sold, distributed, broken up, repaired, processed, salvaged, tested, stored, or destroyed
- Storing your goods in an FTZ can help in making prompt deliveries, thus avoiding the possible cancellation of an order due to delays in shipment
- There are no duties or excise taxes to be paid if the merchandise is re-exported to another country or to another FTZ. Duties are paid once the goods leave the zone to be sold in the U.S.
- Goods can be shipped to the zone in an unassembled or disassembled condition and then can be assembled or reassembled at the zone
- Re-labeling is allowed in order to conform to the laws of the United States
- There is no time limit on keeping the goods in an FTZ
- FTZ's are considered to be outside the Customs territory. Hence, merchandise for which a quota has been filled may be stored in an FTZ until the quota re-opens
- Other benefits may also be applicable; check with the appropriate office for up-to-date information

NOTE: Export Processing Zones (EPZ) are also established in many countries for the promotion of exports. Check with the appropriate authorities in your country to see what facilities you can utilize in an EPZ. See appendix 1-19A for information on FTZ's in the US and appendix 2-5 for information on EPZ's in Pakistan.

Types of Zones in the USA

General Purpose Zones (GPZ)

Most FTZ's are General Purpose Zones. These are generally located in industrial parks or in port complexes. The user may construct his/her own building on the lot allotted to him/her or may rent a warehouse already constructed in an FTZ.

Sub-Zones

Sub-zones are special purpose facilities for companies that are unable to operate effectively at General Purpose Zones. Sub-zones are designated for an individual company's manufacturing and operating needs. The same rules and regulations are applicable to sub-zones as are to GPZ's. See appendix 1-19B for sub-zones in the US.

Customs Bonded Warehouse

A Customs Bonded Warehouse is a secured area or building where imported goods can be kept for several years without paying any duty. During this period, the goods can be manufactured, altered, modified, etc., at the premises. A duty is not payable unless the goods are withdrawn for sale. If the importer cannot sell the merchandise in the domestic market, the goods can be exported without paying any duties or excise taxes. Partial withdrawal of merchandise may also be possible after paying the customs duty. This duty can be refunded provided the merchandise is used in the goods exported. The laws may vary from country to country.

20 | Chapter Twenty

The United States of America

American Culture

The American people are generally very friendly and courteous and expect the same from you. People in the US come from many different backgrounds, and this diversity leads to a variety of cultural practices. Furthermore, different settings impact behavior. For instance, people in New York City live much more fast-paced lives, than people in smaller, suburban areas. Although cultural differences exist, the people come together to form one American culture. They speak the same language, wear the same clothes, and share many of the same ideals.

In American society, men and women are treated equally; one cannot treat a person differently because of gender, race, ethnicity, background, or any other personal characteristic. American children are also very independent and encouraged to make their own decisions. This process starts from a very early age. Children are usually given independent rooms; even infants sleep in their own rooms. The parents' role is to encourage their children in any positive activity that they are involved in. In short, parents support their children, but at the same time they are raised with independent thinking and self-reliance. As children grow older, parents help them to acquire an education and a vast majority of youths attend colleges or universities. Parents contribute toward the expenses of their children's education to the best of their ability. However, the total burden is not placed on the parents' shoulders. The system of education in the US helps students by providing loans and grants. After graduation, students start paying off their loans. The government and private sector provide all the means necessary to ensure that education is accessible to anyone, regardless of income. They realize that education is essential to a prosperous society.

As a result of the large number of diploma/degree holders in the country, a vast majority of Americans maintain a good standard of living. The majority of men and women work and make up the middle class. There exists a small, very rich class whose income runs into the millions of US dollars each month. The youth also contributes towards the economy by taking part time jobs. Generally, they start working at the age of 16, but some start babysitting or doing other small jobs at an even earlier age. Young men and women take up all kinds of jobs, working in grocery stores, fast-food chains, apparel stores, etc. This not only helps them earn money for themselves, but it also gives them a sense of responsibility, teaches them to manage money, gives them more confidence, and provides them with exposure to the real world. Parents encourage their children to work because their contribution helps the economy and lowers the financial burden on the family. Many retired people also take a job in order to make extra money. In other words, everyone contributes toward building the society. Most importantly, each individual is treated with respect no matter what his or her occupation.

It is worth mentioning that there is strong sense of nationalism that exists in this society. People do a lot of volunteer work to build the society. Rich and financially strong people make contributions in many ways; they make donations to universities, research societies, hospitals, etc. Many people give their entire estates for the cause of the people. People donate their time and money to maintain their society.

On another note, Americans do like to relax. They eat out frequently; dinner is usually eaten around 5 or 6 p.m., followed by time for relaxation. On the weekends, Americans engage in leisurely activities such as gardening, shopping, eating out, day trips with friends and family, doing the housework, etc. Sports and comedy shows on television are also extremely popular in the USA. The Super Bowl, the championship game in American football, is a huge event and many people get together to hold Super Bowl parties.

The exchange of gifts is also very common in this society. There are various occasions during the year when gifts are given, including Christmas, birthdays, Valentine's Day, Mother's Day, Father's Day, etc. Family gatherings are generally held on major holidays such as Christmas and Thanksgiving. The New Year is also celebrated with full enthusiasm and parties are thrown for friends and families.

Like any other society, there are social problems in the US such as crime, divorce, etc. The divorce rate in this society is extremely high because of independent thinking and a lack of dependency on one spouse. Americans are extremely concerned about the divorce rate. The society does not encourage divorce; in fact, there are counseling bureaus where people can get help in resolving their issues. Despite these efforts, they have not been able to achieve much success in controlling this issue. In regards to crime, in metropolitan cities the crime rate is high and the society is again very concerned. The crime rate is generally high in poorer areas. Poverty leads to crime; thus, the key to controlling crime in any country would be to solve economic issues.

Business

It is important to understand the American culture in order to develop a healthy business relationship with your counterparts in the USA. Like anywhere else, the first impression plays an important role in establishing relationships. If you know what is expected of you, then you will do better. Americans tend to follow schedules and punctuality is very important. All appointments are pre-fixed, and people expect you to arrive well in time.

Being polite and humble is the key to success. In business, people are generally honest and straightforward, but this does not mean that there are no deceitful people. You need to assess how truthful a person is before engaging in any kind of business.

Attire

Formal business suits are widely worn in the US, and it is recommended that a foreign traveler be formally dressed when attending a meeting. However, business casual attire is now also gaining popularity in some companies.

The Mentality

American business people are intelligent and knowledgeable. They are generally able to seize any available opportunities. Your attitude must be flexible and accommodating because rigid policies will break a deal that might have otherwise materialized.

Haggling is usually not appreciated, though limited negotiation is acceptable. "No" generally means "No" and putting pressure unnecessarily will probably not work.

The American businesspeople are knowledgeable owing to a number of reasons:

* Education level
  * The literacy rate in the US is extremely high. The people have access to all kinds of media and other sources of information. This helps them gain a better understanding of the world around them
* Exposure to different cultures
  * America is full of multi-national communities. There are people from virtually every race and country in the US. This again helps American business people to have a better understanding of other nations
  * Many large companies hire people from different countries who have settled in the US. This helps them to eliminate language and cultural barriers, and leads them to negotiate a better deal. For example, if a company in the US wants to do business in China, they may hire a Chinese person living in the US. In doing this, they can better communicate with the Chinese company, thus helping their own business
* Travel
  * Americans tend to travel a lot. Traveling in itself is an education because it increases exposure to new places, people, cultures, and ideas

Women

Women play a vital role in day-to-day life. They are equally involved in business and work side by side with men. Many women run their own companies or are the head of their department. Currently, women generally earn less wages than men, but this gap is being reduced. They are capable of making independent decisions, so do not underestimate their authority. In short, they are treated at par with men in the USA, so treat them accordingly. Never say or indicate that you are more comfortable negotiating with men, it will immediately put an end to your negotiations. The role of women in the USA is important to know because in many Asian and underdeveloped societies, women play a secondary role in society.

Wages in the USA

Full time jobs require approximately 40 hours a week of work. Currently, minimum wage is US $5.15 (February 2001) per hour. Adjustments to the minimum salaries are made as and when needed. The wages may be paid weekly, fortnightly, or monthly. Management executives are generally paid on a monthly basis. The starting salary for a junior management executive is between US $20,000 to US $45,000 per year, depending upon the company, the city it is located in, and the qualification/experience of the employee.

World Factbook

The World Factbook is prepared by The Central Intelligence Agency (CIA). It is available on CD-Rom, the Internet, and in print. Printed copies and the CD-Rom can be purchased from the Superintendent of Documents. See appendix 1-20A for the World Factbook web site.

Facts

- *Official Name*: United States of America
- *Capital*: Washington, DC
- *Total States*: 50

- *Independence Day*: 4 July 1776
- *Total Area*
  - ◆ 9,629,091 sq km (land: 9,158,960 sq km, water: 470,131 sq km; includes only the 50 states and District of Columbia)
  - ◆ World's third-largest country
- *Climate*
  - ◆ Mostly temperate; tropical in Hawaii and Florida; arctic in Alaska; semiarid in the great plains west of the Mississippi River; arid in the Great Basin of the southwest
  - ◆ Low winter temperatures in the northwest are ameliorated occasionally in January and February by warm chinook winds from the eastern slopes of the Rocky Mountains
- *Natural Resources*
  - ◆ Bauxite, coal, copper, gold, iron, lead, mercury, molybdenum, natural gas, nickel, petroleum, phosphates, potash, silver, timber, tungsten, uranium, zinc
- *Population*: 275,562,673 (July 2000 est.)
- *Population Growth Rate*: 0.91% (2000 est.)
- *Age Structure*
  - ◆ 0-14 years: 21.25% (male 29,956,875; female 28,597,880)
  - ◆ 15-64 years: 66.11% (male 90,345,154; female 91,827,471)
  - ◆ 65 years and over: 12.64% (male 14,472,865; female 20,362,428) (2000 est.)
- *Net Migration Rate*: 3.5 migrant(s) / 1,000 population (2000 est.)
  - ◆ At birth: 1.05 male(s) / female
  - ◆ Under 15 years: 1.05 male(s) / female
  - ◆ 15-64 years: 0.98 male(s) / female
  - ◆ 65 years and over: 0.71 male(s) / female
  - ◆ Total population: 0.96 male(s) / female (2000 est.)

- *Life Expectancy at Birth*
  - ◆ Total population: 77.12 years
  - ◆ Male: 74.24 years
  - ◆ Female: 79.9 years (2000 est.)
- *Ethnic Groups*
  - ◆ White 83.5%, Black 12.4%, Asian 3.3%, Amerindian 0.8% (1992)
  - ◆ Note: A separate listing for Hispanics is not included because the US Census Bureau considers Hispanic to mean a person of Latin American descent (especially of Cuban, Mexican, or Puerto Rican origin) living in the US who may be of any race or ethnic group (white, black, Asian, etc.)
- *Languages*: English, Spanish (spoken by a sizable minority)
- *Literacy*
  - ◆ Definition: age 15 and over can read and write
  - ◆ Total population: 97%
  - ◆ Male: 97%; Female: 97% (1979 est.)
- *Government Type*: federal republic; strong democratic tradition
- *GDP*
  - ◆ Per capita GDP: $33,900
  - ◆ Purchasing power parity: $9.255 trillion (1999 est.)
  - ◆ Real growth rate: 4.1% (1999 est.)
  - ◆ Composition by sector: agriculture 2%; industry: 18%; services: 80% (1999)
- *Population Below Poverty Line*: 12.7% (1999 est.)
- *Household Income or Consumption by % Share*: Lowest 10%: 1.5% ; Highest 10%: 28.5% (1994)
- *Inflation Rate* (consumer prices): 2.2% (1999)
- *Labor Force*
  - ◆ 139.4 million (includes unemployed) (1999)

♦ Managerial and professional 30.3%; technical, sales and administrative support 29.2%; services 13.4%; manufacturing, mining, transportation, and crafts 24.5%; farming, forestry, and fishing 2.6% (1999) Note: Figures exclude the unemployed
♦ Unemployment rate: 4.2% (1999)
• *Budget*
♦ Revenues: $1.828 trillion
♦ Expenditures: $1.703 trillion, including capital expenditures of $NA (1999)
• *Industries*
♦ Leading industrial power in the world, highly diversified and technologically advanced
♦ Petroleum, steel, motor vehicles, aerospace, telecommunications, chemicals, electronics, food processing, consumer goods, lumber, mining
• *Industrial Production Growth Rate*: 2.4% (1999 est.)
• *Exports*
♦ $663 billion (f.o.b., 1998 est.)
♦ Commodities: capital goods, automobiles, industrial supplies and raw materials, consumer goods, agricultural products
♦ Partners: Canada 23%, Mexico 12%, Japan 8%, UK 6%, Germany 4%, France 3%, Netherlands 3% (1998)
• *Imports*
♦ $912 billion (c.i.f., 1998 est.)
♦ Commodities: crude oil and refined petroleum products, machinery, automobiles, consumer goods, industrial raw materials, food and beverages
♦ Partners: Canada 19%, Japan 13%, Mexico 10%, China 8%, Germany 5%, UK 4%, Taiwan 4% (1998)
• *Debt-external*: $862 billion (1995 est.)
• *Currency*: 1 United States dollar (US$) = 100 cents
• Telephones

- ◆ Main lines in use: 178 million (1999)
- ◆ Mobile cellular: 55.312 million (1997)
- *Radio Broadcast Stations*: AM about 5,000, FM about 5,000, short wave 18 (1998)
- *Television Broadcast Stations*: more than 1,500
- *Internet Service Providers* (ISPs): 7,600 (1999 est.)
- *Ports and Harbors*
  - ◆ Anchorage, Baltimore, Boston, Charleston, Chicago, Duluth, Hampton Roads, Honolulu, Houston, Jacksonville, Los Angeles, New Orleans, New York, Philadelphia, Port Canaveral, Portland (Oregon), Prudhoe Bay, San Francisco, Savannah, Seattle, Tampa, Toledo
- *Airports*
  - ◆ 14,572 (1999 est.)
  - ◆ With paved runways: 5,174
  - ◆ With unpaved runways: 9,398
  - ◆ Heliports: 118 (1999 est.)

PART 2

Import from Pakistan

1 | Chapter One

Brief Introduction to Pakistan

I am beginning Part 2 of this book by providing you with some background information on Pakistan. The first two chapters cover the culture, the people, and the major cities of Pakistan. After this introduction, I will then discuss how to go about importing apparel and textiles from Pakistan.

The Islamic Republic of Pakistan is located in South Asia. It borders India on the east, China on the northeast, Iran on the southwest, and Afghanistan on the northwest edge. To the south of Pakistan, lies the Arabian Sea. The capital of Pakistan is Islamabad. Pakistan is a parliamentary democracy; the President is the head of the state and Prime Minister is the head of the Government. At present, the Chief Executive is the head of the government. The Parliamentary set up consists of two Houses, the Senate (Upper House) and the National Assembly (Lower

House). These Houses consist of 87 and 217 members, respectively.

Chief of Army Staff and Chairman of the Joint Chiefs of Staff Committee, General Pervez Musharraf suspended the Constitution and took title of Chief Executive, after a military takeover on October 12, 1999. The Parliament and the Constitution have been under suspension since October 15, 1999. The head of the state is President Mohammad Rafiq Tarar (since December 31, 1997).

Pakistan is a country with its own history and rich cultural heritage. Pakistan is comprised of four provinces: Punjab, Baluchistan, Sind, and the North-West Frontier Province (NWFP). The terrain varies from sandy deserts, plateaus, and fertile plains to mountains with beautiful valleys and snow-covered peaks. The second highest mountain in the world, K-2, is in Pakistan. Many mountaineers come to Pakistan for exploration and adventure. Pakistan is also rich in natural resources (discussed later in this chapter).

There are four well-marked seasons in the country. Spring lasts from March to April, Summer from May to September, Fall/Autumn from October to November, and Winter from December to February.

Summers are extremely hot in the plains, where as the winters are mild. Summer temperatures can reach as high as 45C / 113F in central and southern parts of the country. In the mountainous regions, the weather is very pleasant during the summers, and bitterly cold in the winters. The monsoon season arrives between July and August, and heavy rains sometimes bring floods to certain parts of the country.

Winters are nice in some cities, including Lahore, Faisalabad, Sialkot, Gujranwala, and Islamabad. Karachi is in a coastal region and has a moderate climate for much of the year, although the summers are very hot and humid.

Pakistani Culture

Pakistan has a very rich culture. People are hospitable and friendly towards each other and foreigners. Men play a vital role in daily life and are the decision-makers in the family. Families are close-knit, and the young are expected to give the proper respect to their elders. The people of Pakistan are hardworking. The majority of the Pakistani people are Muslims and are con-servative in nature. Those who live in bigger cities and are more exposed to Western society tend to be less conservative.

The traditional dress for both men and women is shalwar (pants) and kameez/kurta (knee-length shirt). In the summer, the working attire for men is generally either a lightweight shalwar and kameez/kurta with a waistcoat, or a Western-style shirt with pants. In the winters, the attire is usually either, a woolen shalwar and kameez with a waistcoat, or a Western-style suit. The working attire for women is a shalwar and kameez/kurta or a saree (wrap-around). The traditional dress has evolved over time and in cities, it has been given a modern and sophisticated look. In metropolitan cities, a very small minority of women wear Western style clothing, but not as working attire. In general, Pakistan's dress is conservative in nature.

Most women in Pakistan are housewives, but a very small percentage of women do work or own businesses. The trend towards working women is increasing in today's society. In villages, women are married at an early age, where as in cities, women marry between the ages of 20 and 25. Arranged marriages are common. A wedding is celebrated with a lot of enthusiasm and effort. The ceremonies last over 5 days with each day representing a different function. Preparation for the marriage takes months and sometimes even years, depending upon the resources of the family. The success rate in marriages is very high and divorce is not common.

The class system does exist in the society, and people are status conscious. The majority of the people in Pakistan are poor, but a very small extremely rich class does exist. In cities, the middle and upper middle class enjoy the greatest luxuries of life; nice houses, vehicles, air-conditioners, refrigerators, and other modern day amenities.

Pakistani Food

Pakistanis are fond of eating delicious and spicy food. Main cities including Lahore, Karachi, Islamabad, Rawalpindi, Gujranwala, Quetta, Peshawar, and Sialkot all have excellent eating spots where people can go and enjoy delicious meals.

In Pakistan, people eat three meals a day: breakfast, lunch, and dinner. The main meals are lunch and dinner. Pakistan offers a variety of foods, ranging from curries to grilled foods. Pakistanis like to eat spicy food, which is mouth watering, provided you like spices. The many specialties that can be found here include tikkas, kababs, chicken tikka, karahi gosht, etc. Sajji is a very popular dish in Quetta. Pakistanis love curries, such as quormah, nihari, siri pai, and aaloo gosht. Pakistanis are also big meat eaters, as such a large variety of meat is made in a variety of ways. Chicken, mutton, beef, and fish can be cooked separately or mixed with vegetables. Rice and roti (pita bread) are also a part of the main meal.

Food is supplemented with dips and sides, such as raita (made of yogurt), chutney, and pickles. These items are excellent appetizers. Snacks such as samosas, pikoras, and chaats may also be served along with tea.

Chinese food is popular among Pakistanis. In addition, Western food is also gaining popularity, especially among the younger generation. Multinational restaurants such as Kentucky Fried Chicken, Pizza Hut, and McDonald's have recently opened branches in Pakistan.

In regards to drinks, plain water and soft drinks are quite common. The most popular hot drink is tea; drinking coffee is not as common.

Finally, deserts are served after the main meal. Popular deserts include kulfi, kheer, ice cream, and firni.

Natural Resources

Pakistan is country with many natural resources. It is a cotton growing country and produces one of the top qualities of cotton in the world. Textile and garments is one of the largest sectors of export from Pakistan.

All factors needed for export of apparel are available in Pakistan:

- Raw materials
- Skilled labor and unskilled labor
- Machinery
- Competitive prices
- Support from the government

Visitor Tips

Some tips for visitors to the country:

- Do not address business owners or executives with first names. Always use Mr. or Ms./Madam/Miss
- Be respectful and courteous towards both men and women
- Do not refuse gifts or an invitation
- Avoid discussion on religion or other controversial topics
- Do not criticize Pakistan or its people
- Be polite and nice
- Follow the host's level of formality
- Do not discuss sex or other such topics, particularly in the presence of women
- Do not conduct meetings in casual attire
- Female visitors should not wear short skirts or shorts, to show respect for the culture

Facts

- *Official Name*: Islamic Republic of Pakistan
- *Language*
  - ◆ Urdu is the official language. English is widely used in government and business
  - ◆ Different regional languages are also spoken such as Punjabi, Sindhi, Pushto, Baluchi, Seraiki etc. There are numerous local dialects
- *Population*
  - ◆ 135.28 million (95% Muslims, 5% others)
  - ◆ The population of Pakistan consists of Punjabi, Pathans, Baluch, and Sindhis. Punjabis are the largest in number
  - ◆ Population Growth Rate: 2.71 % (2000 est.)
- *Currency*: Pak Rupee
- *Climate*

- ♦ Mostly hot, dry desert; temperate in northwest; arctic in north
- ♦ During summers, temperatures can rise up to 114 F/ 46C in many parts of the country
- *Independence Day*: 14th August 1947
- *Time Zone*: 5 hours ahead of GMT
- *Area*: 796,095 Sq. km
- *Area Breakdown*
  - ♦ Punjab: 205,344 sq. km
  - ♦ Sind: 140,914 sq. km
  - ♦ North-West Frontier Province: 74,521 sq. km
  - ♦ Baluchistan: 347,190 sq. km
  - ♦ Federally Administered Tribal Areas: 27, 220 sq. km
  - ♦ Islamabad (Capital): 906 sq. km
- *Rivers*
  - ♦ The Indus: 2896 km (1799 miles)
  - ♦ Jhelum: 825 km (513 miles)
  - ♦ Chenab: 1242 km (772 miles)
  - ♦ Ravi: 901 km (559 miles)
  - ♦ Sutlej: 1551 km (964 miles)
- *Deserts*: Thar (Sind Province), Cholistan (Punjab Province), Thal (Punjab Province)
- *Major Dams*: Mangla Dam (Punjab Province), Tarbela Dam (North West Frontier Province), Warsak Dam (North West Frontier Province)
- *Business Hours*
  - ♦ Private businesses
    - Mondays through Thursdays and Saturdays: 09:00-17:00; Fridays: 09:00-12:00
  - ♦ Banks
    - Mondays thorough Thursdays and Saturdays: 09:00-13:30; Fridays: 09:00-12:30
  - ♦ Government offices
    - Monday through Thursdays and Saturdays: 08:00-15:00; Fridays: 08:00-12:00

- ◆ Closed on Sundays and national holidays
- ◆ Shorter business hours are observed during the fasting month of Ramadan
- *Common Federal and Local Holidays*
  - ◆ Pakistan Day-March 23
  - ◆ May Day-May 1
  - ◆ Independence Day-August 14
  - ◆ Defense Day-September 6
  - ◆ Iqbal Day-November 09
  - ◆ Birthday of the founder of Pakistan Quaid-e-Azam, Mohammad Ali Jinnah, and Christmas-December 25
  - ◆ Death Anniversary of Quaid-e-Azam-September 11
  - ◆ Eid-ul-Fitr: Religious festival celebrated at the end of the fasting month. The day of celebration differs ever year
  - ◆ Eid-ul-Azha: The day of celebration differs ever year
  - ◆ Eid-e-Milad-un-Nabi: Birthday of Holy Prophet Hazrat Mohammad (Peace Be Upon Him)
- *Weight and Measures*: the Metric system
- *Fiscal Year*: July 1-June 30
- *GDP*
  - ◆ Purchasing power parity-$282 billion (1999 est.)
  - ◆ Real growth rate: 3.1% (1999 est.)
- *Per Capita Income*: US $460 per annum
- *Labor Force:* 37.15 million
  - ◆ Agriculture sector: 47% (1997-98)
  - ◆ Manufacturing and mining sector: 10.50%
  - ◆ Others: 42.50%
- *Aggregate Market Capitalization/Capital of Companies on the Stock Exchange*: US$8.036 billion
- *Major Sources of Energy*: oil, coal, hydro, thermal, nuclear and liquid petroleum gas
- *Wapda's Power Generation Capacity*: 11, 246 MW
- *Electricity*: 220 V, 50 Hz AC. (Two or three pin plugs are in use)

- *Extraction of Crude Oil*: 53665 US barrels per day
- *Cargo Handled at Karachi port* (main sea port): 16.727 million tons
- *Cargo Handled at Port Qasim*: 6.850 million tons
- *Roads*: 228,206 kilometers
- *Total Number of Vehicles on the Road*: 2.6 million
- *Railway Tracks*: 8775 kilometers
- *Telephones*: 2.47 million connections
- *Post Offices*: 13,380
- *Telegraph Offices*: 427
- *Literacy Rate*
  - ◆ 38.9% (1997 est.)
  - ◆ More men than women are literate
  - ◆ Number of primary schools: 150,963
  - ◆ Number of middle schools: 14,595
  - ◆ Number of high schools: 9,808
  - ◆ Number of arts and science colleges: 798
  - ◆ Number of professional colleges: 161
  - ◆ Number of universities: 35 (10 in private sector)
- *Media*
  - ◆ Pakistan television: 5 TV centers in Islamabad, Lahore, Peshawar, Quetta, and Karachi covering 87% of the population; 115 million viewers
  - ◆ Radio stations: 23 stations
  - ◆ Newspapers and magazines: published throughout the country in English, Urdu and other regional languages; 424 daily; 718 weekly; 107 fortnightly; 553 monthly
  - ◆ News Agencies: APP is official news agency; PPI and NNI are private news agencies
- *Sea Ports*: Karachi (International), Port Qasim (International), Gawadar (Domestic), Pasni (Domestic), Minora (Domestic)
- *Shipping Company*: Pakistan National Shipping Company (PNSC). See appendices 1-17C and 2-6H for information about shipping

- *Dry Ports*: Lahore, Rawalpindi, Sialkot, Faisalabad, Peshawar, Multan, Quetta
- *International Airports*: Karachi, Lahore, Islamabad, Peshawar, Quetta
- *Fisheries*: In 1997-98 GDP contribution of this sector was 0.9%
- *Forestry*: In 1997-98 GDP contribution of this sector was 0.1%
- *Livestock*: In 1997-98 GDP contribution of this sector was 8.4%
- *Manufacturing*: In 1997-98 GDP contribution of this sector was about 18.3%. It employed 10% of the labor force. In 1997-98, the value added in manufacturing sector grew by 7%
- *Mining*: In 1997-98 GDP contribution of this sector was 0.4%
- *Tourism*: This sector has great potential for growth. K-2, Kara-Koram highway, Gilgit, Skardu, Harrapa, Moenjo-Daro, and many historical buildings and sites, are some of the greatest attractions in Pakistan. The Kara-Koram highway has led to an increase in the number of tourists traveling by road along the ancient silk route, and has opened up the northern mountains to increase visitors
- *Main Exports*
  - ◆ Raw cotton, cotton yarn, cotton cloth, cotton waste, apparel, tents, towels, hosiery, synthetic textiles, other made-ups, oriental hand knotted rugs, leather and its products, foot wear, sporting goods, fish and its products, wheat, rice, sugarcane, molasses, sugar, vegetables, fruits, pharmaceutical products, surgical instruments, chemicals, fertilizer, steel, electric goods, cement, petroleum and petro-chemicals, etc.

- *Main Imports*
  - ♦ Raw materials, machinery, paper and board, petroleum and its products, edible oil, tea, non-electrical equipment, chemicals, fertilizer, transport equipment, iron and steel products, electrical goods, drugs and medicines, etc.
- *Major Importing Countries of Pakistani Goods*: United Arab Emirates, Saudi Arabia, Hong Kong, Japan, USA, U.K., Germany, Italy, France
- *Major Exporting Countries, Sending Goods to Pakistan*: USA, Japan, Germany, U.K., Saudi Arabia, Kuwait, China, Netherlands, Switzerland, Malaysia

Textile Exports from Pakistan in Millions of US Dollars

Product Description	1996-97 Exports	1997-98 Exports
Textile Manufactures	5,554.5	5,467.1
Cotton Yarn	1,411.5	1,159.3
Cotton Fabrics	1,262.4	1,234.3
Knitwear	688.9	687.3
Bedwear	456.3	501.7
Towels	194.1	199.4
Cotton Bags/Sacks	27.6	22.9
Ready-made Garments	736.4	739.9
Tarpaulin & Canvas Goods	36.2	55.4
Tule, Lace Embroidery, etc.	14.7	8.8
Synthetic Textile Fabrics	512.2	607.2
Other Textile Made-ups (Excluding Towels & Bed wear)	208.7	244.5
Waste Material of Textile	5.5	6.4

2 | Chapter Two

Traveling to Pakistan

For information on travel and tourism in Pakistan, see appendix 2-2A.

Mode of Travel

Air travel is the only way to reach Pakistan from the USA. It is important to note that generally, Pakistan International Airlines (PIA) has direct flights from New York to Karachi, Lahore, and Islamabad, whereas American, European, and Middle Eastern airlines provide connections to Pakistan. Most flights arrive in Karachi, but Lahore, Islamabad, and Peshawar also have international airports.

Entry

Americans and most Europeans require a visa in order to enter Pakistan. Visas must be obtained prior to departure. A visitor can enter Pakistan within six months from the date the visa is endorsed in his or her passport. Generally a continuous stay of up to three months is allowed from the date of entry. A registration with a Foreigners' Registration Office may be required if the stay is longer than 30 days. A single or multiple entry visa may be issued. Contact the embassy of Pakistan in Washington DC or consulates in New York or Los Angeles for up to date information. See appendix 2-6G for the Embassy of Pakistan.

General requirements for obtaining a visa:

- Completed application form
- Valid passport
- Two passport-size photographs
- Confirmed return/onward air-ticket (if traveling by air)
- Proof of sufficient amount of foreign currency
- All policies must be checked with the embassy or the consulate at the time of obtaining a visa

Bringing in Foreign Currency

There are no restrictions on bringing in any amount, but the currency must be declared at the time of arrival. Any unspent balance can be taken out of the country at the time of departure. However, rules are subject to change and must be checked at the time of departure/arrival.

Duty-free Items Upon Entry

The complete list of items that can be brought in to Pakistan duty-free can be obtained from the Pakistan embassy or consulates in the USA and the Pakistan Customs office. Liquor cannot be brought into the country, however non-Muslim foreign visitors can purchase liquor for personal consumption at luxury hotels.

Your Security and Safety in Pakistan

There are some misconceptions about the security and safety in Pakistan. The negative views on this matter have been exaggerated. Although, there have been some negative incidents in the past, these have only been highlighted by the media and do not happen everyday and in every location. Demonstrations or processions can occur, and some places may be less safe than others. However, it is important that you use your best judgement. In addition, the Government of Pakistan is making continuous efforts to maintain law and order. You must use your common sense and street smarts regardless of the country you are visiting. Most of the luxury hotels are located in nice, safe areas. If you are not familiar with these areas, get advice from the concierge at your hotel, or travel with a local.

Cities and Accommodations

Islamabad / Rawalpindi

Islamabad is the capital of Pakistan and is a well-planned, modern city. Its construction started in the early 1960's; thus, it is the most modern city in the country. This city is 177km (110 miles) from Peshawar and 275 km (171 miles) from Lahore. All Federal offices such as the Ministry of Finance and the Ministry of Commerce are based in this capital. The city also has some industrial units and a stock exchange.

Islamabad is a beautiful city nestled in Margalla, the foothills of the Himalayas. Many tourists come to Islamabad to visit areas such as Taxila, Gilgit, Skardu, Hunza Valley, K-2 (the second highest mountain in the world), and Karakoram Highways (gateway to China, which goes through some of the most spectacular areas in the world). The Murree hills and Abbotabad are summer resorts very close to the city. Rawal Dam is also one of the popular picnic spots in the area. In addition, the city offers attractive parks, the beautiful Shah Faisal Mosque, luxury hotels, and some shopping centers where one can buy beautiful hand knotted Pakistani Persian rugs and handicrafts, among other things.

Islamabad is 30 minutes away (driving) from Rawalpindi. Rawalpindi also has some industrial units and Pakistan's Army headquarters are located here. Rawalpindi and Islamabad are also known as the "twin cities."

Although Rawalpindi and Islamabad have some industries in the area, they are not major industrial cities. In Rawalpindi, a dry port has been set up to facilitate export. Export shipments are custom cleared at the Rawalpindi dry port and then sent to Karachi for loading onto the carrier.

Islamabad Airport

One airport serves both cities, Islamabad and Rawalpindi. This is an international airport. There is a flight to Islamabad from New York that takes about 16 to 18 hours of flight time. There are many flights between Islamabad and the other major cities of Pakistan, and also some international flights. Facilities at the Islamabad airport include a restaurant, shops, a bank and post office, etc. Many luxury hotels provide free shuttles between the hotel and the airport. Car rental and taxis are also available at the airport and at other locations. In addition, buses and coaches run between downtown and the airport or other areas.

Luxury Hotels in Islamabad and Rawalpindi

For a list of luxury hotels in Islamabad and Rawalpindi, see appendix 2-2B and 2-2C.

Quetta

Quetta is the capital of Baluchistan, the largest province in Pakistan. It is home to the Quetta Staff College, a reputable military officer academy. The famous R.C.D. highway links Quetta with Karachi. Main items exported from Quetta include traditional mirror work and handicrafts.

Export shipments are custom cleared at the Quetta dry port and then sent to Karachi for loading onto the carrier.

Quetta Airport

This is a small airport. The airport is 15 to 20 minutes (by car) away from the downtown area. There are daily flights between Quetta and the other major cities of Pakistan.

Four Star Hotel in Quetta

There is only one four star hotel available in Quetta. See appendix 2-2D for the address.

Main Cities for Trade Activities

Karachi

This is the capital of the province of Sind and is the largest city in Pakistan. Karachi is a metropolitan city with a variety of people to meet, and places to visit. Getting around is fairly easy here; travel by taxis is cheap, costing approximately US$ 0.20

per kilometer, although taxi drivers charge higher for travel during late hours. Chauffeur driven cars are also available from car rental companies at very reasonable prices.

In regards to sightseeing and leisure, Karachi offers sunny beaches, golfing, sailing, shopping, historical sites, and a lot more. The historical sites include Thatta and the city of Moen-Jo-Daro near Karachi. Karachi is also home to different types of architecture that are both colonial and modern.

Karachi is an excellent shopping center! High quality hand knotted area rugs (Pakistani Persian rugs are considered one of the top quality rugs in the world), handicrafts, shoes, apparel, fashion accessories, souvenirs, etc. can be found here. It's a paradise for buying Pakistani made products.

In regards to food, there are many elegant restaurants offering local and international cuisine in Karachi. Some American fast-food chains are also available here.

Quaid-e-Azam Mohammad Ali Jinnah, Founder of Pakistan and Dr. Akhtar Hameed Khan, a renowned social scientist and founder of the Orangi Pilot Project and Rural Academy of East Pakistan (now Bangladesh Academy for Rural Development, BARD) are buried in this city.

Karachi is the largest industrial city of Pakistan. It is the biggest center for manufacture and export of textile/apparel and other industries. It has industrial areas and export processing zones where many industrial units are located. Trading companies and small manufacturing units are scattered all over Karachi. All types of textile manufacturing units including those for yarn spinning, weaving, dyeing, printing, knitting, and the production of hosiery and apparel can be found here. Many textile and apparel manufacturing units are equipped with the latest machinery.

Karachi is a custom port and all import/export shipments are sent through its seaport and airport. It is the busiest seaport and airport in the country. Importers and exporters from other parts of the country also use Karachi's ports. Karachi is known for its commercial activity.

Most of the Pakistani banks also have their headquarters in Karachi. Many international banks, including US banks such as Citibank, Bank of America, Chase Manhattan, and American Express, have branches here.

Karachi Airport

This is an international airport, and is the busiest airport in Pakistan; both international and domestic flights land and take off from here. All major airlines from various countries around the world fly to Karachi.

The facilities at the Karachi airport include duty-free shops, a bar/restaurants, a bank, a post office, shops, etc. Many luxury hotels provide free shuttles between the hotel and the airport. Car rental and taxis are available at the airport as well as at other locations. Buses and coaches also run between the airport, downtown, and other areas. Travel time by taxi to the city is approx. 30 to 50 minutes, depending upon the traffic. See appendix 2-6K for the web site of the Karachi Airport.

Luxury Hotels in Karachi

For a list of luxury hotels in Karachi, see appendix 2-2E.

Lahore

Lahore is the capital of the Punjab province. It is the second largest city in Pakistan and is one of the largest industrial centers in Pakistan. The distance between Lahore and Islamabad is about 330 km (205 miles), which takes approx. 3.50 to 4 hours by car. Both cities are connected with a newly built highway (the Motorway). The city is located 1305 km (811 miles) to the northeast of Karachi, and is approximately 1.5 hours by plane from Karachi. Travel by taxi is again very cheap, although taxi drivers charge higher for travel during late hours. Chauffeur-driven cars are available at very reasonable prices from car rental companies. Rickshaws and tongas (a horse-drawn carriage) are also used.

Lahore is the academic and cultural center of Pakistan. The people of Lahore are famous for their hospitality and courtesy. In regards to entertainment and tourism, Lahore offers golfing, shopping, historical sites, and more. Lahore is a huge shopping center and is a haven for oriental rugs, handicrafts and Pakistani products! All types of items, including clothing, jewelry, handicrafts, etc., are available here. Lahore is the largest sector of the country where high quality hand knotted area rugs are produced and exported to the US and other parts of the world. One can get excellent bargains in Lahore. The city of Lahore also offers beautiful restaurants that serve delicious domestic and international cuisine. Lahore is considered to be one of the best places for its quality and variety in foods. American fast food chains are also available if you do not like spicy foods.

Lahore is "the city of gardens" and is an ancient town, rich in historical monuments and mosques. All types of architecture can be found in Lahore. One can find palaces, tombs, and forts built during the Mughal Empire, as well as buildings from the British regime. Many historical places such as the Shalimar

Gardens, Badshahi Mosque, the Royal Fort, the tombs of Emperor Jehangir, Empress Noor Jehan, Asif Jah, and Anarkali can be found here.

Allama Mashriqi, founder of the Khaksar Tehrik (Movement), is buried at the compound of the Tehrik's headquarters. The Tehrik was founded in 1930, in attempts to gain freedom from the British and revive the lost glory of the Muslims. It played a vital role in the creation of Pakistan.

Lahore is one of the biggest centers for manufacture and export of textile/apparel and other industries. Trading companies and small manufacturing units are scattered all over Lahore. All types of textile manufacturing units including those for yarn spinning, weaving, dyeing, printing, knitting, and the production of hosiery and apparel can be found here. Many manufacturing units are equipped with the most modern machinery.

Lahore is ideally located; it is close enough for a day trip to other industrial cities involved in apparel and textiles manufacturing. These include Faisalabad, Gujranwala, Sialkot, Kasur, and Sheikhpura. Many visitors use Lahore as their base for visiting neighboring cities, because Lahore offers more luxury accommodations and other attractions than any of the neighboring cities.

Lahore is a custom port and many import/export shipments are sent through its airport and dry port.

All types of Pakistani banks have branches here; many also have their headquarters or zonal headquarters in the city. A number of international banks, including US banks such as Citibank, Bank of America, Chase Manhattan, and American Express can also be found in Lahore.

Lahore Airport

This is an international airport. There are many domestic flights and some international flights that land and take off from Lahore. There is also a direct flight to Lahore from New York.

Facilities at the Lahore airport include restaurants, shops, a bank, and a post office. Many luxury hotels provide free shuttles between the hotel and the airport. Car rental and taxis are available at the airport and at other locations. Buses and coaches also run between the airport, downtown, and other areas. Travel time by taxi between the airport and the city is approx. 20 to 30 minutes, depending upon the traffic.

Luxury Hotels in Lahore

For a list of luxury hotels in Lahore, see appendix 2-2F.

Faisalabad

Faisalabad is situated approximately 140 kilometers (87 miles) west of Lahore. Visitors from Lahore prefer to travel by road to this city, as it is only 3 hours (approximately) away.

Faisalabad is also one of the largest industrial centers in Pakistan. It's one of the biggest and the most important centers for manufacture and export of textile/apparel and other industries. Trading companies and small manufacturing units are scattered all over Faisalabad. All types of textile manufacturing units including those for yarn spinning, weaving, dyeing, printing, knitting, and the production of hosiery and apparel can be found here.

Export shipments are custom cleared at the Faisalabad dry port and then sent to Karachi for loading onto the carrier.

Faisalabad Airport

This is not an international airport, but connecting flights to this city are available from Karachi and other major cities. This is a very small airport with a few flights landing and taking off every day. Car rental and taxis are available at the airport and at other locations.

Four Star Hotel in Faisalabad

There is only one four star hotel in Faisalabad. See appendix 2-2G for the address.

Multan

Multan is believed to be the oldest existing city in South Asia. It is approximately 966 km (600 miles) from Karachi and is in the center of the country. It takes about 7 hours (by car) to reach Multan from Lahore. It is an ancient city whose historical sites and monuments are a great tourist attraction.

Multan is a fast growing industrial city. Its leading products are cotton, textiles, handicrafts, hand-woven carpets, silk, leather, pottery, etc. Trading companies and small manufacturing units are scattered all over Multan. Many types of textile manufacturing units including those for yarn spinning, weaving, and the production of apparel can be found here.

Export shipments are custom cleared at the Multan dry port and then sent to Karachi for loading onto the carrier.

Multan Airport

This is not an international airport, but connecting flights to this city are available from Karachi and other major cities. This is a very small airport with a few flights landing and taking off every day. Car rental, rickshaws, buses, and coaches are available at various locations.

Luxury Hotel in Multan

For the address of a luxury hotel in Multan, see appendix 2-2H.

Gujranwala

This is a small city with some industrial units. It is approximately one hour away from Lahore by car. Gujranwala is on the way to Sialkot.

Trading companies and small manufacturing units are scattered all over Gujranwala. Many types of textile manufacturing units including those for yarn spinning, weaving, knitting, and the production of apparel can be found here.

The city has no airports or luxury hotels. However, rickshaws, buses, horse carriages, and coaches are available.

Sialkot

This is a small industrial city, but is the largest manufacturing center for surgical and sporting goods in Pakistan. Trading companies and small manufacturing units are scattered all over Sialkot. Apparel and textile made-ups are also manufactured in the area.

Export shipments are custom cleared at the Sialkot dry port and then sent to Karachi for loading onto the carrier. Exporters from Sialkot also use the Lahore dry port and airport facilities.

The city is small and has no airports or luxury hotels. However, rickshaws, buses, and coaches are available.

Hyderabad

Hyderabad is situated approximately 164 km (102 miles) northeast of Karachi. A highway connects Hyderabad and Karachi and the road travel time is about three hours. This is a historical and cultural city; the birthplace of the great Mughal emperor, Akbar is nearby.

Although it has some textiles, apparel, and hosiery manufacturers, Hyderabad's primary industries include colorful handicrafts, glass bangles, glazed tiles, lacquered wood furniture, handloom cloth called "soussi", block-printed "ajrak", shoes, and stainless steel utensils. Folk and traditional dresses are also exported from Hyderabad.

Hyderabad Airport

Hyderabad has a small airport with a few flights. The airport is about 20 minutes from downtown. Car rental, rickshaws, buses, and coaches are available.

There are no luxury hotels in Hyderabad.

Peshawar

Peshawar is the capital of the North-West Frontier Province (NWFP). It is approximately 172 km (107 miles) west of Islamabad and Rawalpindi, and is about six hours from Islamabad by car. The city borders Afghanistan.

Peshawar is also well known for its historic and cultural value. It offers attractions such as the Balahisar Fort, Qissa Khawani Bazaar, Chowk Yaadgar, Mahabat Khan Mosque, Khyber pass, etc. The city has delicious domestic and Afghan cuisine. Their specialties include chappal kababs and green tea.

Peshawar's industries include textiles, apparel, hosiery, food processing, furniture, pharmaceuticals, cigarettes, etc. The city offers goods, including costume jewelry, oriental rugs, and handicrafts, from Pakistan, Afghanistan, and central Asia.

Trading companies and small manufacturing units are scattered all over Peshawar. Many types of textile manufacturing units including those for yarn spinning, weaving, knitting, and the production of apparel can be found here.

Export shipments are custom cleared at the Peshawar dry port and then sent to Karachi for loading onto the carrier.

Peshawar Airport

This is an international airport, with the majority of flights coming in from the Middle East. This is a very small airport with a few flights landing and taking off every day. Connecting flights between Peshawar and other main cities are available. Car rental, rickshaws, buses, and coaches are available.

Luxury Hotel in Peshawar

For the address of a luxury hotel in Peshawar, see appendix 2-21.

Comment on Dry Ports in Pakistan

Because the processing/transit time at dry ports is longer, sometimes exporters prefer to send their sea/air shipments directly to Karachi (where they are custom cleared). This is usually done when exporters are short on time and need to have their goods shipped quickly.

Tips for Visiting Faisalabad, Gujranwala, Sialkot, and Hyderabad

These cities are not as developed as Karachi, Lahore, and Islamabad. If you are visiting these cities for business reasons, you may take day trips from Lahore or Karachi, as these cities do not offer luxury hotel accommodations. Faisalabad does offer one four star hotel. Faisalabad, Gujranwala, and Sialkot are closer to Lahore, whereas Hyderabad is closer to Karachi. The distances are easily manageable for a day trip.

Distances Between Main Cities

Kilometers / Miles

	Karachi	Islamabad
Rawalpindi	1510 / 938	20 /12
Lahore	1290 / 802	290 / 180
Gujranwala	1360 / 845	230 / 143
Sialkot	1420 / 882	270 / 168
Faisalabad	1180 / 733	370 / 230
Hyderabad	170 / 105	1410 / 876

Note: Only main cities for textile and apparel production have been included. Keep in mind that textile and apparel manufacturing is also done in many other smaller cities and towns of Pakistan, however, it is not possible to include all the cities.

Travel Within Pakistan

Currency

Most transactions are done in Pak Rupees. Major hard currencies can be converted into Pak Rupees at commercial banks, luxury hotels, or through authorized money exchangers. Rates may vary from one money exchanger to another. The US dollar is convertible at all major cities in Pakistan at banks, currency exchanges, and luxury hotels.

Most transactions in Pakistan require cash, as credit cards are not widely accepted. American Express is the most widely accepted card. Mastercard, Visa, and Diners Club are acceptable at some places. All luxury hotels accept credit cards. However, it is better to check with the hotel, airline, or any other place before making any kind of reservations or purchases.

Air Travel

This is the best and most convenient way of travel in Pakistan. The airlines are as follows.

Pakistan International Airlines (PIA)

PIA is the national carrier and operates on domestic and international routes. It offers many flights during the day connecting major cities of Pakistan. Smaller towns may have fewer daily or weekly flights. Pakistan International Airlines covers 55 international and 38 domestic stations. Major airports include Karachi, Lahore, Islamabad, Faisalabad, Quetta, and Peshawar. PIA offers passenger and cargo services.

Shaheen Airlines

This airline offers passenger services. It flies domestically and to the Middle East.

Bhoja Air

This airline offers domestic and international routes. It offers passenger and cargo services.

Aero Asia

This airline flies domestically and to the Middle East.

See appendix 2-2J to see the contact information for the airlines listed above.

Railways

This is one of the most common modes of travel in Pakistan. Pakistan has over 12,700 km (7,892 miles) of railways that connect both major and smaller cities. There are 8,775 km (5,453 miles) of tracks with 781 railway stations. Trains run on a daily basis. Both air-conditioned and non air-conditioned coaches are available for travel. This is the second best mode of travel in terms of safety and punctuality. The main railway network runs north to south. See appendix 2-2K for more information on railways.

Travel by Land

Pakistan's road network connects both big and small cities. With the exception of some newly built highways, the road system is not at par with the developed world. However, for the most part, it is acceptable. The Lahore-Islamabad Motorway is the most recently built modern highway. It is comparable to the highways of the developed world. Other motorway projects are also under consideration. Traffic in Pakistan is not very organized. All traffic runs on the left side of the road. An international driver's license is valid. The speed limit is 65 km (40 miles) per hour on most roads and highways and 120 km (75 miles) per hour on motorways. The total roads cover a distance of 228,206 km (141,807 miles).

Travel by car, public buses, taxis, rickshaws, vans, and minibuses is quite common. Tongas (a horse-drawn carriage) are also used in designated areas of some cities. The standard of buses is not as high as in the developed countries, but nicer air-conditioned coaches also operate in Pakistan, particularly on longer routes.

Taxis are available. Some run on meters while others may negotiate the price, depending upon the distance and time. Chauffeur-driven cars are also available from auto rental companies. These can be air-conditioned and non-air-conditioned. Rental services are available at all major airports, luxury hotels, and downtown areas in major cities. Check the yellow pages, tourist information, or ask the concierge at the hotel in order to find car rental companies. Because traffic is disorganized and runs on the left side of the road, new visitors who are unaccustomed to these conditions are not recommended to drive on their own. See appendix 2-2A for the Pakistan Tourism Office.

Insurance

All kinds of insurance companies are available in Pakistan. For travelers' insurance, foreign visitors are advised to get insurance in their own country before departure.

Medical Facilities

Good medical facilities with qualified doctors and staff are available in all major cities of Pakistan. Both modern hospitals and private clinics are available for any medical assistance. The medical facilities are much cheaper than in the developed world. Hospitals are either government run or privately owned.

Mailing Facilities

Pakistan's postal service provides domestic and international mailing services. The Pakistan Postal Service provides the following facilities and services: public telephones, fax, telex, local express service, worldwide urgent mail service, air express and international speed post, surface air lifted mail including parcels, etc. The transit time for airmail letters between the US and Pakistan is about eight to ten days. However, delivery through courier services such as Federal Express, UPS, and DHL is very fast. Correspondence through e-mail is also becoming very popular. See appendix 1-17D for courier services and appendix 2-2L for the Pakistan Postal Service.

Communication

Pakistan offers a fairly well established communications system. Direct calls to anywhere in the world can be made from the home or office. Twenty-four hour telephone and fax services are also available at luxury hotels and post and telegraph offices. Cellular phones are becoming very popular in all major cities.

The use of the Internet is also becoming very common in major cities in Pakistan.

Telephone Area Codes

Telephone codes for the cities of Pakistan are listed on the Pakistan Telecommunication Company Ltd. web site. See appendix 2-6K under Pakistan Telecommunication Company Ltd. for their web site.

Drinking Water

Tap water is unsafe to drink. Bottled mineral water is available in major towns and at most tourist attractions. Visitors may also use water-purification tablets to drink regular tap water.

Tipping

Tipping 10% to 20% of the total amount of a bill is commonly practiced.

Shopping

All types of items are available in Pakistan. However, handmade oriental rugs (Pakistani Persians), handicrafts, etc. are the best. Pakistan produces top quality handmade oriental area rugs. Pakistan's area rug industry has developed a strong manufacturing base; they produce high quality goods that have become very popular among consumers in the US and the rest of the world. The hand looms on which these carpets are made are scattered all over the country, especially in remote villages. They are not only purchased for décor, but also as an investment. The different knots, designs, wools, etc. determine the price of the rug. Prices may be negotiated between the buyer and the seller.

Prices in Pakistan are also much lower than if you buy at a retail store in the USA. Many rug dealers accept major credit cards or cash. Hand-knotted area rugs are available in all major cities, including Karachi, Lahore, Islamabad, Rawalpindi, and Peshawar. However, Lahore is the number one wholesale center for oriental area rugs, followed by Karachi. The procedure for bringing rugs into the USA is very simple; area rugs can be brought by air as accompanied or unaccompanied baggage. There is a small customs duty on area rugs. The rate of duty can be checked with US Customs.

Sightseeing

Pakistan has lots to offer and there are many places worth visiting. The tourist office can provide you with any information you may need. Pakistan offers a variety of attractions for different types of tourists with different tastes. For those who prefer the outdoors, all types of terrain including high mountains, plains, and deserts can be found in Pakistan. Outdoor activities include mountaineering, trekking, jeep tours of the mountains, bird watching, jeep safaris, desert safaris, and trout fishing.

There is also an abundance of history everywhere. Many important historical sites can be found in Lahore, Multan, Taxila, Harappa, Thatta, Moenjodaro, Swat, Rawalpindi, Hyderabad, and Peshawar. The ancient silk route, which connects Central and South Asia provides attractions for all. The Karakoram Highway connects Pakistan with China. This route provides great opportunity for travelers to explore the magnificent and unparalleled beauty of this area. One can find beautiful mountains, valleys, and glaciers in the area. The height of mountains can reach 8000+ meters (26246 ft.). The world's second highest peak, K-2 (8611 meters/28,250 ft) is found in Pakistan. In addition, the Indus Valley Civilization, Mughal history, and early Muslim and Gandhara heritage are all excellent historical attractions for tourists.

Famous Mountain Peaks

- K-2 (Mt. Godwin Austin): 28,250 ft./8611 m (2nd highest in the world)
- Nanga Parbat: 26,660 ft./8126 m (8th highest in world)
- Gasherbrum-I: 26,470 ft./8068 m (11th highest in world)

Famous Mountain Passes

- The Khyber Pass, The Kurram Pass, The Tochi Pass, The Gomal Pass, The Bolan Pass, The Lowari Pass, The Khunjrab Pass

Lakes

- Manchar (Sind Province), Keenjar (Sind Province), Hanna (Baluchistan Province), Saif-ul-Maluk (NWF Province), Satpara (Northern Areas), Kachura (Northern Areas)

Famous Glaciers

- Siachin: 75 km (47 miles)
- Batura: 55 km (34 miles)
- Baltoro: 62 km (38 miles)

To find information on historical places, art galleries, museums etc., see appendix 2-2A.

3 | Chapter Three

The Textile Sector

Pakistan is one of the best producers of cotton in the world, and this is one of its major exports. Pakistan is the fourth largest cotton producing country in the world. Its products include 100% cotton and blended yarn, fabrics, and apparels. These can be woven or knitted. All textile products are consumed in the domestic and international markets. The main cities where garment and textiles are produced are Karachi, Faisalabad, Lahore, Multan, Gujranwala, Sialkot, Hyderabad, and Peshawar.

At the time of independence in 1947, Pakistan's textile industry was very small. There were only 78,000 spindles and 3000 looms. Now it is one of the largest sectors of Pakistan's economy. In 1996-97 it had over 440 textile mills/units, 8.23 million spindles, and 143 million rotors. Despite the tremendous growth in all the sectors of the textile industry, including cotton, ginning, spinning, processing and made-up sectors, this industry has not yet attained its optimum potential. There is still room for growth and Pakistan is working hard to produce even better quality cotton and textiles.

Export of Yarn and Textiles from Pakistan

Pakistan exports large quantities of cotton yarn, which includes all varieties ranging from coarse to fine. Countries such as Japan, Hong Kong, and South Korea are the main buyers.

Pakistan also produces large quantities of 100% cotton, blended, knitted, woven, gray, printed, and dyed fabrics for the domestic and export market. Its exports include T-shirts, vests, jogging suits, sports shirts, undergarments, hosiery, bathing suits, shirts, blouses, trousers, shorts, robes, bed linens, pajama suits, and other made ups.

Pakistan's weaving industry consists of everything from basic looms to the most sophisticated shuttle-less looms. The shuttle-less looms are both produced in Pakistan and imported from other countries. The Pakistani weaving sector produces quality fabrics, which are marketed around the globe in gray, bleached, and finished form. The latest finishing and printing mills and units are available in Pakistan and are capable of producing excellent designs, color shades, texture, and luster. Pakistan produces quality fabrics with lustrous texture and great color combinations and designs.

Since good quality cotton is grown in Pakistan, it has an edge on quality and prices over many other countries. However, with the upcoming abolition of the textile quota, Pakistan needs to further improve its quality in order to stay competitive. Right now, Pakistan is working under the protected textile quota system of the world. There will be tremendous room for growth after the quota system is abolished in the upcoming years, when everyone is able to compete in the open market. Although there is some expansion in the industry, Pakistan is capable of achieving much higher growth.

Advantages of Buying from Pakistan

* Pakistan produces one of the top qualities of cotton in the world
* It has an excellent textile and apparel manufacturing infrastructure
* Spinning mills in Pakistan produce top quality ring spun and open end yarn in carded and combed cotton. The yarns can be produced in 100% cotton or in different blends, such as polyester cotton
* It offers the latest weaving, knitting, dyeing, printing, and finishing plants
* Modern, well-organized garment factories are based in Pakistan
* Labor intensive work including hand embroidery is available
* An abundance of skilled and unskilled labor is available for reasonable wages
* Joint venture possibilities are available
* All types of laboratory tests can be done in Pakistan. These include fiber composition, count of yarn, density per inch, color fastness, weight per square yard/meter, shrinkage, etc.

Production and Export of Cloth

Period	Mill Sector 000 Sq. Meter	Non-Mill Sector 000 Sq. Meter	Total Production 000 Sq. Meter	Export Quantity 000 Sq. Meter	Value 000US$
1996-97	333,495	3,447,700	3,781,195	1,257,430	1,262,389

Export of Cotton & Cotton Manufacture

Cotton Manufacture (Million US $) 1989-90

Cotton Yarn	833.70
Cotton Cloth	559.0
Towels	129.8
Bedwear	190.8
Other Made-ups	78.2
Garment	393.8
Hosiery	273.7

Country Rankings According to the Production of Cotton

Rank (1996-97)
1. China
2. USA
3. India
4. Pakistan

Country Rankings According to the Production of Yarn

Rank (1996-97)
1. China
2. USA
3. India
4. Pakistan

Textile Quota

The textile quota applies to textile and garment imports from Pakistan; however, traditional apparel and handmade textile made-ups may be imported quota free. Details must be checked with the concerned US Customs Office and/or the Pakistan Export Promotion Bureau (EPB).

A quota policy is announced at the beginning of every year. The policy is announced by the Export Promotion Bureau, which works under the Ministry of Commerce of Pakistan. The Quota Supervisory Council then ensures proper utilization of the quota. Relevant trade associations execute the quota policies. See appendix 2-3 for the Quota Supervisory Council and appendix 2-4B for the Export Promotion Bureau.

Some of the Pakistani Items Under Textile Quota

Item	Category
Duck cotton & MMF	219
Play suits & sunsuit etc.	237
Infants wear of cotton	239
Cotton sheeting	226/313
Cotton poplin and broad cloth	314
Cotton print cloth	315
Cotton/MMF twill/satin	317/617
Gloves and mittens	331/631
Other coat M & B	334/634
Coat W and G	335/635
Dresses	336/636
Knitted shirts M & B	338
Knitted shirts and blouses W&G	339
Shirts not knitted M & B	340/640
Shirts and blouses not knitted W & G	341/641
Skirts CMMF	342/642
Trousers, slacks, and shorts M & B	347/48
Nightwear and pajamas	351/651
Underwear	352/652
Other cotton apparel coverall & overalls	359/ 659 C
Pillow Cases	360
Bed sheets	361
Terry and other pile towels	363
Flat dish towels, pile dish towels	369(FP)
Bar mops	369 (R)
Shop towels	369 (S)
Sheeting/poplin and broad cloth MMF	613/614
Print cloth	615
Print cloth	626
Poplin and broad cloth	625
Sheeting	627
Twills and Satins	628
Other MMF	629
Knit shirts M&B	638/639
Trousers, slacks, and shorts M & B MMF	647/648

An up-to-date list of items under textile quota can be obtained from the Office of Textiles and Apparel in the US or the Quota Supervisory Council or Export Promotion Bureau of Pakistan.

4 | Chapter Four

Finding Manufacturers & Exporters of Textiles & Apparel in Pakistan

Take the following steps:

- The main cities in which you can find manufacturers and exporters are Karachi, Lahore, Faisalabad, Multan, Sialkot, Gujranwala, Hyderabad, and Peshawar
- Contact the New York Trade Office and get directories/lists of exporters. The trade office can provide the following: trade data, a free trade bulletin, list of exporters in Pakistan, information on investment opportunities, opening branch offices, and joint ventures in Pakistan. See appendix 2-4A to contact the New York Trade Office for up-to-date information

- Contact the Export Promotion Bureau (EPB), relevant trade associations, and Chambers of Commerce and Industry in Pakistan and get directories/lists of exporters. See appendices 2-4B, 2-4C, and 2-4D for contact information
- Although there are no world known apparel and textile trade shows held in Pakistan, many Pakistani companies exhibit in various outside trade shows. Contact the New York Trade Office, EPB, trade associations, and the Chambers of Commerce in Pakistan, to see if they are going to have a pavilion for Pakistani exporters in the USA or in trade shows in other countries you plan to visit. Single country exhibitions are also organized by the EPB. Also ask show organizers if there are any exhibitors from Pakistan at the show
- Ask the EPB and other relevant trade promotion agencies to circulate your trade inquiry. Generally this service is free. These circulars are sent to exporters all over the country
- Research manufacturers and exporters on the Internet
- Contact buying agents in the USA or Pakistan. See appendix 2-6F for a list of some buying agents
- Buy trade directories to find manufacturers and exporters. See appendix 2-4E for publishers
- Advertise in major English and Urdu (the national language of Pakistan) newspapers. See appendix 2-6E for newspapers, periodicals, and magazines

Reaching the Right Company

- Pakistan has all kinds of manufacturers and exporters, varying in products and size
- After you have received lists of companies, write to the exporters and ask for brochures and samples
- Select potential manufactures and exporters

- Make appointments and visit the manufacturers and/or exporters, whether small or large, to see their workmanship. This will help you determine if they are producing up to the standards that you expect. A visit will also help you build a better relationship with the supplier
- Purchases can be made directly or through buying agents based in the USA and Pakistan. If you are working with a known company, you may not require an intermediary. However, if you need to work with small companies, it is recommended that you work through a buying agent. If you need products, which require handmade work, working through an agent might be better
- Evaluate the company and its products
- Make a decision

Note: As in many other developing countries, systems in Pakistan are sometimes not as organized as in the US. In the beginning, one may find it harder to find the right companies. However, this should not discourage you! A little extra effort and energy in finding the right companies will be worth it. If you do not wish to handle everything yourself, one suggestion is to appoint a buying agent. Agents in the US or in Pakistan are experienced and can handle all types of inquiries.

Other Things to Know

Business Negotiations

Pakistani businessmen are very enthusiastic and hardworking. As with any other businessmen, they want the best deal. They are used to negotiating the price, as such it is not improper to negotiate for a better price. However, too much of a price squeeze is not recommended, as this can lead to compromising for a lower quality product.

Sub-contracting in Pakistan

In the apparel industry, sub-contractors are very common. These services are utilized by trading companies, buying agents, large manufacturers, and exporters. Large companies tend to receive big orders, and often hire smaller companies to manufacture some of their orders for them. Since the large companies have expertise in the industry, they are able to monitor production and ensure quality of the products. Sub-contractors are based in almost every major city of Pakistan.

Advertising in Pakistani Newspapers

As mentioned earlier, advertising in daily or trade newspapers is one of the sources available for reaching manufacturers and suppliers. There are a number of popular newspapers in Pakistan in English and in Urdu (the national language of Pakistan). Display advertisements must be placed in order to contact such companies. Smaller ads would not reflect a good image of the importer.

The following papers are quite popular:

- The Business Recorder (English trade newspaper published in Karachi)
- Dawn (English newspaper published in Lahore and Karachi)
- The Pakistan Times (English newspaper published in Lahore and Islamabad)
- The Nation (English newspaper in Lahore)
- The News Islamabad (English newspaper published in Islamabad)
- The Jang (Urdu newspaper published in Karachi and Rawalpindi)
- Nawai-Waqat and Mashriq (Urdu newspapers published in Lahore)

5 | *Chapter Five*

Customs Ports

Merchandise for export is cleared through customs at authorized sea and dry ports. The Karachi seaport is the main seaport and handles 98% of the cargo. Another port in Karachi is Bin Qasim, but this port handles a lot less cargo.

Dry ports in the country are at various locations including Lahore, Faisalabad, Sialkot, Rawalpindi, Multan, Quetta, and Peshawar. For other locations check with the appropriate authorities in Pakistan, such as the Export Promotion Bureau. See appendix 2-4B for the Pakistan Export Promotion Bureau.

Free Trade Zones

Free Trade Zones (FTZ) or Export Processing Zones can be found in Karachi, where there are many manufacturing units.

The government is also opening these in other parts of the country. The FTZ in Karachi was set up to help export-oriented industries. Joint ventures with foreign companies are welcomed in this zone.

The FTZ's basic infrastructure includes fully developed roads, warehouses, telephone lines, water system, sewerage system, and other facilities.

Export Processing Zones in other cities are also under consideration. A complete infrastructure will be provided in these areas along with a package of incentives and facilities. See appendix 2-5 for contact information for EPZ's.

Some incentives to invest in an EPZ in Pakistan:

- 100% ownership rights
- Tax holidays
- No import restrictions
- Pakistan's foreign exchange control regulations do not apply
- Imports of equipment, machinery, and material are duty free
- No limits on investment
- One window operation for handling applications for setting up industries
- Safety of all domestic and foreign workers will be the responsibility of the government
- 100% repatriation of capital, profits, and dividend is allowed to foreign investors
- Electricity and gas bills are exempt from sales tax
- Outdated machinery and equipment can be sold in the domestic market after applicable duties are paid

- Goods and material entering into the EPZ from the tariff area are considered to be exports from Pakistan. These exports are entitled to all benefits allowed on exports to other countries
- Many items used in the construction of the factory, such as steel and cement, are exempt from excise duty
- Better labor laws
- A certain percentage of defective goods can be sold in the domestic market after applicable duties are paid
- Vehicles may be imported duty free. These can be sold in the domestic market after a certain number of years, and after the payment of duty on the depreciated value
- In the case of a bilateral agreement, exemption from double taxation is possible
- The above incentives are generally available, but check with the appropriate authority for the most up-to-date information

The Karachi Export Processing Zone

This is located adjacent to the Landhi Industrial area. It is 30 km (19 miles) from the Karachi seaport and 20 km (12 miles) from Port Qasim. It is ideally located to supply the markets of the Central Asian republics, the Middle East, Asia, Africa, Europe, and the Americas. Pakistan's strategic location provides easy and convenient access to many countries. A distribution center for re-export, imports, and warehousing can also be setup in the zone. The Government of Pakistan has provided great incentives to Pakistanis/foreign investors who set up their industries in the zone.

6 | Chapter Six

Frequently Asked Questions (FAQ) and Miscellaneous

* What are the sources of reaching manufacturers and exporters in Pakistan?
  ♦ The following sources can be used for finding such companies:
    - The Pakistan Trade Office in New York. See appendix 2-4A
    - The Export Promotion Bureau of Pakistan. See appendix 2-4B
    - Trade Associations in Pakistan. See appendix 2-4C
    - Buying agents. See appendix 2-6F
    - Trade directories. See appendix 2-4E
    - The Internet

- Advertise in Pakistani newspapers. See appendix 2-6E for Pakistani newspapers, periodicals, and magazines.
- What is the share of textile exports from Pakistan?
  ◆ Textiles play a dominant role in Pakistan's economy and 60% of its exports are comprised of cotton based products.
- When is the trade policy announced?
  ◆ The trade policy is announced in May or June of each year. For trade policies, contact the Pakistan Trade Office in New York (see appendix 2-4A).
- What types of banks are in Pakistan?
  ◆ There are all types of banks in Pakistan, including Commercial Banks (domestic and foreign), DFI/ Specialized banks, and Investment Banks. Many commercial banks have branches in Pakistan and in other parts of the world. See appendix 2-6A for a list of banks in Pakistan.
- Do Pakistani banks have corespondent-banking arrangements with banks in the USA?
  ◆ Yes, all commercial banks in Pakistan have correspondent banking arrangements with major US banks.
- Is one allowed to open a liaison office in Pakistan?
  ◆ Opening a liaison office in Pakistan is allowed, provided the office is for the purpose of export. More details can be obtained from the Pakistan Board of Investment Office (see appendix 2-6B).
- What are the common modes of payment in Pakistan?
  ◆ Letter of Credit, D/A or D/P, Advance Payment
- Is leather apparel exported from Pakistan?
  ◆ Yes, export of leather is one of the fastest growing sectors of the economy. There are approximately 400 tanneries in Pakistan. Leather apparel and goods are exported all over the world. Leather is being used in

the manufacture of many items, such as all types of garments, fashion accessories, small leather goods, sporting goods, footwear, and gloves.

- Are computers and the Internet used in businesses?
  - ◆ Yes, use of computers and modern technology is growing in every field.
- Are offices air-conditioned?
  - ◆ Yes, use of an air conditioner in an office is quite common, particularly in big cities.
- Where can I get information on investing or joint ventures in Pakistan?
  - ◆ Contact the Pakistan Board of Investment. Its services include providing information on setting up a business in Pakistan and the incentives available. See Pakistan Board of Investment in appendix 2-6B.
- What are Pakistan's major exports to the USA?
  - ◆ Over the past 30 years, there has been growth in trade with the USA. However, there is still room for further growth, and US companies can visit or contact the relevant authorities to see how they can profit from this growing economy.

Pakistan's Major Exports to the USA

Pakistan exports many items to the USA. The main items include apparel, textiles, oriental rugs, surgical instruments, rice etc.

Pakistan's Major Imports from the USA

Pakistan's main imports from the USA include wheat, fertilizers, vegetable oil & fats, machinery & parts and chemicals.

Miscellaneous

- For a list of web site addresses for miscellaneous Pakistan Government Offices, see appendix 2-6C
- For a list of stock exchanges, see appendix 2-6D
- For a list of newspapers, periodicals, and magazines, see appendix 2-6E
- For a list of buying agents, see appendix 2-6F
- For addresses of Pakistan and US embassies, see appendix 2-6G
- For information on shipping, see appendix 2-6H
- For a list of textile journals, see appendix 2-6I
- For a list of market research firms, see appendix 2-6J
- For miscellaneous information, see appendix 2-6K

Appendix 1

1-2. Formulas and Ratios

Break-even Point

Fixed Costs divided by selling price minus variable cost = Break-even point.

Break-even Point in Sales

This formula calculates the amount of sales you need at a certain percentage of gross profit to break even.
Higher sales will be needed if the gross profit is lower and vice versa.
Break-even Point = Fixed expenses divided by percentage of gross profit
For example: 100,000 (fixed expenses) divided by 50% (gross profit) = 200,000 sales. (According to this example when the fixed expenses are of 100,000 and gross profit is at 50%, then we need sales of 200,000 to reach the break-even point.)

Break-even Point in Production

This formula calculates the number of units to be sold to reach the break-even point.
Fixed Cost (FC) divided by price per unit minus variable cost = Break-even Point
For example:
$100,000 (FC)
$40 Unit Price minus $20 variable cost = $20
100,000 divided by 20 = 5000 units to be sold for reaching break-even point.

Cost of Goods Sold

Cost of Goods Sold = Opening Inventory plus Purchases minus closing inventory

Cubic Inches to Cubic Meters

Length x Width x Height divided by 1728 and again divide the remainder by 35.312
For example: 40" x 40" x 40" = 64,000 divided by 1728 and then divide the remainder with 35.312 = 01.05 Cubic Meters.

Dimensional Weight Formula

This formula is used by airlines/couriers for freight charges. Freight is charged on volume or weight, whichever is greater. For international shipments:
Dimensional Weight (lbs) = Length x Width x Height divided by 144
For example: 10 x 10 x 10 divided by 144 = 06.94 lbs.

An airline will charge you for 6.94 lbs., even if the actual weight of the package is less. Ask for the formula applied in the country of export. This will help you in preparing the cargo accordingly, thus, saving cost on freight.

For air shipments within the USA:
Dimensional Weight (lbs) = Length x Width x Height divided by 194
For example: 10 x 10 x 10 divided by 194 = 5.15 lbs.

An airline in the USA will charge you for 5.15 lbs. even if the actual weight of the package is less. Ask for the formula applied in the country of export. This will help you in preparing the cargo accordingly, thus, saving cost on freight.

Gross Profit

Total sales minus cost of goods sold = Gross Profit

Gross Profit Margin

Gross profit minus cost of goods sold divided by gross profit = Gross Profit Margin
For example: 400-200 divided by 400 x 100 = 50% Gross Profit Margin

Gross Profit Percentage

Gross Profit divided by total sales multiply by 100 = Percentage of Gross Profit
For example 400 divided by 1000 multiply by 100 = 40%

Mark Up

Selling price minus cost of goods divided by cost of goods multiply by 100 = Mark up percentage
For example: 400-200 divided by 200 multiply by 100 = 100% Mark up

Net Profit

Total Sales minus cost of goods sold minus expenses = Net Profit Before Taxes

For example: 200,000-150,000-25,000 = 25,000 Net Profit Before Taxes

Financial Ratios

Current Ratio

This measures the short-term financial obligations of a company. In other words, it measures whether a business has enough current assets to meet its current debts.

Current Ratio = Total Current Assets divided by Total Current Liabilities

Debt Ratio (DR)

This measures long term financial obligations of a company. In other words, whether a business has enough current assets to meet its current debts.

Debt Ratio = Liabilities divided by Assets

Inventory Turnover Ratio (IT)

This measures the number of times the inventory has been sold in a given period.

Inventory Turnover = Net sales divided by Average Inventory at cost

Return on Equity (ROE)

This measures the profitability of a company after income taxes.

Return on Equity = Net Income divided by equity

Return on Investment (ROI)

This measures the profitability of an investor after income taxes.

Return on Investment = Net income divided by Investment

Quick Ratio/Acid Test

This measures a company's current liabilities to current assets.

Quick Ratio/Acid Test = Current assets minus Inventory divided by current liabilities

1-3A. Export Promotion Offices / Trade Promotion Agencies

Export Promotion Bureau Of Pakistan
Government of Pakistan
P.O. Box No. 1293
5th Floor, Block A, Finance & Trade Centre, Shahrah-e-Faisal,
Karachi 75200, Pakistan
Tel: 92 21 920 6487
Fax: 92 21 920 5769
Email: epb@epb.kar.erum.com.pk
Web Site: http://www.epb.gov.pk

Pakistan Trade Offices, USA
Consulate General of Pakistan, (Commercial Section)
12 East, 65th Street,
New York, NY 10021, USA
Tel: 212 472 6123, 212 472 6143
Fax: 212 472 6780
Email: paktrade@mail.idt.net
Web Site: http://www.paktrade.org

1-3B. Trade Associations

American Apparel Manufacturers & Footwear Association
1601 North Kent Street, Suite 1200
Arlington VA 22209, USA
Tel: 1 800 520 2262, 703 524 1864
Fax: 703 522 6741
Web Site: http://www.americanapparel.org
http://www.apparelandfootwear.org

American Exporters & Importers Association
51 East 42nd Street, 7th Floor
New York, NY 10017, USA
Tel: 212 983 7008
Fax: 212 983 6430
Web Site: http://www.aaei.org

American Importers Association
710 Peachtree Street NE, Suite 1410
Atlanta, GA 30308, USA
Tel: 404 873 0861
Fax: 501 421 9552
Email: info@americanimporters.org
Web Site: http://www.americanimporters.org

American Textile Machinery Association
111 Park Place
Falls Church, VA 22046, USA
Tel: 703 538 1789
Fax: 703 241 5603
Web Site: http://www.atmanet.org

California Fashion Association (CFA)
515 South Flower Street, 32nd Floor
Los Angeles, CA 90071, USA
Tel: 213 688 6288
Fax: 213 688 6290
Email: cfa@californiafashion.org
Web Site: http://www.californiafashion.org

Fashion Association of America
475 Park Avenue South, 9th Floor
New York, NY 10016, USA
Tel: 212 683 5665
Fax: 212 545 1709
Web Site: http://www.thefashion.org

Fashion Group International
Tel: 212 593 1715, 212 242 7140
Fax: 212 593 1925
Web Site: http://www.fgi.org

Federation of International Trade Associations
11800 Sunrise Valley Drive, Suite 210
Reston, VA 20191, USA
Tel: 1 800 969 3482
Fax: 703 620 4922
Email: info@fita.org
Web Site: http://www.fita.org

Golden Gate Apparel Association
12925 Alcosta Blvd., #7
San Ramon, CA 94583, USA
Tel: 925 328 1122
Fax: 925 328 1119
Email: info@fashionsanfrancisco.com
Web Site: http://www.fashionsanfrancisco.com

International Mass Retail Association
1700 North Moore Street, Suite 2250
Arlington, Virginia 22209, USA
Tel: 703 841 2300
Fax: 703 841 1184
Web Site: http://www.imra.org

International Textile and Apparel Association
Web Site: http://www.itaasite.org

San Francisco Fashion Industries
1000 Brannan Street, Suite 206
San Francisco, CA 94103, USA
Tel: 415 621 6100
Fax: 415 621 6384
Email: sffi@dnai.com
Web Site: http://www.sffi.org

Textile Association of Los Angeles (Tala)
Tel: 213 627 6173
Fax: 213 627 0015
Email: talausa@cyberconcepts.com
Web Site: http://www.textileassociation.org

Textile Distributors Association
469 7th Ave., 2nd Floor
New York, NY 10018, USA
Tel: 212 869 6300
Fax: 212 869 2346

United States Association of Importers of Textiles and Apparel
13 East 16th St.
New York, NY 10003, USA
Tel: 212 463 0089
Fax: 212 463 0583
Email: quota@aol.com
Web Site: http://www.usaita.com

1-3C. Chambers of Commerce and Industry

US Chamber of Commerce
1615 H St. NW
Washington DC 20062, USA
Tel: 202 659 6000
Fax: 202 463 3190
Web Site: http://www.uschamber.org
http://www.chamberbiz.com

1-3D. Trade Promotion Agencies in Europe

Denmark

Danish Import Promotion Office for Products from Developing Countries (DIPO)
Boersen
DK-1217 Copenhagen K., Denmark
Tel: 45 33 95 05 00
Fax: 45 33 12 05 25
Email: dipo@commerce.dk
Web Site: http://www.dipo.dk

Germany

BFAI
Import Promotion Office, Germany
Tel: 49 221 2057 359
Email: bus.contacts@bfai.com
Web Site: http://www.bfai.com

Netherlands

Center for the Promotion of Imports from Developing Countries (CBI)
P.O. Box 30009
3001 DA Rotterdam, Netherlands
Tel: 31 10 2013434
Fax: 31 10 4114081
Email: cbi@cbi.nl
Web Site: http://www.cbi.nl

Norway

Norwegian Import Promotion Office for Products from Developing Countries (NORIMPOD)
Tollbugaten 31, P.O. Box 8034 DEP 0030
Oslo, Norway
Tel: 47 2231 4400
Fax: 47 2231 4403

Sweden

Import Promotion Office for Products from Developing Countries (IMPOD)
P.O. Box No. 7508,
Norrmalmstorg 1,
S-10392 Stokkholm, Sweden

1-3E. American Embassies

US Department of State
Web Site: http://www.usembassy.state.gov
Services: On this web site you can find US Embassies around the world.

1-3F. Trade Magazines/Trade Directories/ Mailing Lists

American Sportswear and Knitting Times
307 Seventh Avenue, Suite 1601
New York, NY 10001, USA
Tel: 212 366 9008
Fax: 212 366 4166
Email: yarn-cad@interport.net
Web Site: http://www.asktmag.com
Services: Trade magazine.

Apparel Industry Magazine
1115 Northmeadow Parkway
Roswell, GA 30076, USA
Tel: 1 800 241 9034, 770 569 1540
Fax: 770 569 5105
Web Site: http://www.aimagazine.com
Services: Trade magazine.

Apparel News
CaliforniaMart, 110 E. 9th Street, Suite A-777
Los Angeles, CA 90079, USA
Tel: 213 627 3737
Fax: 213 623 1515, 213 623 5707
Email: webmaster@apparelnews.net
Web Site: http://www.apparelnews.net

Apparel Strategist
PO Box 406
Fleetwood, PA 19522, USA
Tel: 610 944 5995
Fax: 610 944 5149
Email: editor@apparelstrategist.com
Web Site: http://www.apparelstrategist.com
Services: Trade magazine.

Bobbin Magazine/La Bobina Magazine
PO Box 1986,
Columbia, SC 29202, USA
Tel: 1 800 845 8820, 803 771 7500
Fax: 803 799 1461
Email: Bobbin.PubsInfo@mfi.com
Web Site: http://www.bobbin.com
Services: Trade magazine.

Body Fashions/Intimate Apparel
Web Site: http://www.bfia.com

DNR for Men's Fashion
Fairchild Publications
7 West 34th Street
New York, NY 10001, USA
Tel: 1 800 630 4700, 212 630 4231
Fax: 212 630 4201
Web Site: http://www.dnrnews.com
Services: Trade magazine.

Embroidery/Monogram Business
1199 S. Belt Line Road, Suite 100,
Coppell, TX 75019, USA
Tel: 1 800 527 0207, 972 906 6500
Email: embmag@mfi.com
Web Site: http://www.embmag.com
Services: Trade magazine.

Fairchild Publications
7 west 34th St
New York, NY 10001, USA
Tel: 212 630 4000
Fax: 212 630 4201
Web Site: http://www.fairchildbooks.com
Services: Publisher of Trade magazines, etc.

Impressions Magazine
P.O. Box 612288,
Dallas, TX 75261, USA
Tel: 1 800 527 0207, 972 906 6500
Fax: 972 906 6671
Email: impressions@mfi.com
Web Site: http://www.impressionsmag.com
Services: Trade magazine.

International Dyer
Email: info@worldtextile.com
Web Site: http://www.internationaldyer.com
Services: Magazine for textile printing, dyeing, and finishing.

Printwear Magazine
PO Box 1416,
Broomfield, CO 80038, USA
Tel: 303 469 0424
Fax: 303 469 5730
Web Site: http://www.nbm.com/printwear
Services: Trade magazine.

Sports Trend Magazine
Email: tdaversawilliams@sportstrend.com
Web Site: http://www.sportstrend.com
Services: Trade magazine.

Textile World
Intertec Publishing
6151 Powers Ferry Rd. NW
Atlanta, GA 30339, USA
Tel: 770 955 2500
Fax: 770 955 0400
Email: john_mccurry@intertec.com
Web Site: http://www.textileworld.com
Services: Trade magazine.

Women's Wear Daily (WWD)
7 W 34th Street
New York, NY 10001, USA
Tel: 1 800 289 0273, 212 630 4800
Fax: 212 630 4786
Web Site: http://www.wwd.com
Service: Trade magazine.

World Trade Venue (sm)
4207 Streamwood Drive
Liverpool, New York 13090, USA
Tel: 315 622 4498, 315 652 6402
Fax: 315 622 0205
Email: wtv@wtvusa.com
Web Site: http://www.worldtradevenue.com
Services: Trade directories, mailing lists, web pages, Internet advertising, etc.

1-3G. Web Sites on the Apparel Industry

Fabrics.com
Web Site: http://www.fabrics.com
Services: Textile related web site.

Fashion Icon
Web Site: http://www.fashion-icon.com
Services: Fashion Icon brings you fashion news.

Fashion Institute of Technology, New York
Web Site: http://www.fitnyc.suny.edu
Services: An institute for the apparel industry.

Frederick's of Hollywood
Email: custserv@fredericks.com
Web Site: http://www.fredericks.com
Services: Frederick's is for bras, panties, lingerie, and women's apparel.

Hong Kong's Clothing Industry
Web Site: http://www.tdctrade.com/main/industries/ipclot.htm
Services: Provides overview, trends, and performance of Hong Kong's clothing industry.

InfoMat Inc.
Email: info@infomat.com
Web Site: http://www.infomat.com
Services: Fashion industry search engine on the Internet.

International Fashion Web
Web Site: http://www.intlfashionweb.com
Services: Information on textile & apparel import industry.

NY Style
Web Site: http://www.nystyle.com
Services: A web site on fashion.

Textile Clothing Technology Corporation
Web Site: http://www.tc2.com
Services: Textile Clothing Technology Corporation is a demonstration, education, and research & development resource for the soft goods industry.

TextileWeb
Email: info@textileweb.com
Web Site: http://www.textileweb.com
Services: A source for professionals in the textile industry.

The Look On-Line
Web Site: http://www.lookonline.com
Services: A New York fashion industry Internet magazine.

The Virtual Garment Center
Web Site: http://www.garment.com
Services: This web site is a source for the apparel, textile and fashion industries. It includes a searchable database and a place where information can be posted and read.

The World Fashion Centre, Netherlands
Email: management@worldfashioncentre.nl
Web Site: http://www.worldfashioncentre.nl
Services: Fashion center in Amsterdam, Netherlands.

1-3H. The Office of Textiles and Apparel (OTEXA)

Office of Textiles and Apparel
US Department of Commerce
14th and Constitution NW
Room 3119, Washington DC 20230, USA
Web Site: http://otexa.ita.doc.gov

1-3I. US Textile and Apparel Category System

US Textile and Apparel Category System
Web Site: http://otexa.ita.doc.gov/corr.stm

1-3J. US Customs

U.S. Customs Service
Department of the Treasury
Washington, D.C. 20229, USA
Web Site: http://www.customs.ustreas.gov

1-3K. World Trade Centers

World Trade Centers Association
Web Site: http://www.wtca.org

1-3L. Other Sources of Information for Trade

Foreign Trade Statistics
Web Site: http://www.census.gov/ftp/pub/foreign-trade/www

Harmonized Tariff Schedule
Web Site: https://orders.access.gpo.gov/su_docs/sale/prf/
ordinfo.html
http://www.customs.ustreas.gov/imp-exp/rulings/harmoniz/
index_old.htm
http://www.usitc.gov/taffairs.htm

North American Industry Classification System (NAICS)
Web Site: http://www.census.gov/epcd/www/naics.html

Standard Industrial Codes (SIC)
Web Site: http://www.census.gov/epcd/www/sic.html

Tariff Affairs and Related Matters
Web Site: http://www.usitc.gov/taffairs.htm

Textile and Apparel Quota Embargoes
Web Site: http://infoserv2.ita.doc.gov/otexemb1.nsf/TEXTILE-
AND-APPAREL-EMBARGOS

**United Nations Conference on Trade and Development
(UNCTAD) Web Site on Generalized System of Preferences
(GSP)**
Web Site: http://www.unctad.org/gsp/index.htm
http://www.unctad.org/gsp/usa/Default.asp

United Nations Statistics Division
Web Site: http://www.un.org/Depts/unsd

US Generalized System of Preferences (GSP)
Web Site: http://www.ustr.gov/reports/gsp/
http://www.ustr.gov/reports/gsp/faq.html

US International Trade Commission Interactive Tariff and Trade Data Web
Web Site: http://www.dataweb.usitc.gov

USA TRADE™
Web Site: http://www.usatradeonline.gov

USA Trade Online
Web Site: http://www.usatradeonline.gov

1-4A. Selecting Your Company Logo

International Trademark Association
Web Site: http://www.inta.org

US Copyright Office
Web Site: http://lcweb.loc.gov/copyright

US Patent and Trademark Office
Web Site: http://www.uspto.gov

1-4B. Selecting a Brand Name / Trademark

Brand Institute, Inc.
200 S.E. 1ˢᵗ Street, 12ᵗʰ Floor
Miami, FL 33131, USA
Tel: 305 374 2500
Fax: 305 374 2504
Web Site: http://www.brandinst.com

1-5. World Trade Venue(sm)

World Trade Venue (sm)
4207 Streamwood Drive
Liverpool, New York 13090, USA
Tel: 315 622 4498, 315 652 6402
Fax: 315 622 0205
Email: wtv@wtvusa.com
Web Site: http://www.worldtradevenue.com

1-9A. US Census Bureau

US Census Bureau
Web Site: http://www.census.gov

1-9B. American Apparel Size Charts

Women				
Size	Dress	Size	Bust -Waist	Hips
P	5-9	28-32"	22-24"	30-34"
S	8-12	30-33"	24-27"	34-36"
M	14-16	31-38"	26-30"	36-40"
L	18-20	36-42"	29-36"	40-44"
X	22-24	40-46"	35-40"	44-48"
2X	26-28	44-51"	40-46"	48-52"
3X	30-34	50-57"	45-50"	52-56"
Men				
Size	Chest	Waist	Hips	Neck
P	30-33"	24-27"	34-36"	13.5"
S	34-36"	28-30"	35-37"	14"
M	37-40"	32-34"	38-41"	15"
L	41-44"	35-39"	42-45"	16"
X	45-48"	40-44"	46-49"	17"
2X	49-52"	45-48"	50-53"	18"
3X	53-56"	50-52"	54-57"	19"

Note: The above size charts should not be used for production. They are for reference only. Sizes vary largely in the US. You must contact the buyers and ask them to provide you with the size specifications for production.

1-9C. Figures and Details on Apparel/Textile Imports into the US

Major Shippers Report
Web Site: http://otexa.ita.doc.gov/msrpoint.stm
Services: This report provides general import statistics organized by date of import.

Major Shippers Report: Section One
Web Site: http://otexa.ita.doc.gov/catss.htm
Services: Textiles and apparel imports organized by category in category units.

Major Shippers Report: Section Two
Web Site: http://otexa.ita.doc.gov/ctryname.htm
Services: Textile imports in square meters organized by country.

1-10A. Forecasting Services

Mode Information
Heinz Kramer GmbH
Pilgerstrabe 20
D-51491 Overath, Germany
Tel: 49 22 066 0070
Fax: 49 22 066 00717
Email: info@modeinfo.com
Web Site: http://www.modeinfo.com
Services: Forecasting information for Germany/Europe.

Pantone, Inc.
590 Commerce Boulevard
Carlstadt, NJ 07072, USA
Tel: 1 888 726 8663, 201 935 5500
Fax: 201 896 0242
Web Site: http://www.pantone.com
Services: For colors.

World Trade Venue (sm)
4207 Streamwood Drive
Liverpool, New York 13090, USA
Tel: 315 622 4498, 315 652 6402
Fax: 315 622 0205
Email: wtv@wtvusa.com
Web Site: http://www.worldtradevenue.com
Services: Contact them for fashion & color forecasting information.

1-10B. Labeling Requirements

Federal Trade Commission
Web Site: http://www.ftc.gov
http://www.ftc.gov/bcp/conline/pubs/buspubs/thread.htm
http://www.ftc.gov/bcp/conline/pubs/buspubs/carelabl.htm
http://www.ftc.gov/bcp/conline/pubs/buspubs/cotton.htm

Textile Industry Affairs
6803 Quail Knob Court,
Frederick, MD 21702, USA
Tel: 301 898 3191
Fax: 301 898 0241
Email: Info@TextileAffairs.com
Web Site: http://www.textileaffairs.com/acsguide.htm
Services: Textile industry affairs.

1-11A. *Apparel Centers*

Atlanta Apparel Mart
250 Spring Street NW, Suite 2S-339,
Atlanta, GA 30303, USA
Tel: 404 220 2446
Fax: 404 220 2397
Web Site: http://www.americasmart.com
Services: A center for importers, distributors, wholesalers, etc.

CaliforniaMart
110 East 9th Street, Suite A727
Los Angeles, California 90079, USA
Tel: 213 630 3693
Fax: 213 630 3708
Email: international@californiamart.com
Web Site: http://www.californiamart.com
Services: A center for importers, distributors, etc. with around
1,200 permanent showrooms.

Chicago Apparel Center
Suite 470, 200 World Trade Center
Chicago, IL 60654, USA
Tel: 1 800 677 6278, 312 527 7600
Web Site: http://www.merchandisemart.com/pages/apparel.html
http://www.mmart.com
http://www.chicagostyleshow.com
Services: They have permanent and temporary show rooms with
apparel companies. A trade show is also organized at this center
under the name "The Chicago Style Show."

Dallas Market Center
2100 Stemmons Freeway
Dallas, TX 75038, USA
Tel: 1 800 325 6587, 214 655 6100
Fax: 214 749 5479
Email: sdumas@dmcmail.com
Web Site: http://www.dallasmarketcenter.com/dmc/index.htm
Services: A center for importers, distributors, wholesalers, etc.

Denver Merchandise Mart
451 E. 58th Avenue # 470,
Denver, CO 80216, USA
Tel: 1 800 289 6278, 303 292 6278
Fax: 303 297 8473
Email: info@denvermart.com
Web Site: http://www.denvermart.com

Fashion Center
249 West 39th Street,
New York, NY 10018, USA
Tel: 212 764 9600
Fax: 212 764 9697
Web Site: http://www.fashioncenter.com
Services: A center for importers, distributors, wholesalers, etc.

Miami International Merchandise Mart & Radisson Center
711 NW 72nd Avenue
Miami, FL 33126, USA
Tel: 1 800 333 3333, 305 261 2900
Fax: 305 261 7665
Email: mimm@mimm.com
Web Site: http://www.mimm.com
Services: A center for importers, distributors, wholesalers, etc.

The New Mart
127 East Ninth Street
Los Angeles, CA 90015, USA
Tel: 213 627 0671
Fax: 213 627 1187
Web Site: http://www.newmart.net
Services: A center for importers, distributors, wholesalers, etc.

1-11B. Large Apparel Retail/Department Stores and Designers

Chain Department Stores

Bloomingdales
Web Site: http://www.bloomingdales.com

Bonton
Web Site: http://www.bonton.com

Dillards
Web Site: http://www.dillards.com

Famous-Barr
Web Site: http://www.mayco.com/fb/index.jsp

Federated Department Stores
Web Site: http://www.federated-fds.com

Foley's
Web Site: http://www.mayco.com/fo/index.jsp

Hecht's
Web Site: http://www.mayco.com/wb/index.jsp

JC Penny
Web Site: http://www.jcpenney.com

Kaufmann's
Web Site: http://www.mayco.com/kf/index.jsp

L.S. Ayres
Web Site: http://www.mayco.com/ls/index.jsp

Lord & Taylor
Web Site: http://www.mayco.com/lt/index.jsp

Macys
Web Site: http://www.macys.com

Meier & Frank
Web Site: http://www.mayco.com/mf/index.jsp

Nordstrom
Web Site: http://www.nordstrom.com

Robinsons-May
Web Site: http://www.mayco.com/ca/index.jsp

Sears
Web Site: http://www.sears.com

Strawbridge's
Web Site: http://www.mayco.com/sc/index.jsp

The Jones Store
Web Site: http://www.mayco.com/js/index.jsp

Discount Chain Department Stores

Ames Department Stores
Web Site: http://www.amesstores.com

Burlington Coat Factory
Web Site: http://www.burlingtoncoatfactory.com

Kmart
Web Site: http://www.kmart.com

Marshall's
Web Site: http://www.marshallsonline.com

Mervyns
Web Site: http://www.mervyns.com

Sam's Club
Web Site: http://www.samsclub.com

Target
Web Site: http://www.target.com

TJ Maxx
Web Site: http://www.tjmaxx.com

Wal-mart
Web Site: http://www.wal-mart.com

Retail Chain Stores

Banana Republic
Web Site: http://www.bananarepublic.com

Dressbarn
Web Site: http://www.dressbarn.com

Gap
Web Site: http://www.gap.com

Old Navy
Web Site: http://www.oldnavy.com

Talbot
Web Site: http://www.talbots.com

The Limited
Web Site: http://www.limited.com

Victoria's Secret
Web Site: http://www.victoriassecret.com

Fashion Designers

Bugle Boy
Web Site: http://www.bugleboy.com

Cherokee
Web Site: http://www.cherokeeusa.com

Donna Karan
Web Site: http://www.donnakaran.com

Esprit
Web Site: http://www.esprit.com

Etienne Aigner
Web Site: http://www.etienneaigner.com

Guess
Web Site: http://www.guess.com

Hagger
Web Site: http://www.haggar.com

Jordache
Web Site: http://www.jordache.com

Lee
Web Site: http://www.leejeans.com

Levi's
Web Site: http://www.levi.com

Liz Claiborne
Web Site: http://www.lizclaiborne.com

Nautica
Web Site: http://www.nautica.com

Phillips-Van Heusen
Web Site: http://www.pvh.com

Tommy Hilfiger
Web Site: http://www.tommy.com

Wrangler
Web Site: http://www.wrangler.com

Yves Saint Laurent
Web Site: http://www.yslonline.com

1-11C. Hong Kong Convention and Exhibition Center

Web Site: http://www.hkcec.com.hk

1-12A. List of Trade Shows

List of some trade shows in the US:

Name of Show: Heimtextil Americas
Type of Show: Fabrics, Towels, Bed Linen, and Household Textiles
Organizers:
Messe Frankfurt, Inc.
1600 Parkwood Circle, Suite 515
Atlanta, Georgia 30339, USA
Tel: 770 984 8016
Fax: 770 984 8023
Email: info@usa.messefrankfurt.com
Web Site: http://www.heimtextil.de

Name of Show: International Fashion Fabric Exhibition & Conference (IFFE)
Type of Show: Textiles, Fashion Services, and Trimmings, suppliers of CAD/CAM
Organizers:
International Fashion Fabric Exhibition & Conference (IFFE)
New York, NY 10016, USA
Tel: 1 888 964 5100, 1 800 421 9567, 917 326 6237
Fax: 212 951 6666
Email: info@magiconline.com
Web Site: http://www.magiconline.com
http://www.fabricshow.com

Name of Show: International Kids Fashion Show (IKFS)
Type of Show: Children's Garments
Organizers:
Magic Kids
One Park Avenue
New York, NY 10016, USA
Tel: 1 888 964 5100, 1 800 421 9567, 917 326 6237
Fax: 212 951 6666
Email: info@magiconline.com
Web Site: http://www.magiconline.com
http://www.kidsshow.com

Name of Show: Magic Kids Las Vegas
Type of Show: Children's Apparel
Organizers:
MAGIC Kids
201 Sandpointe Avenue, Suite 600
Santa Ana, CA 92707, USA
Tel: 949 489 2101
Fax: 949 489 2104
Email: info@magiconline.com
Web Site: http://www.magiconline.com

Name of Show: MAGIC Las Vegas
Type of Show: Men's Apparel
Organizers:
MAGIC Corporate
6200 Canoga Ave., Suite 303
Woodland Hills, CA 91367, USA
Tel: 818 593 5000
Fax: 818 593 5020
Email: info@magiconline.com
Web Site: http://www.magiconline.com

Name of Show: The New York Home Textile Show
Type of Show: Towels, Bed Linen, and Household Textiles
Organizers:
George Little Management, Inc.
10 Bank Street,
White Plains, NY 10606, USA
Tel: 1 800 272 7469, 914 421 3200
Fax: 914 948 6180
Web Site: http://www.glmshows.com/glmshows/textiles

Name of Show: WWWD Magic Las Vegas
Type of Show: Women's Apparel
Organizers:
MAGIC Corporate
6200 Canoga Ave., Suite 303
Woodland Hills, CA 91367, USA
Tel: 818 593 5000
Fax: 818 593 5020
Email: info@magiconline.com
Web Site: http://www.magiconline.com

List of some of trade shows in other countries:

China

Name of Show: Asia Pacific Leather Fair
Type of Show: Fashion & Finished Products
Organizers:
Asia Pacific Leather Fair Ltd.
Room 102-5, Stanhope House
738 King's Road
Quarry Bay, Hong Kong
Tel: 852 2827 6211
Fax: 852 2827 7831
Email: info@aplf.com
Web Site: http://www.aplf.com

Name of Show: Hong Kong Fashion Week
Type of Show: Apparel
Organizers:
Hong Kong Trade Development Council
38th Floor, Office Tower, Convention Plaza
1 Harbour Road, Wanchai, Hong Kong
Tel: 852 2584 4333
Fax: 852 2824 0249
Email: hktdc@tdc.org.hk
Web Site: http://www.tdctrade.com

Name of Show: Interstoff Asia
Type of Show: Fabrics
Organizers:
Messe Frankfurt (H.K.) Ltd.
1809 China Resources Building
26 Harbour Road, Wanchai, Hong Kong
Tel: 852 28 02 77 28
Fax: 852 25 98 87 71
Email: textile@hongkong.messefrankfurt.com
Web Site: http://www.hongkong.messefrankfurt.com
http://www.interstoff-asia.com

France

Name of Show: Prêt à Porter
Type of Show: Women's Ready-to-Wear/Fashion Accessories
Organizers:
Sodes
5 rue de, Caumartin
Paris 75009, France
Tel: 33 1 4494 7000
Fax: 33 1 4494 7005
Email: exhidept@pretparis.com
Web Site: http://www.pretparis.com
http://www.pretaporter.com

Germany

Name of Show: CPD Dusseldorf
Type of Show: Corporate Fashion, Formal Wear, Coats, Blazers,
Jackets, Suits, Skirts, Trousers.
Organizers:
Igedo Internationale Modemesse Kronen GmbH
Stockumer Kirchstr. 61
D-40474 Dusseldorf, Germany
Tel: 49 211 4396
Fax: 49 211 4396
Email: corporate-fashion@igedo.com
Web Site: http://www.igedo.com

Name of Show: Heimtextil Frankfurt
Type of Show: Fabrics, Towels, Bed Linen, and Household Textiles
Organizers:
Messe Frankfurt
Ludwig-Erhard-Anlage 1
60327 Frankfurt am Main, Germany
Tel: 49 69 7575-0
Fax: 49 69 7575-64 33
Web Site: http://www.heimtextil.de

Name of Show: Import Shop Berlin
Type of Show: Garments, Home Textiles, Leather Goods, Gift Items, and Home Accessories.
Organizers:
Messe Berlin GmbH
Messedamm 22, D-14055, Berlin
Tel: 49 30 3038-0
Fax: 49 30 3038-2325
Email: central@messe-berlin.de
Web Site: http://www.importshop-berlin.com

Name of Show: InterJeans
Type of Show: International Casualwear and Young Fashion
Organizers:
Herren-Mode-Woche
Messeplatz 1-50679 Cologne, Germany
Tel: 49 221 821 3837
Fax: 49 221 821 2762
Email: info@koelnmesse.de
Web Site: http://www.koelnmesse.de
http://km.nexum.de/asp/index.asp?EXPO=hmw-ij&LANG=english

Name of Show: International Baby to Teenager Fair Cologne
Type of Show: International Baby and Teenager Fair
Organizers:
Messeplatz 1-50679 Cologne, Germany
Tel: 49 221 821 2740
Fax: 49 221 821 2704
Email: info@koelnmesse.de
Web Site: http://www.koelnmesse.de/kuj
http://km.nexum.de/english/index.html

1-12B. Other Information and Sources Relevant to Trade Shows

Trade Show Information

American Trade Show Directory on Line
Web Site: http://www.tradeshowbiz.com

ExpoBase
Web Site: http://www.expobase.com

EXPOguide
Web Site: http://www.expoguide.com

ExpoWorld
Web Site: http://www.expoworld.net

Trade Show News Network
Web Site: http://www.tsnn.com

TSCentral
Web Site: http://www.tscentral.com

-YOUS

Trade Show Organizers in Germany

Deutsche Messe AG
Web Site: http://www.messe.de

Messe Munich International
Web Site: http://www.messe-muenchen.de

Trade Show Organizers in Hong Kong

TDC Exhibitions
Web Site: http://hktdcfairs.tdc.org.hk

Trade Show Organizers in Taiwan

Taipei Trade Shows
Web Site: http://www.taipeitradeshows.com.tw

1-12C. Interpretation and Translation Services

American Translators Association
225 Reinekers Lane, Suite 590
Alexandria, VA 22314, USA
Tel: 703 683 6100
Fax: 703 683 6122
Email: ata@atanet.org
Web Site: http://www.atanet.org
http://www.americantranslators.org/tsd_listings

Translators and Interpreter Guild
2007 North 15th Street, Suite 4
Arlington, VA 22201-2621, USA
Tel: 1 800 992 0367, 703 522 0881
Fax: 703 522 0882
Email: ttig@mindspring.com
Web Site: http://www.trans-interp-guild.org

1-13A. Major Holidays in the US

New Years Day: January 1
Martin Luther King, Jr. Day: 3rd Monday in January
President's Day: 3rd Monday in February
Memorial Day: Last Monday in May
Independence Day: July 4
Labor Day: 1st Monday in September
Columbus Day: 2nd Monday in October
Veterans Day: November 11
Thanksgiving Day: 4th Thursday in November
Christmas Day: December 25

1-13B. World Time Zones

Time Information

CNN
Web Site: http://www.cnn.com/WEATHER/worldtime

Worldtimezone.com
Web Site: http://www.worldtimezone.com

Yahoo
Web Site: http://dir.yahoo.com/Science/Measurements_and_Units/Time/Time_Zones

1-13C. Hotels in the USA

Best Western Hotels
Web Site: http://www.bestwestern.com

Crowne Plaza Hotels & Resorts
Web Site: http://www.crowneplaza.com

Days Inn
Web Site: http://www.daysinn.com

Double Tree Hotels, Suites, Resorts, Clubs
Web Site: http://www.doubletree.com

Embassy Suites
Web Site: http://www.embassy-suites.com

Hampton Inn
Web Site: http://www.hampton-inn.com

Hampton Suites
Web Site: http://www.hamptoninn-suites.com

Hilton Hotels
Web Site: http://www.hilton.com

Holiday Inn Hotels & Resorts
Web Site: http://www.holiday-inn.com

Homewood Suites
Web Site: http://www.homewood-suites.com

Howard Johnson Hotels & Inns
Web Site: http://www.hojo.com

Hyatt Hotels & Resorts
Web Site: http://www.hyatt.com

Intercontinental Hotels
Web Site: http://www.interconti.com

Marriott Hotels, Resorts & Suites
Web Site: http://www.marriott.com

Radisson Hotels
Web Site: http://www.radisson.com

Ramada Hotels
Web Site: http://www.ramada-hotels.com

Red Lion Hotels & Inns
Web Site: http://www.redlion.com

Renaissance Hotels & Resorts
Web Site: http://www.renaissancehotels.com

Ritz Carlton Hotels
Web Site: http://www.ritzcarlton.com

Sheraton Hotels & Resorts
Web Site: http://www.sheraton.com

Westin Hotels & Resorts
Web Site: http://www.westin.com

Wyndham International
Web Site: http://www.wyndhamintl.com

1-13D. Other Hotel and Travel Reservation Related Information

#1 Hotel Finder
Web Site: http://www.1hotelfinder.com

American Hotel Search
Web Site: http://www.americanhotelsearch.com

Hotel America
Web Site: http://www.hotelamerica.com

Hotel Discounts
Web Site: http://www.hoteldiscounts.com

Hotel Resource
Web Site: http://www.hotelresource.com

HotelBook
Web Site: http://www.hotelbook.com

Hotelguide.com
Web Site: http://www.hotelguide.com

HotelNet Discount
Web Site: http://www.hotelnetdiscount.com

Internet Lodging Directory
Web Site: http://www.usa-lodging.com

Priceline
Web Site: http://www.priceline.com

Travelocity
Web Site: http://www.travelocity.com

USA Hotel Guide
Web Site: http://www.usahotelguide.com

World Hotels Yellow Pages
Web Site: http://www.worldhotelsyellowpages.com

1-13E. Car Rental Companies

Ace Rent A Car
Web Site: http://www.acerentacar.com

Alamo Rent A Car
Web Site: http://www.alamo.com

Avis Rent A Car
Web Site: http://www.avis.com

Budget Rent A Car
Web Site: http://www.drivebudget.com

Dollar Rent a Car
Web Site: http://www.dollar.com

Hertz Rent a Car
Web Site: http://www.hertz.com

National Car Rental
Web Site: http://www.nationalcar.com

Payless Car Rental
Web Site: http://www.800-payless.com

Rent A Wreck
Web Site: http://www.rent-a-wreck.com

Thrifty Car Rental
Web Site: http://www.thrifty.com

1-13F. Major Airlines in the USA

American Airlines
Web Site: http://www.aa.com

Continental Air Lines
Web Site: http://www.continental.com

Delta Air Lines
Web Site: http://www.delta-air.com

Northwest Airlines
Web Site: http://www.nwa.com

United Airlines
Web Site: http://www.ual.com

US Airways
Web Site: http://www.usairways.com

1-16A. Machinery Suppliers

Almurtaza Machinery Co (pvt) Ltd.
Shaheen View, A-18,
Block-6, P.E.C.H.S.,
Sharah-e-Faisal, Karachi-75400, Pakistan
Tel: 92 21 4543060
Fax: 92 21 4546555, 92 21 4540558
Email: amcl@super.net.pk
info@almurtaza.com
Web Site: http://www.almurtaza.com
Services: Apparel machinery distributor. They can also provide
a list of buying agents in Pakistan.

Bobbin Show
Bobbin Group of Bill Communications
P.O. Box 612768,
Dallas, TX 75261, USA
Tel: 1 800 789 2223, 972 906 6800
Fax: 972 906 6890
Email: bobbin_expo@vnuexpo.com
Web site: http://www.bobbin.com
Service: An apparel machinery trade show for finding suppliers.

Juki Sewing Machines
Juki Corporation
8-2-1, Kokuryo-cho, Chofu-shi, Tokyo 182-8655, Japan
Tel: 81 3 3480 1111
Email: webmaster@juki.co.jp
Web Site: http://www.juki.co.jp

1-16B. Apparel Testing Laboratories

ACTS Testing Labs, Inc.
25 Anderson Road
Buffalo, NY 14225-4928, USA
Tel: 716 897 3300
Fax: 716 897 0876
Web Site: http://www.actstesting.com
Services: This company provides quality assurance testing for textiles and garments.

ETC Laboratories
40 Ajax Rd.
Rochester, NY 14624, USA
Tel: 716 328 7668
Fax: 716 328 7777
Web Site: http://www.etclabs.com
Services: A testing lab for apparel etc.

SGS US Testing Company Inc.
291 Fairfield Ave.
Fairfield, NJ 07004, USA
Tel: 1 800 777 8378
Fax: 973 575 7175
Email: mitchell_kase@sgsgroup.com
Web Site: http://www.ustesting.sgsna.com
Services: A testing lab for apparel, etc.

STR Inc.
10 Water Street STR, Inc.
Enfield, CT 06082, USA
Tel: 860 749 8371
Fax: 860 749 7533
Web Site: http://www.strlab.com
Services: It conducts physical and chemical tests for apparel
and textiles.

Vartest Laboratories Inc.
19 West 36th St., 10th Floor
New York, NY 10018, USA
Tel: 212 947 8391
Fax: 212 947 8719
Email: avarley@vartest.com
Web Site: http://www.vartest.com
Services: A testing lab for apparel etc.

1-17A. Freight Forwarders

A.N. Deringer
11 East Hawthorne Avenue
Third Floor, Valley Stream, NY 11580, USA
Tel: 1 800 523 4357, 516 256 4780
Fax: 516 256 4781
Web Site: http://www.anderinger.com

Also see Raaziq International (Pvt) Ltd. and Taq Cargo (freight forwarders in Pakistan) in appendix 2-6H.

1-17B. Customs Brokers/Clearing Agents

The National Customs Brokers & Forwarders Association of America, Inc.
1200 18th Street, NW, #901
Washington, DC 20036, USA
Tel: 202 466 0222
Fax: 202 466 0226
Email: staff@ncbfaa.org
Web Site: http://www.ncbfaa.org
Services: Contact the association for a list of companies.

1-17C. Shipping

Web sites containing shipping schedules and information:

Air Cargo World
Web Site: http://www.aircargoworld.com

International Air Transport Association (IATA)
Web Site: http://www.iata.org
http://www.iataonline.com

Schedule On Line
Web Site: http://www.schednet.com

ShippingMag.com
Web Site: http://www.shippingmag.com

Traffic World
Web Site: http://www.trafficworld.com

World Wide Shipping
Web Site: http://www.wwship.com

1-17D. Courier Services

Airborne Express
Web Site: http://www.airborne.com

DHL
Web Site: http://www.dhl.com

FedEx
Web Site: http://www.fedex.com

Roadway Express
Web Site: http://www.roadway.com

TNT
Web Site: http://www.tnt.com

UPS
Web Site: http://www.ups.com

1-18. Credit Reporting Services/Debt Collection Agencies

American Collectors Association
P.O. Box 39106
Minneapolis, MN 55439, USA
Web Site: http://www.collector.com
Services: Association of companies that provide debt collection services.

Dun & Bradstreet
Web Site: http://www.dnb.com
Services: Dun & Bradstreet offers mailing lists, credit history, debt collection, and other services. Please contact the Dun & Bradstreet office in your own country for more information. If there is no office in your country, then contact the office in your region. For example, if you live in Pakistan, your regional office would be in Singapore. This information is available on their web site. Also, most of their services can be ordered over the Internet.

1-19A. Foreign/Free Trade Zones

National Association of Foreign-Trade Zones
1000 Connecticut Avenue, NW
Suite 1001
Washington, DC 20036, USA
Tel: 202 331 1950
Fax: 202 331 1994
Email: info@naftz.org
Web Site: http://www.naftz.org

US Customs Service Information for Foreign Trade Zones
Web Site: http://www.customs.gov
http://www.customs.gov/imp-exp2/comm-imp/ftz/ftstart.htm

US Department of Commerce Foreign Trade Zones Board
Web Site: http://ia.ita.doc.gov
http://ia.ita.doc.gov/ftzpage

1-19B. Sub-zones

Foreign Trade Zones Board List of Subzones
Web Site: http://ia.ita.doc.gov/ftzpage/szlist.htm

1-20A. World Factbook

The Internet version of the World Factbook may be accessed at the following web sites:

World Factbook
Web Site: http://www.odci.gov/cia/publications/factbook/index.html
http://www.cia.gov/cia/publications/factbook/index.html

Enterprise Data Access
Web Site: http://www.enth.com/index.asp
Services: Source of data and information including demographics and population.

Appendix 2

2-2A. Travel and Tourism in Pakistan

Pakistan Tourism Development Corp.
House No. 170-171, Street 36,
F-10/1, Islamabad 44000, Pakistan
Tel: 92 51 294790-2
Fax: 92 51 294540, 92 51 292672
Email: ptdc@tourism.gov.pk
Web Site: http://www.tourism.gov.pk

2-2B. Luxury Hotels in Islamabad

Holiday Inn
G6 Civic Centre, P.O. Box 1373
Islamabad-44000, Pakistan
Tel: 92 51 827311
Fax: 92 51 273273
Email: holiday@isb.comsats.net.pk
Web Site: http://www.holiday-inn.com

Marriott Hotel
Agha Khan Road-Shalimar 5-P.O. Box 1251
Islamabad, Pakistan
Tel: 92 51 2826121
Fax: 92 51 2820648
Web Site: http://www.marriott.com/marriott/ISBPK
http://www.marriott.com.pk

2-2C. Luxury Hotel in Rawalpindi

Pearl Continental Hotel
The Mall Road, P.O. Box 211
Rawalpindi, Pakistan
Tel: 92 51 566 01
Fax: 92 51 563 927
Email: pcisb@pchotels.com
Web Sites: http://www.pchotels.com/pcr-home.htm

2-2D. Four Star Hotel in Quetta

Hotel Quetta Serena
Shahrah-e-Zarghoon,
Quetta, Pakistan
Tel: 92 81 820071
Fax: 92 81 820070
Email: mktg@serena.co.ke
Web Site: http://www.serenahotels.com/content_qu.html

2-2E. Luxury Hotels in Karachi

Avari Towers
Fatima Jinnah Road, P.O Box 15503
Karachi-75530, Pakistan
Tel: 92 21 5660100
Fax: 92 21 5680310
Email: towers@avari.com
Web Site: http://www.avari.com/towers.htm

Holiday Inn
Crowne Plaza Karachi, Shahrah-e-Faisal
Karachi, Pakistan
Tel: 92 21 5660611
Fax: 92 21 5683146
Web Site: http://www.holiday-inn.com

Marriott Karachi
9, Abdullah Haroon Road
Karachi 10444, Pakistan
Tel: 92 21 568 0111
Fax: 92 21 568 0981
Web Site: http://www.marriott.com.pk
http://www.marriott.com/marriott/KHIPK

Pearl Continental Hotel
Club Road, P.O. Box 8513
Karachi, Pakistan
Tel: 92 21 568 5021
Fax: 92 21 568 1835
Email: pckhi@pchotels.com
Web Site: http://www.pchotels.com

Sheraton Karachi Hotel and Towers
Club Road, P.O. Box 3918
Karachi, Pakistan
Tel: 92 21 568 1021
Fax: 92 21 568 2875
Web Site: http://www.sheraton.com
http://www.sheraton.com/property.taf?prop=448&lc=en

2-2F. Luxury Hotels in Lahore

Avari Lahore
87 Shahrah-e-Quaid-e-Azam
Lahore-54000, Pakistan
Tel: 92 42 6310646
Fax: 92 42 6365367
Email: lahore@avari.com
Web Site: http://www.avari.com/lahore.htm

Holiday Inn
25-26 Egerton Road
Lahore 54000, Pakistan
Tel: 92 42 6310077
Fax: 92 42 6314515
Email: holiday@brain.net.pk
Web Site: http://www.holiday-inn.com

Pearl Continental Hotel
Shahrah-e-Quaid-e-Azam
PO Box # 983
Lahore, Pakistan
Tel: 92 42 6360 210
Fax: 92 42 6362 760
Email: pclhr@pchotels.com
Web Site: http://www.pchotels.com

2-2G. Four Star Hotel in Faisalabad

Faisalabad Serena Hotel
Club Road, P.O. Box 433
Faisalabad, Pakistan
Tel: 92 41 600436
Fax: 92 41 629235
Email: serena@biruni.erum.com.pk
Web Site: http://www.serenahotels.com

Pakistan Sales Office for Serena Hotels:
Serena Hotels, Clifton, P.O. Box 3877
Karachi-75600, Pakistan
Tel: 92 21 587 3789, 92 21 587 3791
Fax: 92 21 587 3812
Email: serena-sales@cyber.net.pk

2-2H. Luxury Hotel in Multan

Holiday Inn Multan
76-Abdali Road
Multan 60000, Pakistan
Tel: 92 61 5877 7795
Fax: 92 61 513033
Email: holiday@mul.zoooom.net.pk
Web Site: http://www.holiday-inn.com
http://www.holidayinn.com.ru/holiday-inn?_franchisee=MUXPK

2-2I. Luxury Hotel in Peshawar

Pearl Continental Hotel
Khyber Road, P.O. Box 197
Peshawar, Pakistan
Tel: 92 521 276 361
Fax: 92 521 276 465
Email: pcpsw@pchotels.com
Web Site: http://www.pchotels.com/pcp-home.htm

2-2J. Air Travel

Aero Asia International (Private) Ltd.
Karachi, Institution of Engineers Building
177-2, Fowler Lines, Shahra-e-Faisal,
Karachi, Pakistan
Tel: 92 21 7782851
Fax: 92 21 7782833
Web Site: http://www.aeroasia.com

Bhoja Air
Court View Building, Court Road
Karachi, Pakistan
Tel: 92 21 5683475, 92 21 5682337
Fax: 92 21 5682793
Email: khictob4@aol.net.pk
Web Site: http://www.bhojaair.com.pk

Pakistan International Airlines Corporation (PIAC)
Quaid-e-Azam International Airport
Karachi 75200, Pakistan
Tel: 92 21 4572011, 92 21 4576881
Fax: 92 21 4572225, 45770419
Email: info@fly-pia.com
Web Site: http://www.piac.com.pk

Shaheen Airlines
Ali Complex, 23 Empress Road
Lahore, Pakistan
Tel: 92 42 6316855 59
Email: sair@sai.col.com.pk
Web Site: http://www.shaheenair.com

2-2K. Railways

Pakistan Railways
Allama Iqbal Road
Lahore, Pakistan
Tel: 92 42 6365460
Fax: 92 42 6367673
Web Site: http://www.pakrailway.gov.pk

2-2L. Mailing Facilities

Pakistan Postal Service
Web Site: http://www.pakpost.gov.pk

2-3. Textile Quota

International Development Systems Inc. (IDS)
Web Site: http://www.ids-quota.com

Office of Textiles and Apparel
Web Site: http://otexa.ita.doc.gov

PKTex.com
Web Site: http://www.pktex.com

Quota Supervisory Council
Web Site: http://www.qsc.com.pk

TexWorld.com
Web Site: http://www.texworld.com

2-4A. New York Trade Office

Pakistan Trade Offices, USA
Consulate General of Pakistan (Commercial Section)
12 East, 65th Street,
New York, NY 10021, USA
Tel: 212 472 6123, 212 472 6143
Fax: 212 472 6780
Email: paktrade@mail.idt.net
Web Site: http://www.paktrade.org

2-4B. Export Promotion Bureau (EPB)

Export Promotion Bureau
Government of Pakistan
5th Floor, Block A, Finance & Trade Center, P.O. Box No. 1293
Shahrah-e-Faisal, Karachi 75200, Pakistan
Tel: 92 21 9206487
Fax: 92 21 9206483, 92 21 9205769-67
Email: epb@epb.kar.erum.com.pk
Web Site: http://www.epb.gov.pk

2-4C. Trade Associations

All Pakistan Bedsheets & Upholstery Manufacturer Association
20-T Block, New Multan Colony, Maasoom Shah Road,
Multan, Pakistan
Tel: 92 61 552909, 92 61 552488
Fax: 92 61 557981, 552981
Email: apbuma@mul.paknet.com.pk

All Pakistan Cloth Exporters Association
30/7, Civil Lines, Near State Bank
Faisalabad, Pakistan
Tel: 92 41 644750
Fax: 92 41 617985, 644773
Email: apcea@fsd.comsats.net.pk

All Pakistan Cotton Power Looms Association
P-107, Street No. 5, 1st Floor, Montgomery Bazar
Faisalabad, Pakistan
Tel: 92 41 612929
Fax: 92 41 613636
Email: apcpa@phone.net

All Pakistan Textile Mills Association
APTMA House, 44-A Lalazar, M.T.Khan Road,
Karachi, Pakistan
Tel: 92 21 5610191
Fax: 92 21 5611305
Email: aptma@paknet3.ptc.pk
Web Site: http://www.paktextile.com
http:// www.textileuniverse.com/aptma

Karachi Cotton Association
The Cotton Exchange, I.I. Chundrigar Road
Karachi, Pakistan
Tel: 92 21 2425007
Fax: 92 21 2413035

Pakistan Art Silk Fabrics & Garments Exporters Association
1st Floor, Ghulam Rasool Building, 60,Shahrah-e-Quaid-e-Azam,
Lahore, Pakistan
Tel: 92 42 6360919
Fax: 92 42 6361291

Pakistan Bedwear Exporters Association
Plot No. 245-1-V, Block-6, P.E.C.H.S.
Karachi, Pakistan
Tel: 92 21 4541149
Fax: 92 21 2851429
Email: nash2@ibm.net

Pakistan Canvas & Tents Manufacturers & Exporters Association
15/63, Shadman Commercial Market, Afridi Mansion
Lahore, Pakistan
Tel: 92 42 7577572
Fax: 92 42 7577572

Pakistan Cloth Merchants Association
4th Floor, Hassan Ali Center, Hussaini Market, Mereweather Tower,
M.A. Jinnah Road, Karachi, Pakistan
Tel: 92 21 2444274, 2401423
Fax: 92 21 2419751, 2427483
Email: pcma@digicom.net.pk

Pakistan Commercial Exporters of Towels Association
PCETA House-7, H Block-6, P.E.C.H.S,
Karachi, Pakistan
Tel: 92 21 4535757, 92 21 4522507
Fax: 92 21 4522372
Email: pceta@cyber.net.pk
Web Site: http://www.towelworld.com

Pakistan Cotton Fashion Apparel Manufacturers and Exporters Association
2nd Floor, Amber Court Shaheed-e-Millat Road
Karachi, Pakistan
Tel: 92 21 4533936
Fax: 92 21 4546711
Email: faf@pcta.brain.net.pk

Pakistan Cotton Ginners Association
1119-1120, 11TH Floor, UNI Plaza, I. I. Chundrigar Road
Karachi, Pakistan
Tel: 92 21 2411406
Fax: 92 21 2423181

Pakistan Gloves Manufacturers Association
Post Box No.1330, 349,Khadim Ali Road,
Sialkot, Pakistan
Tel: 92 432 551847
Fax: 92 432 550182

Pakistan Hosiery Manufacturers Association
P. H. M. A. House, 37-H, Block-6, P.E.C.H.S.
Karachi, Pakistan
Tel: 92 21 4522769/4522685
Fax: 92 21 4543774

Pakistan Knitwear & Sweaters Exporters Association (PAKSEA)
Room Nos. 1014-1016, 10th Floor, Park Avenue, Block-6,
P.E.C.H.S
Karachi, Pakistan
Tel: 92 21 454 4035
Fax: 92 21 4525747
Email: info@pakseaonline.com
Web site: http://www.pakseaonline.com
http://www.paksea.com.pk

Pakistan Readymade Garments Manufacturers & Exporters Association
Mezzanine Floor, Shaheen View Building,
Plot No.18-A, Block-6, P.E.C.H.S., Sharah-e-Faisal,
Karachi, Pakistan
Tel: 92 21 4533327
Fax: 92 21 4539669
Web Site: http://www.prgmea.org

Pakistan Silk & Rayon Mills Association
Room Nos 44,48 &49, 5th Floor, Textile Plaza, M. A. Jinnah Road
Karachi, Pakistan
Tel: 92 21 2410288
Fax: 92 21 2419972

Pakistan Small Units Power Looms Association
2nd Floor, Waqas Plaza, Aminpura Bazar,
Faisalabad, Pakistan
Tel: 92 41 627992
Fax: 92 41 633567

Pakistan Tanners Association
46-C, 21st Commercial Street, Phase II Extension
Defense Housing Authority
Karachi, Pakistan
Tel: 92 21 5611961
Fax: 92 21 5611305
Email: aptma@cyber.net.pk

Pakistan Woolen Mills Association
Republic Motors Building, 87 Shahrah-e-Quaid-e-Azam (Second Floor)
Lahore, Pakistan
Tel: 92 42 6306879
Fax: 92 42 6306879
Email: pwma@pwma.lcci.org.pk
Web Site: http://www.lcci.org.pk/pwma

Towel Manufacturers' Association of Pakistan
12th Floor, Kashif Center, Shahrah-e-Faisal,
Karachi 75530, Pakistan
Tel: 92 21 567728, 92 21 5681953
Fax: 92 21 5677132

2-4D. Chambers of Commerce & Industry in Pakistan

Faisalabad Chamber of Commerce & Industry
2nd Floor, N.B.P.Building, Jail Road,
Faisalabad, Pakistan
Tel: 92 41 616045
Fax: 92 41 615085

Federation of Pakistan Chamber of Commerce & Industry
Federation House, Shahrah-i-Firdousi, Main Clifton, P.O. Box 13875,
Karachi 75600, Pakistan
Tel: 92 21 587 3691
Fax: 92 21 587 4332
Email: fpcci@digicom.net.pk
Web Site: http://www.fpcci.com

Gujranwala Chamber of Commerce & Industry
Aiwan-e-Tijarat Road
Gujranwala, Pakistan
Tel: 92 431 256701
Fax: 92 431 254440
Email: gccibar@compare.com.pk
Web Site: http://www.gcci.org.pk

Hyderabad Chamber of Commerce & Industry
Aiwan-e-Tijarat Road, Saddar
Hyderabad, Pakistan
Tel: 92 221 784973
Fax: 92 221 784972
Email: hcci@paknet3.ptc.pk

Islamabad Chamber of Commerce & Industry
Aiwan-e-Sanat-O-Tijarat Road, Mauve Area, Sector G-8/1
Islamabad, Pakistan
Tel: 92 51 250526
Fax: 92 51 252950
Email: icci@brain.net.pk

Karachi Chamber of Commerce & Industry
Aiwan-e-Tijarat Road, Off: Shahrah-e-Liaqat
P. O. Box 4158, Karachi, Pakistan
Tel: 92 21 2416091
Fax: 92 21 2416095
Email: ccikar@paknet3.ptc.pk
Web Site: http://www.karachichamber.com

Lahore Chamber of Commerce & Industry
11, Shahrah-e-Aiwan-e-Tijarat,
P.O. Box 597, Lahore, Pakistan
Tel: 92 42 6305538, 92 42 6365737
Fax: 92 42 6368854
Web Site: http://www.lcci.org.pk

Multan Chamber of Commerce & Industry
M. D. A. Road,
Multan, Pakistan
Tel: 92 61 41087
Fax: 92 61 570463

Pakistan American Business Council of Pakistan
NIC Building, 6th Floor, Abbassi Shaheed Road, GPO Box 1322
Karachi, Pakistan
Tel: 92 21 5676436
Fax: 92 21 5660135
Email: abcpak@cyber.net.pk

Quetta Chamber of Commerce & Industry
Zarghoon Road, P.O. Box 117,
Quetta, Pakistan
Tel: 92 81 821943
Fax: 92 81 821948
Email: qcci@hotmail.com

Rawalpindi Chamber of Commerce & Industry
Chamber House, 108, Adamjee Road,
Rawalpindi, Pakistan
Tel: 92 51 584397
Fax: 92 51 586849
Email: rcci@best.net.pk
Web Site: http://www.rcci.org.pk

Sarhad Chamber of Commerce & Industry
Sarhad Chamber House, G.T.Road,
Peshawar, Pakistan
Tel: 92 91 9213314
Fax: 92 91 9213316
Email: sccip@brain.net.pk

Sialkot Chamber of Commerce & Industry
Shahrah-e-Aiwan-e-Sanat-O-Tijarat, P.O. Box 1870
Sialkot, Pakistan
Tel: 92 432 261881
Fax: 92 432 268835
Email: scci@skt.comsats.net.pk
Web Site: http://www.scci.org.pk

2-4E. Trade Directory Publishers

Publishers of Pakistan Yellow Pages
U.S. Publishers (Pvt.) Ltd.
18 C.P. & Berar Cooperative Housing Society
Karachi 75350, Pakistan
Tel: 92 21 453 6321
Fax: 92 21 4536330
Web Site: http://www.jamals.com

Publishers of Trade Index of Pakistan
Space & Time (Pvt.) Ltd.
Space & Time Center, National Auto Plaza, Marston Road
Karachi 74400, Pakistan
Tel: 9221 7765973
Fax: 9221 7765663
Email: info@fpcci.org.pk
info@PakistanBiz.com
Web Site: http://www.fpcci.org.pk
http://www.pakistanbiz.com

2-5. Export Processing Zones

Export Processing Zones Authority
Government of Pakistan
Landhi Industrial Area, Mehran Highway
Karachi 75150, Pakistan
Tel: 92 21 5082001
Fax: 92 21 5082005
Email: epza@super.net.pk
Web Site: http://www.epza.com.pk

Rawalpindi Export Processing Zone
Cresent Developers Private Limited
Khan Chamber, 60-Canning Road, Saddar
Rawalpindi, Pakistan
Tel: 92 51 568038, 567607
Fax: 92 51 515779
Web Site: http://www.rcci.org.pk/rcci/repz.htm

2-6A. Banks

Commercial Banks

Allied Bank of Pakistan Ltd.
Banks & DFIs N.I.C., Building, 13th Floor Abbasi Shaheed Road
Karachi, Pakistan
Tel: 92 21 5670379, 92 21 5670371
Fax: 92 21 5683312
Web Site: http://www.abl.com.pk

Habib Bank Ltd.
22,Habib Bank Plaza I.I.Chundrigar Road
Karachi, Pakistan
Tel: 92 21 2412128, 92 21 2441542
Fax: 92 21 241491
Email: webmaster@habibbank.com
Web Site: http://www.habibbank.com

Muslim Commercial Bank Ltd.
Ground Floor,Block-C, Finance and Trade Centre, Shahra-e-Faisal,
Karachi, Pakistan
Tel: 92 21 568 7541
Fax: 92 21 567 4829
Email: contact@mcb.com.pk
Web Site: http://www.mcb.com.pk

National Bank of Pakistan
NBP Building I.I.Chundrigar Road
Karachi, Pakistan
Tel: 92 21 9212100
Fax: 92 21 9212180, 92 21 9212235
Email: info@nbp.com.pk
Web Site: http://www.nbp.com.pk

United Bank Ltd.
State Life Building No.1
I.I.Chundrigar Road
Karachi, Pakistan
Tel: 92 21 2417120, 92 21 2417100
Fax: 92 21 2413483
Web Site: http://www.ubl.com.pk

Other Smaller Pakistani Banks

Askari Commercial Bank Ltd.
Web Site: http://www.askaribank.com.pk

Prime Commercial Bank Ltd.
Web Site: http://www.primebankpk.com

Soneri Bank
Web Site: http://www.soneri.com

Union Bank Ltd.
Web site: http://www.unionbank.com.pk

American Banks in Pakistan

American Express Bank Ltd.
Shaheen Commercial Complex, Dr. Ziauddin Ahmed Road,
Karachi, Pakistan
Tel: 92 21 2630249
Fax: 92 21 2631803
Web Site: http://www.americanexpress.com

Bank of America
Jubilee Insurance House I.I.Chundrigar Road
Karachi, Pakistan
Tel: 92 21 2412530, 92 21 2412520
Fax: 92 21 2415371
Web Site: http://www.bankofamerica.com

Chase Manhattan Bank, N.A.
Shaheen Commercial Complex M.R.Kayani Road
Karachi 74200, Pakistan
Tel: 92 21 2633079, 92 21 2633073
Fax: 92 21 2631393
Web Site: http://www.chase.com

Citibank
State Life Building No.1 I.I. Chundrigar Road P.O.Box: 4889
Karachi 74200, Pakistan
Tel: 92 21 2412649, 21 2412641
Fax: 92 21 2418993
Web Site: http://www.citibank.com/pakistan

2-6B. Investing

Industrial Development Bank of Pakistan (IDBP)
State Life Building No.2,
Wallace Road,
I.I.Chundrigar Road, P.O. Box No. 5082,
Karachi-74000, Pakistan
Tel: 92 21 2419160
Fax: 92 21 2411990
Email: idbp@idbp.com.pk
Web Site: http://www.idbp.com.pk

Investment Corporation of Pakistan
5th Floor, N.B.P. Building
I.I.Chundrigar Road
Karachi, Pakistan
Tel: 92 21 2415869
Fax: 92 21 2411684, 92 21 5680035
Web Site: http://www.icp.com.pk

Pakistan Board of Investment
Ataturk Avenue, G-5/1,
Islamabad, Pakistan
Tel: 92 51 9218267
Fax: 92 51 9217665
Email: boipak@isb.compol.com
Web Site: http://www.pakboi.gov.pk

Pakistan Industrial Credit & Investment Corporation of Pakistan
Head Office:
State Life Building No. 1,
I. I. Chundrigar Road, P.O. Box No 5080,
Karachi 74000, Pakistan
Tel: 92 21 2414220
Fax: 92 21 2417851
Email: contact@picic.com
Web Site: http://www.picic.com

Privatisation Commission, Finance Division, Government of Pakistan
5-A, EAC Building Constitution Ave,
Islamabad, Pakistan
Tel: 92 51 9205146
Fax: 92 51 9203076 / 9211692
Email: info@privatisation.gov.pk
Web Site: http://www.privatisation.gov.pk

2-6C. Misc. Pakistan Government Offices

Central Board of Revenue
Email: info@cbr.gov.pk
Web Site: http://www.cbr.gov.pk

Government of Pakistan
Web Site: http://www.pak.gov.pk

Information Technology Commission
Web Site: http://www.itcomm.gov.pk

Ministry of Commerce
Web Site: http://www.paktrade.org

Ministry of Finance
Email: finance@comsats.net.pk
Web Site: http://www.finance.gov.pk

Ministry of Foreign Affairs
Web Site: http://www.forisb.org

Ministry of Science & Technology
Web Site: http://www.most.gov.pk

National Assembly
Web Site: http://www.na.gov.pk

Overseas Pakistanis Foundation
Web Site: http://www.opf.gov.pk

Pakistan Software Export Board
Web Site: http://www.pseb.org

Pakistan Telecommunication Authority
Web Site: http://www.pta.gov.pk

Pakistan Telecommunication Corporation Limited
Web Site: http://www.ptc.pk

Private Power and Infrastructure Board
Web Site: http://www.ppib.gov.pk

State Engineering Corporation Pvt. Ltd.
Web Site: http://www.sec.gov.pk

Other useful Pakistani trade links are available at the following URL:

Useful Links
Web Site: http://www.worldtradevenue.com/useful/pakistan.html

2-6D. Stock Exchanges

Islamabad Stock Exchange
Stock Exchange Building
101-E Fazal-ul-Haq Road,
Islamabad, Pakistan
Tel: 92 51 275045
Fax: 92 51 275044
Email: ise@ise.com.pk
Web Site: http://www.ise.com.pk

Karachi Stock Exchange
K. S. E. Building, Stock Exchange Road,
Off I. I. Chundrigar Road,
Karachi 74000, Pakistan
Tel: 92 21 111 001122
Fax: 92 21 241 0825, 92 21 241 5763
Email: info@kse.com.pk
Web Site: http://www.kse.com.pk

Lahore Stock Exchange (Guarantee) Ltd.
Stock Exchange Building, Khayaban-e-Iqbal,
Lahore-54000, Pakistan
Tel: 92 42 6368000, 92 42 6368522
Fax: 92 42 63638484

2-6E. Newspapers, Periodicals, and Magazines

Business Recorder
531 Business Recorder Road,
Karachi 74550, Pakistan
Tel: 92 21 7210071
Fax: 92 21 7228644
Email: editor@brecorder.com
Web Site: http://www.brecorder.com
Services: Daily English trade newspaper.

Dawn
Haroon House, Dr. Ziauddin Ahmed Road,
Karachi 74200, Pakistan
Tel: 92 21 111 444 777
Fax: 92 21 568 3188
Email: webmaster@dawn.com
Web Site: http://www.dawn.com
Services: Daily English newspaper with trade section.

Pakistan & Gulf Economist
3A, Falcon Arcade, BC-3, Block-7, Clifton,
Karachi, Pakistan
Tel: 92 21 586 9534
Fax: 92 21 587 6071
Email: information@pakistaneconomist.com
Web Site: http://www.pak-economist.com
Services: Weekly English business magazine.

Pakistan Observer

Pakistan Observer, G-8 Markaz,
Islamabad Pakistan
Tel: 92 51 2853818
Fax: 92 51 262258
Email: observer@best.net.pk
Web Site: http://www.pakobserver.com
Services: Daily English Newspaper with trade section.

ShippingMag.com

Email: mahmoodi@cyber.net.pk
Web Site: http://www.shippingmag.com
Services: Shipping and trade magazine on the Internet.

The Nation Group of Publications Pvt. Ltd.

NIPCO House-4 Shahrah-e-Fatima Jinnah,
Lahore, Pakistan
Tel: 92 42 6367580
Fax: 92 42 6367005
Email: editor@nation.com.pk
Web Site: http://www.nation.com.pk
Services: Daily English newspaper.

The News International

Al-Rahman building, I.I. Chundrigar Road,
Karachi, Pakistan
Tel: 92 21 2630611
Fax: 92 21 2418343, 92 42 2418344
Web Site: http://www.jang-group.com
Services: Daily English newspaper.

Also see appendix 2-6I for textile journals in Pakistan.

2-6F. Buying Agents

Ammar Associates
6th Floor Fayyaz Centre, Shahrah-e-Faisal S.M.C.H.S.
Karachi, Pakistan
Tel: 92 21 438 9950
Fax: 92 21 438 9971
Email: info@ammar.com.pk
Web Site: http://www.ammar.com.pk

Conley National Buying Syndicate
1407 Broadway, Suite 12
New York, NY 10018, USA
Tel: 212 730 1890
Fax: 212 730 1895

Fran International Private Ltd.
Godrej Kandawalla Building, M.A.Jinnah Road
Karachi, Pakistan
Tel: 92 21 7211119
Fax: 92 21 7216629
Email: franint@fascom.com.pk
fran@biruni.erum.com.pk

Gia Associates (Pvt) Ltd
Plot No.18, Sector 24, Korangi Industrial Area
Karachi-74900, Pakistan
Tel: 92 21 506 0411, 506 0991
Fax: 92 21 506 3283, 505 4828
Email: giaasso@cyber.net.pk
Web Site: http://www.gia-textiles.com

Giltex Pakistan (Pvt), Ltd
306-307, Amber Estate, Main Sharah-e-Faisal
Karachi, Pakistan
Tel: 92 21 4543073, 92 21 4549626
Fax: 92 21 4545731
Email: giltex@cyber.net.pk

Rosenel Feuer Buying Svc Inc
109 West 38th Street, Suite 802
New York, NY 10018, USA
Tel: 212 869 8010
Fax: 212 840 1916
Email: rosenel@mail.idt.net
Web Site: http://www.rosenel.com

2-6G. Pakistan and US Embassies

Consulate General of Pakistan
10850 Wilshire Blvd., Suite 1100
Los Angeles, CA 90024, USA
Tel: 310 441 5114
Fax: 310 441 9256

Embassy of Pakistan
2315 Massachusetts Ave.,
NW Washington D.C. 20008, USA
Tel: 202 939 6200
Fax: 202 387 0484
Email: info@pakistan-embassy.com
Web Site: http://www.pakistan-embassy.com

Pakistan Trade Offices, USA
Consulate General of Pakistan, (Commercial Section)
12 East, 65th Street,
New York, NY 10021, USA
Tel: 212 472 6123, 212 472 6143,
Fax: 212 472 6780
Email: paktrade@mail.idt.net
Web Site: http://www.paktrade.org

US Consulate General
50, Empress Road
Lahore, Pakistan
Tel: 92 42 6365540
Fax: 92 42 6365177
Web Site: http://usembassy.state.gov/posts/pk2/wwwhamcn.html

US Department of State
Web Site: http://www.usembassy.state.gov
Services: On this web site you can find US consulates and embassies in Pakistan and around the world.

US Embassy in Islamabad
Diplomatic Enclave, Ramna 5
Islamabad, Pakistan
Tel: 92 51 826179
Fax: 92 51 214222
Web Site: http://usembassy.state.gov/posts/pk1/wwwhusis.html

2-6H. Shipping

Delta Shipping Pvt Ltd.
Seedat Chambers, Dr. Ziauddin Ahmed Road,
P.O. Box No. 10062,
Karachi, Pakistan
Tel: 92 21 5687961
Fax: 92 21 5687701
Email: delship@cyber.net.pk
Web Site: http://www.deltashipping.com

Karachi International Container Terminal, Ltd.
Administration Building, Berth 28-30,
West Wharf, Dockyard Road,
Karachi, Pakistan
Tel: 92 21 2316401
Fax: 92 21 2313816
Email: info@kictl.com
Web Site: http://www.kictl.com

Karachi Port Trust
Web Site: http://www.kpt.cjb.net
http://www.shippingmag.com/kpt/index.htm

Oriental Shipping Company
201-203, Muhammadi House, I.I. Chundrigar Road,
Karachi, Pakistan
Tel: 92 21 2411505
Fax: 92 21 2416917
Web Site: http://www.orientalshipping.com.pk

Pakistan Customs
Custom House
Karachi, Pakistan
Tel: 92 21 201155
Fax: 92 21 200492
Web Site: http://www.cbr.gov.pk/customs/auction

Pakistan National Shipping Corporation
Web Site: http://www.pnsc.com.pk

Qasim International Container Terminal
6th Floor, Bahria Complex II, M.T Khan Road,
Karachi-74000, Pakistan
Tel: 92 21 5610583
Fax: 92 21 5610527
Web Site: http://www.qict.net

Raaziq International (Pvt) Ltd.
129-E/1-Main Boulevard,
Gulberg-III,
Lahore, Pakistan
Tel: 92 42 5761977, 92 42 5762891
Fax: 92 42 5712471
Email: raaziq@brain.net.pk
Web Site: http://www.raaziq.com.pk

Taq Cargo
Suite 16-17, Third Floor, Davis Hytes Plaza,
38 Sir Agha Khan Road,
Lahore-54000 Pakistan
Tel: 92 42 630 9281
Fax: 92 42 630 2381
Email: mtm@tlpk.com
Web site: http://www.taq.com.pk

Also see appendix 1-17A for a freight forwarder in the US.

2-6I. Textile Journals

Pakistan Textile Journal
D-16, K.D.A. Scheme No. 1,
Karachi, Pakistan
Tel: 92 21 452 2189
Fax: 92 21 453 3911
Email: ptj@cyber.net.pk
Web Site: http://www.ptj.com.pk

Textile Today
Fourth Floor, Dada Chambers
Hussaini Market, M.A. Jinnah Road
Karachi, Pakistan
Tel: 92 21 2419751
Fax: 92 21 2419751

Also see appendix 2-6E for newspapers, periodicals, and magazines in Pakistan.

2-6J. Market Research Firms

Aftab Associates (Pvt.) Ltd.
5-E/1 Commercial,
Gulberg-III Lahore 54660, Pakistan
Tel: 92 42 5710987
Fax: 92 42 5711020
Email: aal@brain.net.pk

Marketing Association of Pakistan
403, Burhani Chambers Abdullah Haroon
Road, Karachi, Pakistan
Tel: 92 21 7760032
Fax: 92 21 7729952
Email:mapmail@cyber.net.pk
Web Site: http://www.map.org.pk

2-6K. Miscellaneous Information

Central Cotton Research Institute
Old Shujabad Road, P.O. Box 572
Multan-Pakistan
Tel: 92 61 545361
Fax: 92 61 543245
Email: ccri@mul.paknet.com.pk
Web Site: http://www.ccri.org.pk

Online Conversion Tools
Web Site: http://www.sirius.on.ca/running/km_miles.html
http://www.welton.net/nana/misc/us_metric.html

US Government Web Site on Pakistan
Country Commercial Guides: Pakistan
Web Site: http://www.state.gov/www/about_state/business/
com_guides/1999/sa/pakistan99_11.html

Pakistani Insurance Companies

Adamjee Insurance Company Ltd.
Adamjee House, 6th Floor, I.I. Chundrigar Road, Karachi 74000,
Pakistan
Tel: 92 21 241 2623
Fax: 92 21 241 2627
Web Site: http://www.adamjeeinsurance.com

EFU General Insurance Ltd.
8th Floor Business Plaza, Mumtaz Hasan Road
Tel: 92 21 2428969, 92 21 2428965
Fax: 92 21 2428119

Web Sites About Pakistan

Akhtar Hameed Khan: a great social scientist of Pakistan
Web Site: http://www.akhtar-hameed-khan.8m.com

Allama Mashriqi: one of the founding fathers of Pakistan
Web Site: http://www.allama-mashriqi.8m.com

Business & Trade Directory
Web Site: http://www.pak.com

Chowk
Web Site: http://www.chowk.com

Country Watch
Web Site: http://www.countrywatch.com/files/131 cw_country.asp?
vCOUNTRY=131

ePakistan.com
Web Site: http://www.epakistan.com

Get Pakistan
Web Site: http://www.getpakistan.com

Islamabad
Web Site: http://www.islamabad.org

ISO 9000 Directory & Resource Guide of Pakistan
Web Site: http://www.iso9000.com.pk

ISO Certified Exporters of Pakistan
Web Site: http://www.forisb.org/iso-certified.htm

Karachi Airport
Web Site: http://www.karachiairport.com/

Karachi
Web Site: http://www.karachi.com

Lahore
Web Site: http://www.lahore.org

National Fund for Cultural Heritage
Web Site: http://www.heritage.gov.pk

Pak Center
Web Site: http://www.pakcenter.com

Pakistan
Web Site: http://www.pak.org

Pakistan Defence Journal
Web Site: http://www.defencejournal.com

Pakistan Jamal Yellow Pages
Web Site: http://www.jamals.com

Pakistan Meteorological Department
Web Site: http://www.met.gov.pk

Pakistan Page
Web Site: http://www.pakistanpage.net

Pakistan Power Page
Web Site: http://www.pakpowerpage.com

Pakistan Telecommunication Company Ltd.
Web Site: http://www.ptcl.com.pk

Pakistan Travel Web
Web Site: http://www.travel.web.pk

Pakvalley.com
Web Site: http://www.pakvalley.com

Quick Pakistan
Web Site: http://www.quickpakistan.com

Saher
Web Site: http://www.saher.com

The Pak Ranks
Web Site: http://www.pakranks.com

United Nations Web Site on Pakistan
Web Site: http://www.un.org.pk

Web Site of Pakistan
Web Site: http://www.webspak.com.pk

Zarposh
Web Site: http://www.zarposh.com

Glossary

Financial Terms

Accounts Payable
Money, which a company/person owes to another for the products and/or services purchased.

Accounts Receivable
Money, which another company/person owes to you for the product and/or services sold.

Accrual Basis
An accounting system in which income and expenses are accounted for as and when they occur.

Bad Debt
An amount which cannot be collected for any reason.

Balance Sheet
A document which shows the assets, liabilities, and net worth of a company on a particular date.

Capital
The use of cash or goods in order to generate income/benefits.

Cash Flow Statement
A financial statement that shows the receipts and payments during a given period of time.

Fiscal Year
The twelve months of the accounting period.

Journal
A book in which all accounting records are first entered; it provides a chronological record of all business activities.

Ledger
A book in which accounting information from the journal, is entered under specific categories; provides easy access to all information on each company's account.

Petty Cash
The amount kept by a company for meeting day to day small expenses.

Working Capital
The money used for running a business.

Other Terms

Advising Bank
A bank that sends the original Letter of Credit to an exporter/ seller.

ATA Carnet
An internationally recognized custom document for temporary import of goods without paying duty/taxes. "ATA" is an acronym of the French and English words "Admission Temporaire / Temporary Admission."

Bill of Exchange
A document, which directs the drawee to pay a specified amount, on a specific date, to the drawer.

Collecting Bank
A bank that is responsible for collecting payment from the buyer.

Consignee
The person or company named on the Bill of Lading to whom goods are to be delivered.

Certificate of Inspection
This certifies that the goods are inspected and found to be as per the specifications of the order. The certificate of inspection is issued by a third party.

Certificate of Manufacture
A Document confirming that the goods are ready for dispatch to the buyer and are as per the specifications of his/her order.

Certificate of Origin
A document that states the name of the country where the goods have been manufactured.

Collection Papers
Documents submitted, by the seller to the buyer, to receive payment for the goods shipped.

Commercial Invoice
A bill prepared as per the terms and conditions agreed upon by the seller and the buyer.

Correspondent Bank
Any bank that handles the business of a foreign bank, in its own country.

Cost and Freight (C&F)
The seller's price is based on the cost of goods and freight charges up to the named port of destination.

Cost, Insurance, and Freight (CI&F)
The seller's price is based on the cost of goods, insurance, and freight charges up to the named port of destination.

Cost, Insurance, Freight, and Commission (CIF&C)
The seller's price is based on the cost of goods, insurance, and freight charges up to the named port of destination. The price also includes the commission of the intermediary/agent.

Demurrage
The charges/fees paid for the late removal of goods from the dock.

Dock Receipt
This is an acknowledgement of receipt of cargo by the ocean carrier. After the shipment is placed at the specified dock for moving to the final destination, the ocean carrier issues this receipt.

Documents Against Acceptance (D/A)
A method of payment. The title of goods stays with the seller unless the buyer accepts the goods and signs the document for payment.

Documents Against Payment (D/P)
A method of payment. The buyer makes the payment and takes title of the goods. The title of the goods stays with the seller unless the buyer signs the document and releases the payment.

Drawee
A buyer is referred to as drawee, on the documents, in case of documentary collection.

Drawer
A seller is referred to as drawer, on the documents, in case of documentary collection.

Duty Drawback
This is an import duty refund, which an exporter receives upon the export of goods.

Error and Omissions Excepted (E&OE)
Generally mentioned on invoices by the shipper, who does not take responsibility for typographical errors or unintentional omissions.

Ex-factory, Ex-works, Ex-warehouse
The price of the goods is based on the warehouse of the seller and the customer pays all the charges from the warehouse to the point of destination.

Factoring
Selling receivables at a lower price than the face value.

Free Alongside Ship (FAS)
The price is based on the cost of the goods. The exporter is responsible for bringing the goods alongside the ship, but the importer pays loading and other charges. The buyer arranges the space on the ship. The seller's responsibility ends when the goods are placed at the pier to be loaded onto the ship.

Free on Board (FOB)
Price is based on the cost of goods only. It is the responsibility of the exporters to deliver the goods to the port and make them ready for loading onto the ship. All costs up to loading are borne by the exporter. The seller arranges the space on the ship.

Free Port
A port where goods can be imported without obtaining an import license.

General Agreement on Tariff and Trade (GATT)
An international agreement to reduce trade barriers. It deals with trade quotas and tariffs.

Gross Weight
Includes the total weight of the shipment including the weight of the merchandise and packaging.

Hard Currency
A stable and strong currency which is easily convertible. It is generally convertible into gold. US$, the German Mark, and the Japanese Yen, are all examples of hard currencies.

In Bond
A term used for goods on which duty is not paid. They are meant to be kept in a bonded warehouse.

Issuing Bank
A Letter of Credit originates at or is opened by a bank known as an issuing bank.

Long Ton
The equivalent of 2,240 pounds.

Marine Insurance

An insurance that provides protection in case the goods are damaged or lost during shipment. Generally, an "All Risk" insurance is purchased. If the buyer is purchasing the insurance from the time that the goods are shipped until they arrive, then it is recommended that the seller purchase insurance for transport from the warehouse to the port, in order to cover any eventualities.

Metric Ton

The equivalent of 2,204.68 pounds.

Notify

Name of the person/company (on the Bill of Lading) to be notified upon arrival of the shipment.

Packing List

This document carries complete information about the packages being sent. It provides all information including name and address of the shipper, total number of packages, quantity in each package, weight and dimensions of the packages, etc.

Pro forma Invoice

An Invoice issued by the seller prior to shipping the goods, which informs the buyer of the full description of the goods and the terms of the sale.

Promissory Note

A document according to which a person agrees or promises to pay a certain amount to another individual/entity.

Shipped on Board

This means that the goods have been placed on the carrier for onward delivery to the destination.

Short Ton
The equivalent of 2000 pounds.

Sight Draft
This means that payment is to be made by the buyer before he/ she receives the merchandise, usually as soon as the shipment arrives at the port of the destination. The exporter holds the title of the goods until paid. The buyer gets the title after he/she has made the payment.

Through Bill of Lading
If more than two carriers are involved in the shipment of the cargo, a through bill of lading is issued.

Wharfage
A fee charged by the dock authority for handling the incoming or outgoing cargo.

Sources of Information

Part I

- http://www.dol.gov/dol/ilab/public/library/reports/iclp/apparel/main.htm
- http://www.state.gov/www/issues/economic/textile.html
- http://www.odci.gov/cia/publications/factbook/geos/us.htm
- http://www.cia.gov/cia/publications/factbook/index.html
- http://www.ita.doc.gov
- http://ia.ita.doc.gov
- http://www.doc.gov
- http://www.customs.gov
- http://otexa.ita.doc.gov
- http://www.tdctrade.com/main/industries/ipclot.htm
- http://www.qsc.com.pk
- *Standard & Poor Industry Survey* January 2001 VOL., I Chapter Apparel & Footwear Industry Page No. 07

Part II

- http://www.pak.gov.pk/public/govt/basic_facts.html
- http://www.odci.gov/cia/publications/factbook/geos/pk.html
- http://rcci.org.pk/rcci/pakistan.htm
- http://www.privatisation.gov.pk/Introduction/
  Country.asp?q=Stat
- http://www.fpcci.com/pakistan.html
- http://www.finance.gov.pk
- http://www.tourism.gov.pk
- http://www.odci.gov/cia/publications/factbook/geos/pk.html
- http://www.epb.gov.pk/pak02.htm
- http://www.pak.gov.pk/
- http://www.paktextile.com/stats1.shtml
- http://www.pakistaneconomist.com/database1/mics/
  quota.htm
- http://www.epza.com.pk/incentives.html
- http://www.pakboi.gov.pk
- http://www.paktrade.org
- http://www.forisb.org
- http://www.ptc.pk
- http://www.usembassy.state.gov
- http://www.pakistan-embassy.com
- http://www.cbr.gov.pk

Index

A

D

G

N

O

P

S

Styling, 54
Sub-contracting in Pakistan, 283
Substandard shipments, 177
Sub-Zones, 225
Success at the trade show, 142
Superintendent of Documents, 231

T

Target market, 41, 146, 182,
Tariff, 50, 56, 59, 60, 99, 202, 286, 382
Tax holiday, 32
Tazkirah, 12
Tehrik, 11, 22, 259
Television sales, 124
Terms of payment, 142, 170, 173, 207
Terms of sales, 42, 49
Textile, 93, 97, 98, 106
Textile exports from Pakistan, 288
Textile quota, 19, 43, 52, 98, 127, 155, 195, 274, 277, 279
Textile sector, 273
Time draft, 217, 219
Time Zone, 73, 160
Tips for exporters when requesting an L/C, 216
Tips for importers when opening an L/C, 216
Trade and research information, 49
Trade association, 51
Trade body, 107
Trade bulletins, 50, 107, 108,
Trade data on US imports and exports, 58
Trade delegation, 107, 108
Trade directories, 55, 104, 105, 106, 110, 281, 356
Trade fair, 132, 136
Trade libraries, 52
Trade magazines, 55